AND THEN LIKE MY DREAMS

AND THEN LIKE MY DREAMS

{a memoir}

MARGARET ROSE STRINGER

 FREMANTLE PRESS

I dreamed of him last night, as I do all too seldom.

We were ... who knows where? – I never seem to recognise dream locations.

I put my arms around his neck and asked him please not to die before me.

There was a moment, then he smiled; and made a little gesture that encircled us.

He said, 'Isn't it good?'

§

CONTENTS

Dianne McKissock: thank you.

§

ALL OF IT

I dwelt in interior darkness, when I was thirty-one. I lived inside my head without any idea of what was happening to me, fear my only companion.

And then there was light.

Out of nowhere, as if by magic, when I was as low as I had ever been or thought it possible to be, someone came to save me. He offered me unconditional and non-judgemental love, and hoped only for the same from me.

The best part was that I was saving him, too.

It was 1 *anno Carli*, and the world began.

§

Another thirty-one years passed before the light failed.

Very late one terrible night I stood beside the one who had saved me, he who was everything I had ever wanted or needed, my hand resting helplessly on his shoulder as he lay on a wheeled stretcher in a little room off a corridor near Emergency. They had just released him from there, and his back was propped high so that he could breathe.

A few tears drifted slowly down one of his cheeks; and what little measure I had of ability to process thought started to eke away, even as did his tears.

I had no comprehension of how we had got to this: where had my husband gone? – who was this person undergoing such dreadful suffering...?

I was unable to speak to him.

He had so little time left; and I stood there, unable to speak to the man with whom I had stormed heaven.

All I knew was that half my life had been bound to this joy, and it was about to fly away forever.

A gossamer thread of sanity touched me, the contact brief.

I bent and kissed his head.

BACKLIGHT AND FILL

One April day in Melbourne, a bit before the world began, my second-eldest sister summoned me. She knew I was on studio duty that week and not out on film crew, so she phoned me at work and – well, yes, summoned me*. As I was then flatting in South Yarra and she and her husband living in their Warrandyte (semi-)rural idyll, it seemed a bit strange, for these two suburbs are at more than a little distance. But I, with an awful lot of stuff going on in my head, didn't dwell on the strangeness once having remarked it to myself: I merely took a couple of trains and a bus and puffed up the hill, arriving just in time, I hoped very much, for dinner.

No dinner.

Jo wanted to let me know, face-to-face, that on that same ordinary workday morning, over in Perth where we were born, our father had laid his head gently on his desk-blotter and given up the struggle.

He was sixty-four.

There was a long history of cardiovascular problems: no one could be surprised. Our mother had nursed him during the previous ten years, on and off; and I later learned that last rites had been performed on him more than once.

He had been the axis of my unstable world, as my sister, the person to whom I was closest and whom I loved only second-most to Dadda, understood very well. But there wasn't much she could do for me, for her heart, too, was broken. She had a husband and new baby to look after and, being unable to afford herself the luxury of deep grief, couldn't share mine in other than thought.

The sun was setting as my brother-in-law drove me all the way back to South Yarra; and by the time I trudged wretchedly into my flat, darkness surrounded me.

Home had ceased to exist.

§

* if you have an older sister, you'll know how this goes ...

Father's genes had manufactured nothing but X chromosomes, and our extremely clever but emotionally incompatible parents produced nothing but daughters. I was the fourth of five, and for nine years the baby. When the last arrived there was maternal suspicion that she had stolen the wind of 'the littlest' from my sails, but such was far from the case: I adored the beautiful little creature – everyone did.

My mother didn't like me very much, her dislike springing from the unacceptable fact that I was fat. I was the only one to carry excess poundage: the other four were, as well as clever and good-looking, without physical failing. My 'avoirdupois', as it came to be referred to in pseudo-tactful family fashion, varied between regimens: I launched myself or was thrust by Mama upon many, with unfailing success – until I stopped dieting, when every lost ounce would almost instantly reappear and rush to reclaim its old familiar spot, bringing along a few friends.

It seems that from the time I was put into a highchair for my meals I displayed an impressive ability to put away food; and keeping track of the top end of my range developed into a family amusement. In fact, my appetite was often presented as an act when there were other people eating with us:

> Last time Mummy made *galuptzi* Margie
> Rose ate five! – she might eat SIX
> tonight!

I revelled in the attention, and it provided me with an ongoing excuse for being a greedy little girl: Mama served up her amazing meals and I put them away with encouragement and gusto.

I can say with absolute honesty that in my earliest gormandising years I don't remember anyone telling me not to make a pig of myself. That was saved until I was old enough for the avoirdupois to have settled itself with a grateful sigh into all nooks and crannies, creating general convexity – when attempts to be rid of it became very hard yakka indeed. By then cuteness had faded and my hair had stopped being a mass of curls; and it was generally agreed that for me to be fat was not *normal* – for such was the general view, back then.

INT.	BACK BEDROOM	WINTER'S DAY

Mother is stuffing number four daughter, who is finishing off an apple, into her overcoat.

A button flies off.

Reality bites.

> MAMA
> (frustrated; infuriated)
> Just…LOOK AT yourself!
> I'm ashamed to have to be seen on the street with you!

Yes, I do have a memory like an elephant. For some things.

§

I don't mean to paint a picture of a miserable childhood: in fact it was a time of fierce family loyalty. Self-identification was as part of my family, and I was intolerant of those who didn't match the cleverness with which I was habitually surrounded. There was no deliberation on the part of our parents to set up this situation (at least, I don't believe so); but we grew up without mixing with others – except for the family who, by a quirk of fate, lived next-door: being equally intelligent and well-educated, they were totally acceptable.

My family was a kind of closed shop, into association with which only those of a certain level of intellectual capacity were admitted. We children had our school friends, of course; but our parents never socialised with theirs, and we assumed that was how all families operated.

I suspect that, really, my parents' only true common ground was their enormous intelligence; and because of it they put too much emphasis on their children's.

It's from within this very small circle that come all my memories from childhood. There are flashes, for instance, of us kids putting on concerts, for which we erected a kind of curtain across one end of the lounge room: I would stand in front of it and sing, vamping to fill for as long as was required while sisters changed costumes, props, etc., then emerged to perform.

All my childhood joy, I realise now, belongs to that period when I was young enough for my size not to matter.

I was truly happy as a little girl; when those I loved would brush my hair and kiss me.

§

Years later, old enough to understand the baggage that came with being fat, I found I could cloak my shame through force of personality.

My beloved father was one (unwitting) source of this, furnishing me with a lifelong covert: he made me understand that the whole world comprises merely multiples of one person; that it doesn't matter by how many others one is faced, because the sum total is actually just one individual replicated by <X> – *for everyone can only think inside his or her own head*. That's a powerful thing to pass on to a kid, and it became my bulwark against society. However, his intention in giving me this precious knowledge had nothing to do with protecting a vulnerable child, but merely with coaching a daughter about to lead a school debating team. I doubt he was even aware of the vulnerability: my girth had no significance for him. He did call me 'Fatty' occasionally, but so did everyone in the household, for my sisters had labelled me thus in my very early years, with no cruelty intended or felt: it was my identity.

But my mother's declared dislike of my outward

appearance must have made me resentful, I suppose; and eventually I started to counter the didactically-pronounced opinions she was in the habit of uttering, thus breaking the unspoken family rule of going along with her for the sake of peace. I have no idea of the source from which I derived the strength to do this, and it didn't come about until my mid-teens; but at some point I found that smiling and nodding, and then rolling my eyes when her back was turned, just wasn't enough for me. I took to the barricades. So it's probably understandable that she felt as she did: she must have seen me as not only fat and therefore unattractive, but also disagreeable and argumentative. I don't know if my mother ever considered the possibility that my being fat had made me who I was.

Her interpretation of the maternal rôle was to give us every material thing we needed – often at cost to her own ease or leisure – and I will readily admit she never stinted. She was a *cordon bleu* cook; a top-class dressmaker, who made most of our clothes; she cut our hair; she came up with everything we needed for our many and diverse school activities; she dragged us off to the family doctor to have our little arms jabbed with preventative needles for everything she read or heard about – oh, there are far too many things she did for us for me to remember them all! She went back to work in her middle years: with a University of Western Australia arts honours degree and a Dip. Ed. from her youth, she was a brilliant linguist and had mastery over several European modern and ancient tongues. She was awarded the *Ordre des Palmes Académiques* by the French government for services to that country's language*. She later taught it at our school: I studied under her for my last two years, and my much younger sister throughout her education, and she was a very good teacher indeed. My mother was without a doubt the cleverest and most able woman I have ever known.

But I had to find out about puberty by writing to someone

---

* she mostly *thought* in French!

without a name, a so-called nurse at a pharmaceutical company, whose address I found on the side of an empty tampon packet discarded by one of my older sisters. And I wasn't provided at home with a single 'fact of life'.

§

Father, during his leisure hours, was wont to swan about amongst his women – wife, daughters and always a live-in maid – being doted on and scattering the largesse of his formidable wit and charm. Not long after the youngest had become one of the company his audience shrank; for the eldest left to study how to become holy, the second-eldest to teach others how to study, and the third to study how to be married – the rates of success varying. After these departures, Dadda had only me and my little sister for audience, and I suspect the radical change in statistics was hard for him.

The first four of his children adored him (further on in time, the youngest was left on her own, at twelve, to be raised by parents then middle-aged – a whole different ball game, and one that drew her closer to our mother), so I don't know that I can say I loved him most. I liked to think I did. Many years later I decided that his favourite had been my sister Carole, the next one up from me, with whom I shared a bedroom until I was – oh, something like fourteen, I think. She was 'a problem' for most of her short life; and I wondered if he had perhaps filled that rôle in his own family. I don't believe any of us was ever told about his childhood, so that's only surmise.

It was I alone, however, who shared something with him: a particular – I can't think of the right word ... failing? weakness? Whatever it was, he discovered it and understood, doing his best to help me without exposing me to the common gaze (for I think I held up to my father an imperfect mirror). This can only be explained by relating a small anecdote from a period somewhere before my puberty.

The family was on the point of going out to dine at a local hotel – a most unusual event in the context of Mother's brilliant cooking. There's nothing in my memory about why we were going to do this; I know only that matching the strangeness of the imminent outing was what was happening to me – for I was feeling *really* weird.

INT.	LOUNGEROOM	DAY

The child sits on the floor, her back against one end of the big old couch, clutching her knees.

Those family members present are hooling about in normal chaotic fashion, with no one paying her any attention.

She is wondering if, when her head falls off, it will roll as far as the china cabinet…

Suddenly her father is beside her, one hand reaching down to her. She's *compos mentis* enough to realise that he wants to give her something.

FATHER

(softly, out of the side of his mouth)

Take this…

and when the brief transfer is effected she finds she has a tablet in her sweating palm.

She gets instantly to her feet and leaves the room.

I went to the kitchen, got a glass of water and swallowed the pill; and within quite a short time I felt perfectly normal again, all strangeness gone. No other family member had noticed anything.

Whatever that pill was, it must have been his own lifeline to the world, and he threw it to me.

INTO THIS HOUSE WE'RE BORN

Our parents loved us in their fashion. I have to write it like that, for I don't remember them actually saying as much – and yet I feel fairly sure that they did. There seems to be an enormous gap in my memory about all that kind of thing. I can only summon up images like that of myself at sixteen, swearing I would never, *ever* have children, for I might have a daughter who would think about me as I thought about my mother! – but I'm unable to remember the subject of the bitter disagreement of that day.

I do know they were good people and did their best to be good parents: Father was the provider, the senior partner in a Perth legal firm started by his own father; and Mother not only performed all the chores mentioned but assisted with the providing when she went back to teaching in her fifties. I suppose I'm saying I wish I could remember physical contact throughout this good parental care – hugs and kisses given and received as an ongoing part of life. Or that I could look back and see myself as a genuinely loved and wanted part of the family dynamic, rather than having that black hole in my memory with echoes of critical remarks about my size bouncing off its sides. Well: there must be many pleasant memories lurking, and presumably they'll come flooding back before long if what I hear about getting old is true ...

One thing I remember now, and very clearly, was parental drive for us all to achieve. After I gained a less than brilliant matriculation, they made it clear that I had failed them: I was not allowed to go to university, and my father decided on librarianship as a career for me. I'm obliged to admit that after initial brief raging I forgot about what might have been, and settled perfectly happily into my not outstanding career. For two years I had a great job at the public library in Fremantle, followed by another couple of years at the library of a teachers' college not far from where we lived, studying, the while, for exams – passing the first easily, failing the next and then not even sitting. Father attributed this to the boyfriend I by then had (whom he didn't like, so the attribution appealed). If he'd known that my boyfriend had decreed we were to be virgins when we wed but was screwing the wife of a married couple who were part of our group for almost the whole time we were together (as I and the young woman's husband discovered after a couple of years), 'didn't like' wouldn't have covered it.

Nevertheless, he arranged the purchase of my first car: it was a brand-new Mark I Mini – light green, and the pride of my life. I gave no thought to how long it would take to pay off the £763*: it was never my habit to think further ahead than about half an hour. But after several months I pranged it – not entirely my fault, I insist to this day – and split my face open, having to be carried off to hospital, fainting, by some Good Samaritans. My father, driving home from work that day, saw my Mini on the side of the road with its front caved in before anyone had contacted the family: when he eventually arrived in my hospital room he appeared to have aged ten years. This puzzled me a lot, for a while; then I simply forgot about it.

I'd been out of school and working for those four years when he decided to send me away to earn my living in 'the Eastern States': Mama and I had been growing daily more irascible with each other, so irresistible logic says she would've egged him on in taking this fairly draconian step. I'd shown that I wasn't going to be successful at the less interesting aspects of librarianship, and he remained deeply worried about the cause of my accident, believing it associated with my boyfriend. As well, his own poor health meant he needed peace and quiet; and there was parental consensus that all these problems would be solved by the simple expedient of locating Margie Rose somewhere else.

But in spite of breaking up with the boyfriend and facing

---

* this figure popped straight into my head, so it's probably correct

the ongoing difficulty of living with Mother, I had no wish to go: I fought my eviction with everything I had.

It wasn't enough.

Some time after the big party for my twenty-first I was packed off, wanting only to continue living in the loved house in which I'd spent all but my first two years – though there was an undeniably attractive element in getting away from Mother (on both sides, to be sure).

I remember going about the house and the huge garden, taking photos – which I still have – and I remember saying goodbye to it.

There's nothing of the trip to Sydney: it's as if I were beamed across.

The following decade was successful, career-wise: I went without hiccup from job to job, never for a moment considering the possibility of there being none to replace that which I'd just left, nor giving any thought to my future.

But in spite of a succession of entertaining occupations, I was not happy. The unpredictable emotional state of my childhood was still very much in play – it had begun to take over my life, reaching a point where the people I mixed with were sometimes not much more than a distraction from things going on in my brain. I was labouring under killing pressure caused by understanding *nothing* of what was happening to me: it felt as if someone had placed a huge weight on my breast and gone away, leaving me to try to get it off, alone. And although I didn't understand it for a long, long time, that was more or less what had occurred.

A few years later, when I was back home on holidays, Dadda confirmed that he had long since realised I had problems. He told me that he himself had not had a day in his life without anxiety: he'd had to work out how to control and live with it. I never learned anything more – not of his anxiety's origins, nor of its form. He had bared himself to me as much as he was able. He urged me to stay in contact with a good doctor. I told him I had just such a one, whom I saw fairly regularly; and thus he could feel a little less stressed about what his genes had helped create.

He gave no sign of recognising the contradiction in understanding my emotional state while sending me away from my home. I suppose it meant that he didn't fully comprehend my passionate attachment either to himself or to it.

I have no difficulty now in accepting that his number one priority was, and had to be, doing whatever it took to stay sane.

§

When he died I hadn't seen my father for over a year; and our last meeting had not been a happy one. The radio was playing The Doors' 'Riders on the Storm' as I pottered about my flat one evening (St Kilda, in Barkly Street, down past Inkerman – not the most salubrious of areas at the beginning of the '70s), when he turned up unexpectedly. He'd come alone to Melbourne for a work-related visit to a brother who was also at the bar, and that solo trip was a very, very unusual thing for him to have undertaken.

I can remember no more of our meeting than its general tenor.

It's a fact that I started out truly happy to see him; but I believe our short time together ended with my becoming resentful – always the way with young women who see themselves as grown-up and needing no parental oversight. For he made it clear that he didn't like the flat, didn't like me living on my own, didn't like what he saw as a threatening environment. And he was worried about me in general: what was I doing with my life?

There was in fact real reason for parental anxiety: I lived in a charmless, not at all secure ground-floor flat (with double bed) in a most unappealing area, alone. And did I have a single idea regarding my future? – not even the beginning of one.

Later, he went out into the wet St Kilda night having done his best to make contact with the real me. But Dadda no longer knew who he himself really was: Catholicism, faith of his fathers, was an on-again off-again affair – he searched but didn't find, I think. There had been an attempt by each to reach the other, but it had not been done well, not by either of us.

I watched him walk away on the dark street, and in my head Jim Morrison was still singing.

I believe I managed to keep my father from understanding that my anxieties had grown, changed direction and turned into something much more serious. I have always hoped so.

ONSET OF WINTER

My period of banishment had started, as I said, in Sydney, where Jo was living while tutoring at a Sydney University college. She was yanked rudely out of a lovely but small Rose Bay unit to find a place for us to share – a furnished flat in Edgecliff, notable only for the fact that within a few weeks of our arrival, burglars cleaned us out.

Ah, life in a big city.

The job my father had arranged for me had not even lasted a day, because the publishing company was dissolved at much the same hour as my first lunchbreak; and I'd been out selling cookbooks in factories along O'Riordan Street to bring in some cash (a fact my parents were never to know). Thus did the burglary make a deeper impression than it might otherwise have done: Sydney Was Against Me, I felt.

So with something akin to planning, I fronted up to the ABC's then HO on the corner of William and Forbes and applied for a job as a temporary typist. As soon as I was confirmed as an employee I had myself transferred down to Melbourne, waving goodbye to Jo in Edgecliff without a second thought. I knew a bit of that city, because as kids we'd frequently been sent across from Perth during our long school holidays, numbed within thumping old propjet Electras, to stay in Brighton with the family of one of my father's brothers.

Once in Melbourne, I was posted to the ABC's Programmes Department, where I had three bosses who were intelligent, amusing and excellent at their jobs, as well as kind and helpful to a raw kid from the sticks. In a very short time, one arranged for me to be given an audition as a radio announcer with one of Melbourne's commercial stations; but I was unable to read the ads with anything approaching the required sincerity – the first time impatient intolerance was a career downfall for me, and I wish I could say I learned from it. Another then sent me off to the head of the ABC's

Education Department, who gave me a job as a TV script assistant and assigned me to the young man who was to be my producer.

Don was also amusing, intelligent, happy, friendly and skilled; and, as well, gay: we became fast friends, and spent all our time together during the working week.

§

After a shortish period in a furnished room in Middle Brighton, I'd started sharing a flat in Toorak with two other young women: my roommate was a tall, willowy blonde with glasses – extraordinarily beautiful and extraordinarily sexually active, as the photos she delighted in showing us indicated beyond any doubt. It was the first time I'd seen anything like that; and I don't know that I've ever seen anything like it again – certainly not featuring a face (for occasionally one was to be espied) that I knew. It disturbed me greatly. But Diana never made any attempt to entice either Marie or me into her circle or even to discuss it: she just came home waving her photos around with the pride born of achievement.

I got rid of my virginity while living there in Illawarra Crescent, with a visiting (married) ABC journo who was a self-styled professional at the deflowering game; and later I was angry with myself for having undertaken this rite of passage with such a pathetic shit. Possibly with payback as motivation, I very soon became one of those girls who went out in search of a screw, just as did the young men my age. It became a challenge to mark up at least as many hits on my scoreboard as did those of the svelte girls comprising my peer group – so there's motivation for you, I suppose.

It was towards the end of my living there that I first started evincing a strange physical symptom of ... *something*: I would suddenly, in the middle of doing anything at all, find that my breath had been snatched away, and it was very difficult getting it back. I had to go somewhere quiet and simply try to breathe. Of course, I always succeeded; but it was very weird, very inexplicable and very, very frightening. I had a local GP who took it seriously; but no GP had knowledge of symptoms like this, not back in those days. So I would visit him to report yet another attack, and we would sit looking at each other helplessly.

Eventually he sent me to a well-known psychiatrist, who booked me in to an overnight hospital in Kew a couple of times, popping me LSD: and that was as weird as the problem and somewhat less effective than talking with my GP. I lay in a very small room on a very small bed – overlapping it uncomfortably on the non-wall edge, I can still recall – and waited for Insight. Of this there remains only a very small selection of brief family scenes – such as that of my eldest sister, a terrific pianist, charging Beethovenishly up and down the keyboard of the baby grand we once had. These were dutifully delivered to the trendy psychiatrist as he wandered throughout the night between dreamers, eliciting what we all had to tell him; but I don't think my ramblings proved of any analytical value.

There's nothing in my memory even faintly resembling an outcome to this very '70s activity, and I continued along my troubled path.

§

I went home for the festive season. My parents were delighted that I'd become an ABC employee: they saw it as a respectable career. I can't say they were wrong, but nevertheless I begged my father to let me stay home. He pointed out I would never get a position anything like that in Perth, so I was to return at the end of my holiday.

A week or so later there was another of those breath-loss instances, right in the middle of dinner, resulting in the family psychiatrist's being summoned[*]. Peter consigned me

---

[*] that we had one says a fair bit

to hospital under a drug regimen of I know not what; and there I remained, eating a great deal and bored shitless. He eventually pronounced that I was suffering from guilt because of neglecting my religion, having asked me loaded questions and interpreted my responses to suit his Catholic hypotheses. He couldn't have been more wrong: there hadn't been a religious sentiment in my head since my final school year caused me to ask myself – and answer – a few pertinent questions on this topic. But he wanted a diagnosis that would fit my parents' mores: what they made of it, I never heard. Psychiatric intervention, of which this second instance would not be the last, never helped me in the slightest.

After my totally wasted holiday I dutifully went back to Melbourne and to the ABC, where I had a brief but torrid affair with a (married) junior executive and fell pregnant. I had an abortion. He found himself able to be entirely unaware of any of it.

Never did the faintest feeling of guilt assail me on this topic: religious scruples didn't enter the frame; I had no belief in sentience before birth; and it was a fact that any baby of mine would know such confusion and misery as to wish never to have been born. But what terrified me about even the concept of giving birth was my own secondary rôle in the process: although I didn't yet have any understanding of it, the need to be in total control of everything around me was paramount. Measured against that, nothing else even entered the frame.

Back at work, my producer had a huge row with his partner and went home to Brisbane. He was shattered by the breakdown of his relationship and I was shattered by the loss of ours. I was assigned another producer: he was large and boisterous and I didn't respect his intelligence. I moved on.

When the parents eventually discovered that I'd taken a job as the sole employee – a kind of office manager, I suppose – within the Monash University Union's student newspaper, *Lot's Wife*, and abandoned my promising career, they were utterly appalled. Not even my starting a part-time undergraduate degree, a perk of the job, brought them 'round, in spite of my doing well in first year.

One day, to my huge surprise, the boyfriend I'd had since starting at *Lot's Wife* – he'd recently graduated – ended our relationship. There was no other woman, just a need to be without me. Neither of us knew what had gone awry. I understood how difficult it had been for him to do this and we parted without enmity, but there seemed no point continuing on there with all the no-longer-current associations. When I left *Lot's Wife* my studies were summarily brought to a halt, and my brain returned to its normal, non–intellectually stimulated state.

Jo, erstwhile flatmate/carer, got married during this period, which was when she and her husband settled in Melbourne; so I wasn't without a reference point in disturbing times, and I turned to her often.

§

I moved on to a very successful pop music newspaper called *Go-Set* – working on the financial side, dealing with the advertising and handling first-stage bookkeeping. The staff were amazing and amusing, and all greatly tickled by my utter lack of sophistication: they were the nearest thing to total cool I'd ever come across, and probably still are. My formally trained accountant boss Geoffrey had just Discovered Life, at forty, and was busy throwing himself into it with abandon: he introduced me to dope while he was briefly a lodger in my tiny Carlton semi (but we were never more than friends).

Go-Set brought me many adventures and interesting times, and I met lots of people in the entertainment industry whose names resound still and attended some notable industry events, one being the first pop festival ever held in Oz, in Ourimbah (what a *blast!* – you only got to see Billy

Thorpe doing 'Season of the Witch' like that one time). I can remember many a weekend afternoon spent with friends from a particular pop group, all of us stoned and wandering around Carlton eating sugared breakfast cereal from the packet; and many an evening at my place when, straight, we played poker for sums far too large. But at work clever Geoffrey taught me elements of bookkeeping that stood me in good stead later, so these fun years were not a total waste of time.

In terms of men, however, they were: I had resumed my predatory ways, with a good degree of success. But in a couple of years I found myself pregnant again, this time to a (married) policeman; and he, too, found himself able to be entirely unaware of what transpired when I had another abortion. Looking back, I can only think how lucky we were, we young girls of those years, to be spared HIV/AIDS: I was a complete fool – a completely *screwed-up* fool – for getting myself pregnant twice; but if I'd been born not all that many years later, it's a penny to a quid I would've found myself in far deeper shit.

How lucky I was, as well, to have my sister's help: I've often wondered what would have become of me during those lost years had Jo not been there for me ...

§

Around this time I learned that my parents had sold our home, buying another in the same suburb but several blocks inland from the river that formed the rear boundary to the property, and to which I felt a kind of umbilical attachment. I wasn't outraged because no one had seen fit to mention this to me in advance, for that was not how things were done in our family: I was, simply, stunned with sorrow.

Not much later I found out that the purchasers had immediately razed the house. To my savage satisfaction, their architect had botched his plans for their new dwelling, so that they had to live in our old garage for a long while. I could laugh about that; but I was absolutely shattered that my home no longer existed.

From the time I learned what had happened, I've never again been anywhere near where I grew up. In my head our house still exists; and there is not a single vulgar *nouveau riche* 'mansion' to be seen anywhere in Victoria Avenue.

§

Eventually the *Go-Set* phenomenon started to wane and a staff cull loomed. Being merely a cash wrangler I'd be at the front of that; so I didn't hang about and, using the recently inculcated bookkeeping skills, went to work in GTV9's Accounts. While within the Channel 9 precincts I was referred by a kind Garry Stewart – one of the very few in television management never to be madly important in his own eyes – to Crawford Productions.

I got a job at Crawfords by mistake: the personnel manager had fallen in love with a new range of trendy terminology without ascertaining all the meanings, and willingly employed me as what he had just renamed a 'Script Assistant' because my CV showed I'd been there and done that. In fact, what he hired me to do was continuity on film crew; and the relationship between the duties of that job and of an ABC TV script assistant was ... well, the word 'tenuous' springs to mind. Perhaps 'non-existent'? – no: there is a common use of stopwatch. Oh, and *scripts*!

No worries: I was a fast learner back then, happily for us both. Continuity was a far more difficult and exacting job than it has become since the introduction of the video split[*] and the delegation to Wardrobe and Props of responsibility for their own continuity. In the early '70s we who held the title did the lot, and all from memory. Challenging? – you can believe it. Stimulating? – indescribably. And I was teamed up

---

[*] a small video camera providing immediate playback of anything the film camera shoots – now made virtually redundant by the industry's acceptance of digital

with a young director who was to me very like the brother I'd never had. As well, I admired Ian Crawford enormously, having first encountered his intelligence when instructed in a programming aid he'd devised for scheduling TV shooting days: it was complex but incredibly pertinent to the task at hand, and so was Ian. I became devoted to him, and he put up with it.

These seemed happy and fulfilled years: in my usual way, I saw no path leading off into the distance, but simply enjoyed the one I was treading. I had a big bear of a friend on the lighting crew, known as The Black Bastard, and spent a lot of time with his extended Italian family. As well, I reintroduced my erstwhile practice of poker; and crew members and selected actors spent many an evening *chez moi* at this disreputable occupation, amidst much laughter (and, this time, small change).

But my director and his lady decided to leave Oz to move to the UK. To say that I was upset is to put it mildly: I was shaken to the core by losing my rôle as his offsider. New directors followed, in descending order of ability and character, and I became less tolerant as the procession passed.

Before long The Black Bastard and his lady went – somewhere: I don't remember where. Maybe Trieste, his home town. But in any event he, too, was gone.

And then my father died.

I went home for the funeral and found myself the last to join the queue of daughters unable to grieve because Mother was the only one allowed to do that: we all had to rally around and support her, while so very much in need of support ourselves.

IN THE COLD DARK

I came back to Crawfords seeking a way out of the chaos of my life; but the only thing that changed was that I turned into a human dynamo, sexually speaking. I was even screwing some visiting actors – considered totally off-limits by all crew members. Finally, I had a very public row with Ian in a TV studio control room, offending him. To remain there without being in his good books was impossible (he never knew he'd been cast in the rôle of father substitute), so I walked away from the company, my self-esteem in tatters.

For several months I freelanced, on one occasion landing a job unit managing a small film crew travelling around Queensland with a well-known big band, making a doco for the band's corporate sponsor. These were strange weeks: the Sound Recordist and I and half the band spent the entire time ripped off our heads. I have no idea how I managed the various responsibilities of unit manager – I must have been flying on autopilot. I was sleeping with one of the guitarists because he was quite amusing, and I picked up an STI from him – the *shit!* – in Cairns spending many long hours in pain and anxiety, not having a clue as to the cause. Eventually a local GP was found, I was carted off to him by someone (no idea who) and all was fixed, beginning with a very large and very painful hypodermic. And served me right.

Late one night the entourage was moving on to another town in the band's bus, travelling unlit roads through endless cane fields. I was listening to Elton John's 'Rocket Man', and had got up from my seat to stand at the front of the bus, looking out as the black ribbon unrolled. There in the dark, the slide guitar riff wailing and Elton singing that it was gonna be a long, long time, deep loneliness looked back in at me. I shivered uncontrollably. Almost immediately, one of the band members stepped up silently behind me, put his tracksuit jacket around my shoulders and returned to his seat. A thoughtful action like that was typical of him: he was a genuinely nice man. It followed, then, that not long after he got home he died suddenly of a brain haemorrhage – no rare occurrence among front line brass. His funeral at the Rookwood Crematorium was hideous: some children fainted; there was a tide of unhappiness washing through the chapel and sucking at our feet.

I could go to his funeral because I was by then back living in Sydney, working once more at the ABC – same job, but in the Music Department. A couple of months had passed unmemorably after I returned to Melbourne from the tour; then one horrible morning I'd found one of my two beautiful moggies mysteriously dead on the lawn outside my flat. I'd admitted defeat, given away the other cat and gone back to Sydney to have another go.

It's very strange, and very contradictory in terms of the bulk of my emotional problems: but the fact is that even now I can recall the need driving me to explore streets I'd never seen.

§

Things in Sydney seemed OK, initially: a couple very vaguely related to me – the man the ex-husband of a cousin (but no friend) of mine, and the woman to become someone close and loved – asked me to move into their apartment in Neutral Bay to housekeep for him while she went back to England for a family funeral. To assist me with shopping and so forth, he took back from his ex a Mini station wagon he'd lent her in case her charity work required it (it didn't) and bestowed it upon me, to my absolute delight: such pleasure, *and* a Mini!

But then he went interstate on business, and the moment his back was turned the ex threw me out: he had promised the children they could have a holiday in his apartment, she said. I was on the street. With almost no money, I ended up in a horrible kind of boarding house, growing hourly more distressed from living cheek by jowl with people who were strangers in every sense of the word. It was a time of suspended reality, and I was living at several removes.

Upon his return I was immediately reinstated; but my emotional state was dire. I found work somehow, enabling me to get my own digs; and I lived there in Kurraba Road for some months, during which period I think I must have become very like my ex-flatmate Diana and her gang (though my activities were unaccompanied by photographs). Whatever was wrong with me was getting worse, and I'd decided the best way of dealing with it was to be in the company of people who actively sought mine. These were, ninety-nine per cent of the time, men. Where they came from, I have no idea: I suspect I might as well have had emblazoned across my forehead *I'M UP FOR IT*. Men found me, that's all I can say; and I spent a large proportion of my time horizontal.

My major problem was that when on my feet I couldn't manage to actually *go* anywhere: a pendulum in my brain had swung 180°, and from seeking strange streets I was now completely unable to cope with being anywhere I didn't know. I would visit a good friend, the wife of the bass guitarist from the band I'd toured with, and listen with something like horrified awe as her older daughter, still a little girl, spoke of going with mates to a new beach up the coast. It had become incomprehensible to me, as if being discussed in Sanskrit, the concept of travelling strange roads, among unknown houses, to an unfamiliar destination.

I'd drive back to the North Shore from Colleen's flat through the Cahill Expressway tunnel, and feel tension ease with the brightness of the lights, and the firm belief that if I absolutely had to stop there would be people who would also stop, and help me. The unfounded – and, happily, untested – expectation of there being complete strangers around to whom I could turn for help became a frequently used prop during my gradual disintegration.

It was Colleen who gave me three brothers from a litter of tabby kittens, to whom, with great joy, I gave all the love I couldn't give anyone else. But then some *bitches* living in the flat above mine, who had often admired the palest-striped of the trio, moved out one morning around five, taking him with them.

Genuine crisis point. I decided to 'go home': perhaps Mother might even pull her weight and make up for ... well, for history.

§

Back in Perth, it transpired that Mama was fully occupied with her new flat and enforced change in lifestyle, and unable to deal with me or my problems. The latter had coordinated themselves into one; and I have a clear memory of the moment of coalescence.

A friend from my schooldays, now married, had invited me to spend a few days with them – a stay I was happy to undertake. I was there having a shower one morning when something I think I had dreamed came back to claim my head.

It was deep night. I was on a waterway, its high, greenery-covered banks close by, on a jetty that was part of some kind of marina. There were mesh fences, with security padlocks on the gates; and a few lights on very tall poles casting narrow beams down onto the water. No one was there: the stillness and the silence were absolute. It was a reprise of that night on the band's bus, but now I comprehended that I was utterly, fundamentally alone; and as I stood transfixed under the water there came absolute conviction that it would always be so.

I don't remember anything of leaving Katherine's house; but at some point I was back in my own place, crouched on a chair. Terror was there with me, and from then on it had free run of the place, coming and going at will.

What was to be diagnosed as clinical depression found me under the care of an excrescence of a psychiatrist attached to Royal Perth, who was delighted to be able to experiment with the antidepressant *du jour* ... Quaalude? – seems to ring a bell. He was a patronising and irresponsible prick. I should admit, though, that the pills he so readily administered did enable me to fool people into thinking I was a participant in things going on around me, even to the point of holding down an office job.

But that brought its own testing times, as from my strange little rented house in Bicton (very close to the animal quarantine station and thus remembered mostly for the *endless* howling of bored dogs) I had to catch a bus to get to the office; and the bus route had one extremely long hop that tried me to the utmost. I could cope with public transport only if able to leave it at will; so the lengthy stretch along Melville Parade in South Perth, uninterrupted by a single bus stop, was almost intolerable. My palms would have been made to bleed by my fingernails, if I'd had any. Then, as I couldn't hack these daily *Wages of Fear* rides, I threw in the towel and the Bicton house, renting instead a flat near my mother's! – how loud, I think now, must have been my silent cry for help.

In an attempt to maintain a semblance of self-respect, I listed my CV with PIFT, WA's only film industry–related body, hidden away down in Fremantle, and huddled with my moggies within this flat – awaiting anything or nothing and occasionally gracing the hospital shrink with my presence for want of anything else to do.

It's impossible to guess where the uninspired and unvarying treatment he doled out would have got me, had nothing intervened.

HERE COMES THE SUN

INT.	PERTH PRODUCTION OFFICE	DAY

WIDE SHOT: various members of a film crew, lounging
about a big table waiting for a pre-production meeting
and looking like an assortment of extras from Central
Casting. A calendar somewhere shows it to be late 1974.

CUT TO: a door opening. She arrives.

She's a local resident, sort of; whereas, with the
exception of the Camera Assistant, they have all come
from Sydney.

She looks at them.

They look at her.

I hadn't, prior to that moment, come across a more varied
collection of headgear, facial hair, t-shirts and footwear – not
in all my days. Mind you, my own presentation was not a lot
different, now I come to think of it: a floor-length kaftan was
about my normal gear, back then. But I'm pretty sure I was
wearing shoes of some kind – at least sandals, surely?! – for
the meeting.

(cont'd)

M.R.
(nervous as always when amongst
strangers, but hiding it)

Is one of you Pat Clayton?

ATTRACTIVE BEARDED MAN
(in a beautiful, deep voice)

He hasn't turned up yet.

But here's his name on a stand: we could
start the meeting with that…

He positions the little object carefully at the head of the table and adopts an attitude of rapt attention – immediately aped with glee by the rest of the crew.

In fact, we all had to wait a bit for Pat the Production Manager; and I can't remember if I spent any more of that time talking to this delightful man who'd made everyone laugh. But I do know that by the time the meeting was underway, I'd ascertained he was Stills Photographer, Charles Stringer, and he was called Chic (but I had no idea what a stills photographer did on a film crew!).

He was very funny; and, as well, he was kind, helpful and astonishingly knowledgeable about – well, everything. Within a couple of days I'd found him unable to be stumped on anything I could come up with; but he never, ever pretended to knowledge if he didn't have it.

He really was *awfully* attractive ...

I was there as Continuity, of course; inexperienced on a full-sized feature film crew but raring to get up to speed. It was a stressful job, and my neuroses didn't furnish me with the most relevant background, but Chic stopped me from biting my nails within three days.

INT.	FILMING LOCATION	DAY

C.S.
(amused)

Do you have any idea how revolting that habit is?

M.R.
(whipping fingers from mouth)

What habit?!

We were both smokers then, and he would buy my cigarettes without any request from me when he bought his packet of Drum (I was to quit in another couple of years, but he not till he was close to fifty). I remember being overwhelmed by his kindness, but I did nothing more than thank him: a man's being kind as well as funny was not within my sphere, and I wasn't sure how to handle it.

He helped me with my job. He'd been in the industry for a fairly short time, though he was already a top stillsman, having worked on several features; and he'd noted with great interest many of the duties of Continuity. The rest of the crew gave me help too, but often with some irritation that it was needed: Chic gave me ready answers when he could, and used logic when he couldn't, and didn't mock me. And he made me laugh OFTEN – sometimes after the event, as well ...

he taught me how to do this, later!

It took me a matter of days to recognise that my prime motivation had become to get into his pants. He met *all* my criteria: how was this possible?!

Of course he was married: no way a man like that could've escaped the bonds or would have wanted to. But he showed none of the usual signs – the self-satisfaction, the preening, the air of mutual complicity – by which I, the expert, could so easily identify the adventuring married man of the '70s. Thus I felt momentary qualms, even after a crew member who knew him had told me that his marriage seemed one of habit rather than of enjoyment; but they were singularly transient, those qualms. Having weighed up the matter, I opted for putting in whatever hard yards might be required.

None were: by the second week of filming we had become, as used to be said, an item.

INT.   CREW HOTEL   EARLY

WIDE SHOT: assembly of unshaven men and snaggle-haired women, of assorted ages and all looking as if they haven't had enough sleep; for such is – or was then, anyway – the way with film crews.

They are sitting about in attitudes of less than total attention, but are in fact heeding the words of the First – he is shaven – who addresses them while eating a bun and perusing a schedule (chances are he can pat his head and rub his tummy at the same time).

He has lowered his paperwork to survey them over the top of it, grumpily.

                    FIRST ASSISTANT
          (perfectly clearly, although his mouth
          is full of bun)

     OK, you lot… The location is suddenly
     not available for today. The bloody
     council has changed its bloody mind
     again, so Terry and I will have to find
     another one.

     You can stand down till called.

     Don't leave town.

With a snap of his jaws he demolishes the last of his bun
while tossing the overtaken-by-events schedule into a
nearby bin-this bloke is a natural!

C.S.

(unimpressed; to M.R.)

Wanna come and have a cuppa with me?-I
bought some much better teabags than the
hotel gives us.

Her bland expression would fool anyone.

M.R.

(careless)

Nice idea: I've been wondering what the
crew's rooms are like…

I know me: there would've been a variety of scenarios, all
equally shifty, running through my head as we wandered off
in amity towards the lift.

INT.	CREW HOTEL BEDROOM	NOON

From inside looking through lacy curtains to outside
world, where the day is doing what days do. PAN OFF
window with SLOW TILT DOWN to bed.

C.S.

(reaching for watch on bedside table)

Whaa-?!

(looks again, disbelieving)

Give me strength!-we've been fucking
for *four hours*!

It can be seen that this mysterious passage of time astonishes and delights him.

                    M.R.
          My, how time flies!, etcetera.

She stretches in luxurious idleness.

                    M.R.
          Well, it looks like we won't be shooting
          today, so…

CUT TO BLACK.

_____

SHALL WE ...?

INT.	BEDROOM	VERY EARLY

Flashforward to mid-1977.

The sun has risen, but the pair is sound asleep in bed; he is in an old white t-shirt, she in nothing at all (it *fits* so well).

A sound of timid door-knocking is heard in the background.

M.R.

> (gaga)

Mhuhh...?

C.S.

> (sitting up: instant cognition)

You go: if I do, he might start to behave aggressively.

M.R.

> (coming to and grumpy)

You *know* him?! So who is this dickhead who comes and knocks on the door at –

Peers myopically at bedside alarm clock...

M.R.

> – six o-bloody-clock on a fucking Saturday morning?!

C.S.

> (too excited to protest about foul language, nudges her forcefully)

Go on, get out of bed: our fate awaits!

He was right to be excited because, as he had instantly divined, it was the process server come to serve him with The Divorce Papers.

Lousie*, it seems, had grown tired of being rid of her spouse while not having *all* the joys of her newly freed-up state; so she'd decided to put herself in the position of accepting an offer from Mr Someone-Else, were he to make an appearance. And fair enough, too!

In joyous frame of mind, we invited the process server in for a cuppa. He dithered, but eventually decided he was not being lured inside by a devious husband wanting payback. He drank many cups of tea and proved garrulous on all topics. We had to push him out, eventually, as he showed signs of expecting to share our breakfast. And anyway, I was sick of clutching my brunch coat to me (the buttons had long since gone), having no wish to share my extreme generosity of pinkness.

INT.	HALLWAY	EARLY

The wire door has just closed behind the process server, whose diminishing voice can be heard travelling through a range of platitudes as he disappears gradually down the front path. And then there is peace.

The sun streams in, laying a speckled trail of gold down the hallway as they make their way back to the kitchen.

<u>C.S.</u>
(idly, but looking at her sidelong)
So…shall we get married?

She's hit for six.

---

* OKOK, that wasn't actually her name: we were great fans of Denys Parsons' silly typos humour about the Shrdlu family

42

OH!

Collects herself rapidly.

                    M.R.
    You're not sick of it, after thirteen
    years…?

    I know you said the last eight were like
    living in a boarding house with someone
    you know quite well, but…

She trails off for fear of becoming persuasive.

                    C.S.
        (loftily)
    Nup. It'd be entirely different.

                    M.R.
        (offhand)
    Well…why not then?!

They giggle happily, and postpone breakfast in lieu of a
spot of anteconnubial bliss.

---

                    §

When the shoot finished, Chic had reluctantly gone back
to Sydney: he couldn't just not return to Lousie and/or his
career, but he was awfully unhappy to leave me.

I lasted in Perth about a week before deciding that I
couldn't stand it there another day, so I made arrangements
to return once more to Melbourne, where there were people
I knew and concomitant possibility of re-employment. I took
the red-eye special on a night of strangeness, over-sedated in

order to be got onto the aircraft; for not only had I become absolutely terrified of flying since a frightful landing some years previously, but my emotional problems were showing signs of resurfacing.

From Tulla I made my way at an ungodly hour to South Yarra where dwelt the old Goanna, my dear friend from Crawfords days, ostensibly to discuss resettlement. But I realised as we talked that I'd already decided to go back to Sydney – *such* a surprise ...

I did so that very night, by train because I'd exhausted the supply of Valium; and upon arrival next morning threw myself on the mercy of my vaguely relateds, who gave every sign of being pleased to see me. I phoned Chic. He left the photographic studio more or less instantly and, having collected me, drove us to a forest somewhere where we did our best to make up for lost time. This was not fearfully comfortable, as he had a small Suzuki 4WD (a 'Sierra', I think it was: its interior did indeed feel a bit like a mountain range).

We became man and mistress: there was a complete absence of animosity – or anything else at all – between Chic and his wife, but he just couldn't bring himself to walk out on her, not in that early period. But when I had work of some duration, enabling me to cease sponging off my friends and get my own accommodation, he found the determination and did it. And he moved in.

Lousie, it transpired, had zero problems with it all; and it did leave her, post-divorce, with just about everything Chic owned, for he had no stomach for divvying up.

§

We got on as cohabitants like a house on fire from the very start, and that's the truth.

I'd lived solo for almost the whole decade in Melbourne because I really preferred being on my own: to me, sharing meant having people underfoot who do unspeakable things, like ... oh ... wanting to play music that I don't like, or chatting while watching telly – obviously intolerable! Whereas Chic had been married to Lousie for thirteen years; and although they never quarrelled because they weren't interested enough, that was still living with someone.

So you might think that two more disparate lifestyles could scarcely be imagined; but their conjoining brought perfect harmony. From the moment he walked into my flat and put down his car keys in the realisation he would not be picking them up again to go home, we were a settled pair. It was as if we'd always been together. As if we already knew each other inside out from years shared.

And one memorable evening, when he was quite unable to identify something I'd cooked, he decided to take over in the kitchen. O frabjous day! – I no longer had to even approach the stove! I could never have been described as a cook, for Mother's brilliance had not stretched to patiently teaching her daughters: she was one of those 'Oh, for heaven's sake! – here, give it to me: *I'll* do it!' instructors. I produced meals with painful attention to cookbook directions, and didn't enjoy it.

Chic, having been brought up the fourth of four boys in a household of engineers, hadn't exactly wrested the kitchen spoon from his ma during his youth; and he hadn't been the cook when married to Lousie. But he proved instantly to be a natural! He cooked fabulous food – yummy and good: Italian, mostly, with liberal application of extra virgin olive oil. This meant I was unlikely to get any thinner; but he couldn't care less – although he did adjure me, quite often, as follows:

INT.	DINING ROOM	NIGHT

He comes around from the kitchenette to put a plate in front of her. CLOSE-UP on a steaming, delicious-looking serving of pasta, somewhat heaped.

He stands back from this delectable delivery, saying tentatively:

Her face reflects joy (and greed).

                    M.R.
            (lying unhesitatingly)
        Nono! – of course not!

and she lifts the first mouthful with reverence.

   Truth to tell, I didn't know how not to be fat; there's never been a moment in my life when I wasn't self-conscious about my weight. To put out of my mind the criticism and teasing from childhood has always been beyond me, for the lessons society teaches a child early are wholly absorbed.

   Yet the fat thing provided the most enormous contradiction of my life. For when Chic told me that he loved me, I accepted it – without protesting and without turning it into a joke. Amazing…!

   I look back over all those years, reflecting how extraordinary it was that I took his honesty on board and put all my trust in him at the outset of our relationship, thereby doing away with paranoid dithering and time wasting during its development.

   He must also, and from the same point, have wanted it to endure. I believe this was because I brought him something he deeply needed – to look after another person; and my interests and tastes were so astonishingly similar to his …

   It may well have been that he saw through my facade from day one; for I was, quite unknown to myself, simply longing to be looked after. And whether or not he'd set out on a quest for a grail, there it was, to his hand.

That we met at that moment, both in such dire need (and, as it transpired, specifically of *the other*), can be put down to – I know not what.

I have my doubts about kismet.

FRIENDS

INT.	POSH FLAT	NIGHT

Having briefly travelled to the future, we're now back in 1975, in a very up-market apartment in Neutral Bay.

She is bringing C.S. for the first time into the fold of friends who are very much part of the corporate world.

She wonders how he will react to the husband's rather alarming ability to consume alcohol.

ERICA
(adding the mayonnaise she's just made
to the splendidly laid table)

So what time did you tell him to—

She's interrupted by the sound of a doorbell.

M.R.
(over shoulder halfway to apartment
door)

Has Kit gone into hiding?

ERICA

No: he's getting changed. He came home
early from work specially–after all, it
IS only seven-thirty…

M.R. has a momentary image of Kit's emerging in a dinner suit and she's briefly anxious; but her expression changes to plain besottedness as she opens the door.

M.R.

Hello, Stringer, my angel: alas that
you're not wearing a tuxedo.

(grins teasingly)

C.S.

(unfazed)

I was going to. But then I thought, why
bother?

And also, I don't have one.

They can't resist a bit of a smooch, but Erica clears her
throat behind them so they vacate the foyer and move into
the living room.

M.R.

(happily)

This is Chic, Elly: Stringer, here's my
friend Eri-

A very large man distinguished by a silk cravat[*] joins the
little group, and holds out his large hand to C.S..

KCG

(very urbane-his trademark)

Erica Valerie March Game, my wife. How
do you do?-I'm Kit Game.

He was A Presence in his day, Kit Conley Game – a man of
great intellect with a matching taste for the good life; and I
told you a little of him, earlier (for this pair comprises my
'vaguely relateds'). So, having seen him in action many times,
I sat back to see how Chic met the challenge.

This he did by totally nullifying it: he was simply,
disarmingly, himself.

Since this could only reveal his quite extraordinary
breadth of general knowledge, as evinced when Kit subtly
attempted to test his capacity on any unfamiliar topic, and
the way in which he turned to logic if the topic was too

---

* Kit firmly believed the world should keep up with him, and not vice versa

49

unfamiliar, combined with an unassuming niceness and an impressive wine palate, our host was completely won over well before the end of Erica's knockout meal. And although Chic was unable – not to mention unwilling – to go drink for drink with him, Kit had never found anyone who could; so he was quite prepared, with his usual generosity, to overlook this sin of omission.

Erica's cooking was unimpeachable, and impressed Chic greatly, as he told her more than once. They discussed the food and its preparation often while we were at the table; and it was probably this meal that sowed in him the so-very-fertile seeds of culinary interest and activity.

The evening found me beside myself with joy on realising that he bowled over other people on first meeting, too.

§

If you're wondering about the reason for my using his family name to address him, there really isn't one. I think it began back on film crew when we first met: on one never-to-be-forgotten occasion, I called him 'Chuck' rather than 'Chic', and nearly died of shame when the misnomer left my lips – I squirmed with embarrassment for hours, and remember clearly *praying* he would be able to bring himself to speak to me again.

Whatever the origin, once I'd started using his surname I never stopped, and he didn't mind a bit. In fact, he didn't even ask me to stop when the wickedly funny Director of Photography David Eggby spent an entire movie shoot out in Blacktown screeching '*STRING*errr!!!' all over the place, in mockery of me.

He actually liked it – of that I believe I can be sure.

§

Our other close (and 'old') friends, Francis and Sarah, live in Victoria. Francis is number two son in the family who'd lived next-door to us while I was growing up; and thus held a fairly unassailable position even before I'd caught up with him again, when he settled in Melbourne (after some years in the UK), married and a father. No idea how they met, those two: but they were meant for each other. I can't remember when we originally visited them as a pair; but it was the first time of many, during each of which we would occupy various rooms in their lovely sprawling house in Glen Iris and be totally at home.

They found one of Chic's particular attractions to be that he was a good Scrabble player. Francis always won hands-down at Scrabble, and because of this unpalatable fact Sarah and I would usually try to get out of it when a game was suggested. But Chic was not so spineless, and could even sometimes stretch Francis, to a degree. As well, he was able to squash him amusingly whenever Francis uttered one of his ghastly puns. We called our friend 'François the Pun King', and made occasional reference between ourselves to 'going down to Versailles'; and it is a lamentable fact but true that the ghastlier the pun the happier Francis has always been. Chic could make riposte dryly and effectively, and we would all fall about laughing at their singular wit.

Francis' favourite from Chic's witticisms originated as follows:

| INT. | FRIENDS' KITCHEN | DAY |

The other three are chatting at the kitchen table while C.S. is at the stove, reheating some coffee.

He switches off the heat under the pan, and turns to add to the conversation, managing to pour coffee over his thumb.

<u>C.S.</u>
(outraged!)
PAINPAIN***PAIN***!!!

as he rushes to the sink to run cold water on it.

I thought Francis was going to fall off his chair laughing (it was immediately obvious that no serious burning had occurred); and he uses to this day, upon any occasion of minor damage, that concertina word.

Chic was without falseness or pretence of any kind, and blessed with a spontaneous and silly sense of humour: when those he met were of a similar nature, all barriers were down immediately. So Francis and Sarah, extremely silly when in good form, and my friends for so much of my life, became his friends too from the moment they met him. This meant we could all be frightfully rude to each other in true Aussie fashion, and think it amazingly funny.

That was the only kind of rudeness Chic ever indulged in – he was a gentleman and, most definitely, a scholar.

Alas that the same – gender-differentiated, of course! – could not be said of his wife ... but then, the dissimilarity was part of the mutual attraction.

T³

There's something I need to explain: unless he was off working on a shoot, Chic would become part of my employment activities. Oh, not in an insinuating way; but just because he was *there*, with his *amazing brain*; because it brought him happiness to be of whatever help to me he could; and because he knew the joy it gave me for him to be involved in what I was doing. And I've never been able to find a satisfactory way to describe the pleasure it gave me in having him share whatever I did.

I was sitting at my desk at Grundy's*, before lunch, back in the early days, waiting for Chic; and it suddenly occurred to me to think, 'I am really lucky! This man is ... *terrific!!!* Why is he with me? And how is it that I am so confident about him?', but no answer was to be found. I didn't know him well enough then – nor, I probably don't need to add, myself.

More than twenty years and jobs later, I was once again sitting at a desk at lunchtime, when in he came with a parcel. He'd just bought me a couple of pairs of shoes, and wanted to check them in case of needing to change sizes. I have feet really difficult to fit, and was then restricted to one adjustable brand; Chic had passed the shop, seen that a new range was in, liked what he saw and bought me some.

The only one of my colleagues still in the office during this lunchbreak was popeyed: 'Your husband *bought shoes* for you? – for no particular reason? Does he often do things like that?' she asked after he'd gone, disbelieving her own eyes. I was shaken by the realisation of just how different he was from the general run of spouse.

The truth has been there for a very long time; but it's not been all that long since I've come to render it in my head as an image, and bring that to life by populating it.

It was as if a huge tree had started, slowly, to grow, after

---

* then a production (and thus employment) powerhouse

Chic had come into my life and changed it so completely. It had widely spreading branches that cast merciful shade and brought a promise of being there always. I call it 'the truth tree'; and this seems as good a place as any in our story to introduce it.

Its trunk, the part through which everything that makes the tree a living thing must traverse, is represented by something I've already written of, but possibly not all that well:

> **T³** *Chic really, **really** wanted and needed to look after me; and I really, **really** wanted and needed him to do it.*

And in this mutually gratifying and totally satisfactory manner did our relationship flourish.

FUR

This location is a small pink rented house in Naremburn, where our couple is not yet living in sin but merely committing it frequently.

Establish C.S. doing something to the wiring at the back of one of the speakers, with concentration.

> M.R.
> (voice off, calling)
> Stringer, have you seen The Doctor?

> C.S.
> (removing tool from mouth)
> Isn't that him on the couch? – oh no, sorry, it's The Captain. No, he hasn't been around since I've been in here…

Getting on with the job, he swaps the thing in his mouth for something else.

> M.R.
> (entering through the front door)
> I can't find him; and it's – well, unlike him to be anywhere else!

She crosses to a very large tabby curled on the lounge, and picks him up, admonishing him lovingly.

> M.R.
> Where's your brother, Captain? – you're his keeper, dammit!

(somewhat indistinctly around a
screwdriver)

I'll go and have a look for him soon as
I finish this wiring: he can't be far.

But the other of the two tabby moggies was nowhere to be found. And in spite of almost nonstop searching, it was not until the evening of the following day that Chic managed to discover his hiding place, right under the house – his poor little face was smashed in, and he was in a very bad way. Chic got him out with great difficulty (and a lot of filth), tenderly and carefully.

EXT.   REAR OF HOUSE   DAY

C.S.
(disbelief, morphing instantly into
rage)

Someone has done this to him – some
FUCKING BASTARD has hit him in the face
with something, DELIBERATELY!!!

It was I who normally talked like that, not Chic; so I was able to see that he felt about the animals as I did – an entirely unplanned test that he'd just passed. These were my two tabbies, lugged from Sydney to Perth and back to Sydney again; and although there was no doubting that Chic had affection for them, I knew that he'd not been raised as a cat person, but with dogs. I hadn't until then grasped that he accepted and looked on these little creatures as being as much his as mine; and in the midst of my anguish for The Doctor, I was filled with joy.

Note, please!, that we took our mog immediately to a close-by vet who turned out to be a specialist animal surgeon, and Doctor McCoy was fixed up in a fairly short time, considering his injuries, and back to being the other bookend.

Cat-worship is inherent in me: in our family we rarely had less than two moggies. (It was our mother who had made us cat fanatics – a worthwhile trait, amongst others far less admirable, to have passed on to us all; and I'm truly grateful to her for it.) So Chic's joy in these animals was something that pleased me immensely; for a cat-lover he had become, as the rest of our life was to confirm. I have myriad photos of him draped in, being sat or slept on by or, especially, holding/carrying our various cats, all showing evidence of *extreme* affinity. The Doctor was completely devoted to him; I had to sometimes wonder if he actually sensed that his life had been saved by Chic.

that's them ...

It was slowly dawning upon me that I had the power to bring about change in Chic's outlook; and some intimation of my importance to him was beginning to appear, like the first faint rays of the sun creeping up over the horizon. It was only a pale glimmering though; and thus it remained for a long time.

If you're me, you simply can't think about mind-blowing things like that.

§

One memorable day we got our first real Russian Blue – a beautiful, silver-grey, loving animal to whom we gave the informal name of Mr Walker*. (This is a long way further on into our story than The Doctor and The Captain: we got Mr Walker when we bought a house in Annandale, after we moved back to the mainland from the house that Chic built on an island – all of which is still to come.)

Our source for Mr Walker was a breeder who raised these glorious creatures in a very old brick semi in an inner western suburb of Sydney, in absolute squalor. She had her breeding sire in a cage outside her side door – the entrance everyone used – and inside, the whole house was overrun with queens in different stages of pregnancy and kittens of various ages. Though we knew nothing of cat-breeding, we were distressed because it was smelly, and we hated the thought of cats being allowed to get that way. Still, she showed great affection for them, including the great ugly tom in his cage (yep, just the one: what a perfect example of poor gene-pool diversity!).

We fell in love with Mr Walker as soon as we saw him, which is not a wise thing to let happen; for even though he seemed to have a cold, or something of the sort, we wanted him – and so we bought him.

We had had him and loved him utterly for only two years

---

* baby boomers who grew up reading comics should get it

when the illness of his infancy, seemingly so slight a thing at the time, showed itself in its true colours. It transpired that Mr Walker had been born with a deadly congenital disease called FIP – feline infectious peritonitis, of which there are a couple of varieties – and paralysis commenced to creep over him.

We spent unaccountable amounts of money at Sydney Uni's Veterinary Teaching Hospital, to no avail. Mr Walker did not outrun the long reach of this horrible disease: I don't believe any cat has yet been able to do so. We made our awful choice the moment the specialist vet was obliged to admit defeat; and I don't know which of us was the more unhappy.

But before many more months had passed, we found another and genuine breeder of Russian Blues, and from her we found out a whole lot of stuff about how the first woman should have been breeding them and keeping them, and what her lack of hygiene had meant for us. We bought another beautiful kitten, which we named Captain Navarre (from *Ladyhawke*), and he was central to our life for more than twelve years. He too was known as The Captain; but as the two Captains were far apart in our history, the replication of nomenclature* never caused confusion. You will find this one here and there in our story: he made us a family for just over a third of our life, and was the bringer of great joy.

It is to be admitted that after the tragedy of Mr Walker, The Captain's position in the household was grossly overhyped: we were unabashed in referring to him as 'our child', and deeply, *deeply* attached to him.

§

That period was not filled with nothing but light for another reason, as well.

I'd never stopped to wonder how our being a pair had come about; and it was this, I think, that resulted in there

---

* wow! – terrific phrase, eh?!

arising a time during our early days when I decided quite dispassionately to leave him.

He'd just finished working on a feature, and one Saturday (film crews used to work six-day weeks) there was an end-of-shoot party to which, of course, he went. I had no problem with that. But as the hours wore on I became too tired to wait up for him, and went fairly grumpily to bed.

I woke up at six, and he was still not home. I arose, showered, dressed, ate toast then went out to sit on the front step. I commenced Thinking. I thought several things, but prime amongst them was the inescapable fact that he preferred to spend a whole night with other people – with whom most of his time had already been spent over the past couple of months – than be with me. I can't show myself in a kinder light: I could see only that aspect of the situation. I addressed the cats on the topic, quite forcefully: they came and went frequently through the front door as I sat there, rubbing up against me in a consoling manner but contributing not a lot.

Chic arrived home somewhere around eight, extremely tired but perfectly happy – until I started talking. I conveyed to him my thinking, which seemed to point to my being less committed than either of us had realised. It's always been a facet of my character to punt everything on one roll of the dice – I'm not one of your sensible people: this trait had led me to walk out of all kinds of situations, and I appeared to be about to do it again ...

He was panic-stricken at my stated intention of leaving, but I didn't see it – we are talking, after all, of *me*. However, he gathered himself and responded, answering every question and removing all doubt. It would never have taken much to sway my resolve, I think: I wasn't angry so much as puzzled. The whole shemozzle was over and done with inside half an hour.

The moggies got off our feet, where they'd been lying offendedly because of being refused our laps, and wandered happily off as if sensing the clearer air. I remember both of us continuing to sit there silently, holding hands, watching The Captain and The Doctor gobbling from their bowls in the little kitchenette. We turned back to each other at the same moment, smiling; and he said something silly about children and divorce that had us falling about laughing. Although he was very needy of sleep by then, he didn't get any for a bit.

Once having stopped to actually think about what we were doing – about *sharing life*, just for starters – there was actual awareness of each other, something different from the basic mutual attraction. You might even say we put our feet on the first rung of the ladder to maturity on that day.

But as to how high up it we managed to climb ... well, that's something I'll have to leave for others to judge.

LA MÈRE

INT.	LIVING ROOM	DAY

Our lovers are dwelling in a small terrace belonging to
an absent friend for whom they're house-sitting, having
achieved cohabitation status (sinful).

Open on a MID-2SHOT: they are looking in the same
direction.

C.S.

> (pensively)
>
> I don't think I can make this one…

PULL OUT to reveal them involved in a game at a small
pool table that's had to be angled rather oddly to fit
into the living room: in fact, one corner of it seems to
be right up against a window.

The director Terry Bourke introduced us to pool, at his home
in St Ives: Terry held frequent pool evenings when he was in
Sydney, and as Chic was his number one stillsman, we were
always invited. We both took to the game with gusto; although
I aggrievedly discovered that having boobs meant I couldn't
lean over the table with the required élan or effectiveness.
Such was my excuse, anyway.

Terry had an ability to enjoy life that was catching, and
he was an excellent film director, even though his projects
were … well, not exactly Merchant Ivory. Chic liked and
admired him, both because he was competent at his job and
because he always treated his crews well: some directors
looked on and behaved toward their crews as if they were
cattle (whereas, as Mel Brooks made clear in *The Producers*,
it's *the cast* that should be thus classified!).

Our newly acquired pool table was a testament to our

regard for him, and had cost us far more than we could afford.
But we were like that.

(cont'd)

A third person – a short, late-middle-aged woman whose
facial characteristics show her undeniably to be M.R.'s
mother – is turning to leave the room; as she disappears,
they pull long faces at each other.

He moves around to a corner of the table and prepares to
line up the shot: putting down his cue, he picks up a
ludicrously short one, and pushes up the window sash with
the other hand.

Only now is it understood that, in order to play the ball
from that position, HE IS OBLIGED TO HAVE HIS CUE-ARM
ELBOW OUT THE WINDOW…

                         M.R.

               (hissing)

          What can we DO?! – she'll be here till
          doomsday!

C.S. frowns, making 'sshh!' signs.

He bends down, lines up: as he strikes the ball, her
mother walks back into the room carrying a book with
theatrical care. It's probably some Religious Tome: they
have no intention of asking.

                         MAMA

               (brightly)

          Oh, NEARLY, darling*…

He grits his teeth. Closes the window.

M.R.'s mother places her book down reverently before
sitting – yep, one of her R.T.s, all right…

---

* this utterance was immediately added to our list of 'Stringerisms' – things people
said that we quoted, pissing ourselves laughing, whenever we remembered them

MAMA

MAMA
(making herself comfortable)

You know, when I woke up this morning
and put my glasses on, I noticed for the
first time that there's a trapdoor in the
ceiling of my room. What's up there?

He's on the point of giving her a factual response when
a light bulb flashes in his brain, and a beatific smile
spreads across his face. He's so pleased by whatever has
inspired him that he doesn't even register her use of the
possessive adjective.

He swaps cues again, and, to cover his glee, wanders over
to a chair and pats a cat.

M.R.
(sees the subject needs changing)

Erhmm…how about a bit of a walk,
Mither?–Stringer's decided I'm going to
win this game, anyway.

CUT TO C.S. reaction: she's never been within a bull's
roar of beating him.

And after that, it was easy! Mama spoke again over
lunch – as she did almost every day, quite untruthfully – of
wanting to go home to her own cat in Perth: this particular
utterance put the seal on Chic's plan by providing ostensible
rationale for his nefarious intentions[*].

The next morning, when she disappeared into the tiny
bathroom to spend about half an hour (and very possibly
more) in it, he set to with a will. She eventually emerged and
went through to 'her' – originally our – bedroom, to find it
no longer extant!

During her prolonged occupation of the bathroom Chic

---

[*] that's it – I'll never be able to top that one …

had refurbished it as the study, and the study, where we'd been sleeping in a compressed and transient kind of way during her lengthy stay, had become formally our bedroom (which it remained for the rest of our stay in Barbie's house, as we liked sleeping in it much better). He'd effected his little miracle by moving most of the smaller furniture up into the attic – access to which was via the trapdoor referred to, of course – and bringing down some other stuff and rearranging it all, having worked out a complete plan of attack the day before, when she unwittingly gave him the idea.

Mama was momentarily stupefied, but undeniably out-flanked and outgunned; so she booked her 'plane ticket that day with only a half-hearted attempt at her usual load of emotional blackmail, and departed.

She wasn't even too miffed; certainly not enough to prevent her from coming to stay with us in other domiciles on many more occasions.

I was almost speechless with admiration. That may even have been the very first example of the following exchange:

INT./EXT.	ANYWHERE	ANYTIME

She is regarding him with awe.

                    M.R.
         (throws up her arms in amazement)
      I am without words!

                    C.S.
          (very big grin)
      NEVER...!

---

but it was very, very far from being the last.

MEANING

Someone who knows a great deal about memoir-writing suggested I should let the reader in on the early development of our relationship, especially during the period when I was his mistress: 'will he/won't he leave his wife?', and so forth, adding a little tension to the story.

Can't be done. I never had the slightest doubt that he would, before very long, be living with me. There was no tension.

This doesn't mean heavenly skywriters had been at work; or that we had made promises to each other along these lines (in fact, I can't recall a single instance of our ever, *ever* making promises to each other, about anything! – such a requisite never arose). Rather, it means that not thinking was my habitual approach to life.

When Chic and I had been together for several weeks on that first film crew, back in Perth, my mother asked me* one day if I was going to marry him. I laughed rudely, reminding her that he had a wife, and also that I wasn't thinking that far ahead. Both facts were indisputably true, but the latter was the key, and remained so: I never planned anything.

I can't say if he was any more foresighted than I; for something rather strange about our relationship was that we didn't talk about it. We never had what I once described to Jo as 'deep and meaningfuls' – not about ourselves, I mean. We had many deep discussions on every other serious topic under the sun; but we never talked about us (the solitary exception being when we agreed instantly, very early in the piece, that children were not on our event horizon nor ever would be). I can't believe it was deliberate: we were simply the same in living the moment and never thinking about what lay ahead.

Anyone having that philosophy – for want of a better term – sees no need to talk about it. It *is*.

§

---

* hopefully, I should think

It was, it seems to me, a rather extraordinary love story.

How come two grown people, both past youth, came together to meld their lives into one, in complete understanding and total interdependence? How did this pair of unalikes fit as if made expressly for each other into a mould that might have been created by some kindly disposed deity? Where did the immediate joy in each other's company spring from? And why *was* there no tension – not even at the beginning?

Ah, so many questions ...

Too late for answers to any of them.

KEY LIGHT

For the purpose no reader could fail to grasp, my own early years have been fairly exhaustively portrayed; and it would give me enormous pleasure if I could recount Chic's to the same degree. But I can't – no more than he could mine were he writing our story. There was not enough exchanging of details about our childhoods, that's what it boils down to; so what I know is limited.

My husband was the youngest of four boys; and as there was a gap of something like eight and a half years between him and number three, he grew up pretty lonely in his family environment: Chic wasn't ignored or unloved, but his mother, raised in rural Victoria, was practical before everything else, and his father was very tied up with what the war and those conducting it required of him.

Dad was top banana in a big engineering company with a contract to manufacture the bows of supply lighters[*] for the American armed forces, by kind favour of the then Oz government. Because of this latter fact, Chic told me, the family moved something like nine times during his childhood; and he remembered attending at least as many different schools. I shall never forget about the time his mother gave him a note to take to school that contained the address of the next 'home' to which he was to make his way when the bell went to mark the end of the day ...

A couple of years ago, I emailed his remaining brother, Reg, asking if there were any anecdotes about Chic as a child that had stuck in his mind, and he replied:

'One little event you may not know about. It points to his developing ability in engineering skills. At the age of three he was very adaptable, collecting heavy objects such as pieces

---

[*] two other companies looked after the middles and the sterns respectively, and the three bits had all to be shunted to a fourth location to be welded together! – the mind boggles, but in fact with large infrastructure that kind of thing goes on to this day

of steel, etc. He attached a rope to his collection and dragged them all around the garden of our home during his set play times, packing them up ready for the next day.

'That was during the war years: we had a dugout air-raid shelter in the garden in which he stored his treasures.'

Why that's what Reg remembers most easily about his little brother can only be guessed at, even by him. When he sent me that little story, I laughed like anything when I thought how Chic would have reacted to it.

Reg also passed on to me a totally unrelated but delightful story, set in that period when their father was a kind of volunteer factotum to a family named Ferguson, the developers of Victoria's Lake Eildon. Albert Ferguson (to become Weary Dunlop's father-in-law!) had his argyle socks knitted for him in Scotland, in true Laird fashion: when he'd finished with them – who knows what this meant?! – they would be passed on by Dad to his own mother, who would unpick them, wash the wool and reuse it to knit sweaters for her grandsons.

Maybe one of the photos I have of the small Stringer even shows him wearing one – hang on, I'll check ...

with Dad: does that look like an
ex-sock or two?

OKOK, I confess: the socks story – absolutely true! – happened years before that little boy in the photograph was around, but anyone who's at all practical will have worked that out already.

But since it's highly likely that the jumper he's wearing there is a hand-me-down, it probably *is* part of Reg's story!

§

Chic was a dreamer. There were no siblings close enough to provide a peer group, so he read omnivorously all his life.

His mother wasn't keen on piles of books, never having herself grown up with them; so she would get rid of them when he'd finished, saying 'You've read that, now; we'll give it to someone else'. For some reason, this tugged at my heartstrings more than anything else; I could hardly bear to

Douglas, Reginald, Bruce, Charles

think of the little boy reading his beloved *Treasure Island* secretly, so that she wouldn't know how far along he was. But his parents were truly good people; Mum simply didn't comprehend his need to read and re-read, lost in a world of fantasy. (It was she who gave him his nickname, by the way: his father's name was also Charles, and Chic believed they simply ran out of ideas after three boys and plumped for the obvious for number four. Before long the need arose to avoid dual responses, so 'Chick' came into being, as it was a quite common diminutive in those years; and he later dropped the 'k'.)

One of the many things she did comprehend was his left-handedness: at school they tried to force him to write with his right hand, but Mum elicited from him the reason for his being upset, and marched off to front them, totally effectively. No teacher attempted again to put a pencil or pen into Chic's right hand; and he remembered with love her instant and total support of him, in the face of what was then a pretty overpowering school system.

The family lived in Mt Ku-ring-gai for a while, in a house actually backing on to the parkland, and Chic referred to this period more often than any other time in his childhood. It must have been a magical time for him, wandering virtually unfettered throughout the vast, sprawling and beautiful Ku-ring-gai Chase National Park, where he discovered nature, working out for himself whatever he came across that was unknown. I think his ramblings there, giving rise to wondering and puzzling and reflecting, played a big part in the development of his truly awe-inspiring brainpower; for that little boy became an adult who knew everything and could do anything.

Yes, I can see that looks like a ridiculous statement to make; but the number of occasions in a thirty-one-year stretch on which he was unable to provide an answer to a request for information is represented by less than the number of fingers on one hand, with no exaggeration at all. And I'm quite unable to come up with a single thing that went wrong in our various domiciles that he was unable to rectify, nor one we needed that he was unable to create. He was more clever, more able and more erudite than I could ever convey. I *revelled* in it.

The hands-on engineering environment of the men in the family, all extremely able in a variety of ways, must have provided a background of common sense and logic; and as he was the only child amongst them, he could simply listen and soak up. He also taught himself to *look* up: anything he didn't recognise or understand he found in a dictionary or an encyclopaedia; and he would do that for the rest of his life, on the odd occasion that it was needed. He derived immense pleasure from taking out any large volume of our OED and simply reading it.

Chic pressured his parents into letting him leave school well before finishing, so he was mostly self-taught – although he did study architectural drawing, metallurgy and similar technical subjects when he was in the army; and these he utilised frequently later on, both professionally and in our life. He looked back on his short time in the army with loathing, but it did give him something to do; and it did indeed furnish the various kinds of training that were his reason for enlisting. His personal knowledge base put Microsoft's in the shade, though; and there's no way it was all built up during that brief army stint. No, it was simply Chic's astounding brain; and no one is able to explain the vagaries of heredity regarding that organ.

The sibling age difference, I imagine, also taught him not to volunteer information. In all the years we shared, I never once heard him put forward information that hadn't actually been sought – a highly desirable character trait, rarely found (and certainly not in his spouse).

From one of those who loved him:

'The most impressive thing about him was that he was totally unassuming, when he had so much to be assuming about.'

§

Hagiography of my husband is not my intention: our life was not without vicissitudes, and we had some impressive fights. Sometimes he was bossy – not terribly endearing to a person who'd spent her childhood being bossed around. And sometimes I was unreasonable – on second thoughts, we might try 'often': I am my mother's daughter.

In these past few years when I've had so much time to think about so many things, I've realised that on the occasions when Chic played lord and master, issuing orders or refusals, he unknowingly created in his wilful wife great, but at the time unrecognised, resentment – often causing what seemed inexplicable rows. I cast him in the rôle of the leader; I wanted him to take responsibility for and run everything... but at the same time I hated it when he became authoritarian.

I know myself better, now, with the benefit of some reverse engineering, undertaken during all that thinking.

When we were little, Carole and I were often verbally ripped apart for apparent misdemeanours, but we were not allowed to defend ourselves. So in me were sown seeds of rancour that sprouted on later occasions when unappealing authority first made itself felt; but the paradox is that never in my life did it occur to me to refuse to kowtow to such totalitarianism. No: when even obviously silly authority was expressed, I heard and obeyed, with an enormous feeling of injustice but no thought to any lack of sense or logic. A young lifetime in a convent school, obeying without question the meaningless dictates of the day, might provide sufficient explanation for my logic processes having turned to mush. I hope. But when I reflect on the impossible rôle in which I cast Chic, it looks very much as though 'maturity' is a word lacking strong presence in my personal lexicon.

I remember his apologising to me on many occasions after a fight, but can recall only one example of my doing the same. During one of her many visits, I'd discussed with my mother the fact that we girls had never been introduced to opera while growing up: the somewhat heated conversation had resulted in my discovering that, while she claimed to love the art, she had no opera CDs. So I sent her one of ours, *La Forza del Destino*, in which Plácido Domingo sings with Leontyne Price, because I thought Chic had agreed we didn't like Price's strangely husky soprano. But it was a case of me only half-listening: it transpired that he loved that rendition of the opera for the pace of its conducting, and he was deeply upset that I had given it away without even asking him, especially to my mother.

We had a very unpleasant row about this in the middle of the night. But I did apologise without reservation when it became obvious how thoughtlessly I'd behaved, for this meant I couldn't be resentful, and resentment or lack thereof – as established by the reverse engineering – seems always to have been the key to my *modus operandi*.

Still, any deep disagreement we had, regardless of seriousness, lasted only as long as it took for the expressing; and ordinary, day-to-day kind of arguments were simply that, their shelf life transitory.

Looking back on all this kind of thing, I can state categorically that Chic's really major failings were three, and in comparison any others paled into insignificance. He had:

- a habit of waking me up in the middle of the night with anything he felt called for serious discussion;
- an ability to procrastinate skilfully (and indefinitely) regarding things he didn't want to do; and
- a horrid tendency to hoard heaps and *heaps* of technical objects of all shapes, sizes and origins – in spite of our almost total lack of storage space.

Tsk! – such sociopathic tendencies ...
Me? – oh, no failings at all. Then *or* now.

HOW NOT TO WHISTLE

In order to live, one must work. Happy, then, the person who does it over fairly short periods at different jobs, in different places, and with and for different people.

We were both freelancers: when possible, we worked in our respective trades on the same production, but this couldn't always be the case.

Chic had been contracted as a studio photographer to Andrew Warn; and the two of them had set up a company called PRIPP – PR, Industrial and Press Photography – which was all the stuff that Chic shot. But Andrew found it difficult to work around Chic's being so often unavailable when away working on movies, so eventually they split. The breakup meant that Chic now also had periods of unemployment, which he spent with me, to our mutual delight.

At one time, I got that gig with Grundy's, doing research on a television quiz show. The show's producer, Julian Jover, was a really nice bloke, and of considerable industry standing: I must have impressed him with my musical knowledge, for the show was about being able to identify songs. It was hosted by a little jerk we'll call the Whistler. I set to with a will.

My research consisted of unearthing from various sources sheet music with melody lines people could recognise; I had also to come up with info about the songs that provided clues, if such was found necessary*. I would then pass my selections on to a bandleader who would arrange them, and my clues on to Julian, who would dumb them down.

For a while everything was fine, but I began to grow more and more jaded by the standard of the contestants' musical knowledge.

---

* you'd better believe it

The small pink house again. It is night-time.

He is slumped in front of the TV making scoffing noises, while she sits at the dining-room table, ensconced in paperwork and tearing her hair.

M.R.

(flinging down her pencil)

Aaarghh!!! I must've put together forty-three million of these bloody shows: I don't think there are any songs left to use!

He switches off the TV in disgust and starts, reluctantly, to look for his jacket.

C.S.

No you haven't; but you HAVE said that forty-three million times.

And I thought you weren't going to bring your work home, any more?!

M.R.

(big whinge)

Well I can't help it! – it's not MY fault if the contestants can't recognise a single song!

Julian's grumpy because we haven't had a winner for three months. AND that fuckwit host's constantly making snide remarks about my ability...

Pfuh! – what the fuck would he know? – he can only whistle one fucking tune...

TIGHTEN IN on him during this tirade. He opens his mouth to remonstrate and then closes it again, recognising a *crise de nerfs* in the offing.

C.S.

(thinking while donning the eventually
found jacket)

Weren't you going to look for sheet
music of Simon & Garfunkel?

M.R.

(brightening)

Oh, yes – I forgot! What a moron I am!
Thank you, darling! I found 'em last
week! – a whole bloody hardback book of
'em. It must be in here somewhere…

She searches madly, paperwork flying about and books
falling to the floor.

Manic page turning ensues when it's found; while in the
little kitchenette he rinses the coffee mugs.

M.R.

How well-known is 'Bridge Over Troubled
Water', Stringer? – is it just me who
knows every note…?

C.S.

(observing that she's settled, bends
down to kiss her goodbye)

If the bandleader does a halfway decent
arrangement of it, probably even an
idiot couldn't fail to know it. Should
be fine.

Chic had quickly grown confident in handling me: never
controlling, but pointing me in the right direction when I
headed for panic.

This was quite frequently; for as I was not yet entirely free
of hang-ups, I wasn't too hot under pressure.

§

At Channel 7 we put down a week of episodes every taping day, and when he wasn't working, Chic would come in and sit in a dim corner of the studio, unnoticed, taking everything in.

His favourite visit was the day when the Whistler's loathing of me became public (very!) knowledge: it caused great mirth, and the story was retold for years. I honestly don't remember why the man disliked me so much, but I suspect it had to do with my being totally unimpressed by him (and I have never been one to camouflage my opinions).

But neither of us had comprehended *the extent* to which he detested me.

INT.	ATN7 STUDIO	DAY

A taping session: on the set, the host and a contestant are facing each other on a rather second-hand-looking podium.

The ultimate question is being played: the familiar but wordless notes of 'Bridge Over Troubled Water' are heard, and the contestant begins looking outraged at being expected to name so very obscure a piece of music – and, predictably, fails to do so.

His disgust is matched by the host's, who, forgetting all about the clue that might save the contestant from being hauled off, announces to camera (the viewing audience-to-be):

WHISTLER
(flinging down script in dramatic fashion and shrugging helplessly: 'What can one DO?!')

Well, there it is, everyone; the score is now contestants NIL, Margaret Rose ONE!

In the dimness down at the back of the studio they lean on each other in hysterics.

                    M.R.
        (wiping her eyes)

        Bastard, Stringer…! You never told
        me that a total cretin's failing to
        recognise 'Bridge Over Troubled Water'
        would see me exposed to the world on the
        telly!

He does a Yiddish 'This I should know?' with hands and
shoulders, and they collapse laughing in whispers before
creeping out.

There were Repercussions, of course: and the nice Julian
was obliged to ask me to say goodbye, for the Whistler
carried a lot more weight (figuratively) than did I. And it was
an undeniable fact that in the time of my researching songs
for the show there had been only one winner.

Of course the problem was me.

I could remember clearly, music *and* words, songs from as
far back as my early childhood, and found it hard to accept
that people selected to be contestants in a show of that
kind didn't have anything remotely like the same ability. I
wouldn't include in my list once – let alone repeatedly – the
trashy music that they might, just possibly, have been able
to recognise; whereas I should have done, and regularly,
regardless of 'lowering my personal standards'. Yesyes, I
know: beginners' stuff. Terrific thing, hindsight, she said
testily …

I was developing a reputation for being difficult: driven by
the work ethic and finding that the entertainment industry of
the day had less than its fair share, with far too many people
in it through contacts rather than ability or experience*. In
spite of the fact that I laughed a great deal and made others
laugh too, it wasn't all the time: Chic had to pick up the pieces
when there was a real reason for me not to.

---

* I didn't understand, then, that this is how the world works

One very unfunny occasion was when the managing director of TCN9 called me into his august presence to dress me down because I'd been doing my job too well. I was Senior Directors' Assistant, then, brought back to the channel specifically to get all the DAs up to speed across the board. One of my underlings, who belonged to A Family Of Note, had gone directly to the MD to complain because I'd taken her off a show she *liked* being DA on and put her onto *something else*, just for *training*! And who did M.R. *think she was*, coming in and *instructing* her?!

The MD not only knew on which side his bread was buttered but liked to have it laid on with a trowel. And it mattered not a whit to either of the pair that Channel 9's directors were ecstatic about the growing ability of the DAs to support them on anything they directed – he wanted to suck up to her family and she'd been born having her own way. It didn't appear to matter to my boss the Production Manager either, although he'd been reaping the rewards of the work for which he'd hired me: he was revealed, upon my entry, sitting *behind the MD's door*, on a *stool*, for crissake ... And apparently unable to open his mouth on my behalf.

This time, I said goodbye myself, as soon as I was able to work out what the MD was talking about – his circumspection was understandable, as he was trying to threaten me for having improved the effectiveness of his staff. Having flung my ID badge on his desk and stomped out of his office, I left the station in a rage, but pleased on my absent husband's behalf that I hadn't sworn at the idiot once. It made no difference: the delighted gossip around the Channel 9 corridors was that I'd told him to get fucked, for no one could believe otherwise of me (especially in the circumstances).

At home, I raved at my unfortunate captive audience. I'd been enjoying the job, finding satisfaction in the problem-solving aspects of it, and in being able to roster myself back into studio control rooms, every so often. It had been particularly gratifying to be headhunted, for I'd begun to think that amongst the hirers and firers my reputation for being trying would precede me for the rest of my working days rather than merely accompany me. I could scarcely believe that all this, plus the gratifying upward trend of the DAs' abilities, had been thrown out the window by one stupid, arse-kissing little bastard who got off on wielding his authority over lowly staff. His tirade had made it impossible for me to continue: if I didn't resign I'd have to work in acceptance of the fact that my position was lower in the food chain than that of the silly spoilt girl, and omit her from all scheduled training (and how can you be divisional commander of eight-ninths of your division?!).

Chic allowed me to let it all out, and then comforted me; and I wish I could say I remember everything he said. I do recall talking myself to the point of exhaustion and being able to regain some perspective simply through his attentive listening. But he responded, as well: he was always ready to. I can almost hear his voice now, as he looked into what I was saying, dissected it and reordered it, ascertaining what the content actually was as opposed to how it was being presented, and said practical and calming things to his impetuous woman – who would've been raving furiously and waving her arms, something tells me ...

You have to be a strong person to deal with that, and know exactly how to be practical and calming without exacerbating the fury: but he could do it* every time. It was his specialty, I think – compressing my extremely large reactions to the point where they were within the frame and manageable.

---

* practice makes perfect ...

SILVER TONGUE

EXT.	DUPLEX GARDEN	DAY

This is where she lives for a short period that brings up few memories, so the year is uncertain. But it's early in the relationship, for she is as yet 'only' his mistress.

Nice big WIDE SHOT of duplex: she's outside the little fence, attending to plants growing along it. ZOOM IN past her through flat window to LOOSE MID-SHOT of him in the kitchenette making a pot of tea.

C.S.
(calling without looking up)

Darling, don't you think you've done enough pruning? I reckon the hairies above are getting a bit restive that the street frontage is not as leafy as it was before you moved in.

REVERSE through window to see her at fence.

M.R.
(happily waves secateurs)

Heavens, no!!! Just look at these rosebushes! They all have to be opened out from the centre, an–

CUT BACK TO exterior WIDE SHOT, as a window is flung open in the upper storey, and a voice is heard from on high.

TENANT
(passionately)

Are you EVER going to stop cutting down ALL the plants? The garden is for BOTH duplexes, you know; and you didn't ask us if you could denude EVERYTHING!

She looks up; steps back trying to get an eye-line to the utterer of this hyperbolic complaint. The tenant, however, also steps back, so that she can see only fluttering curtains (the wimp!).

                         M.R.
            (bright)
          Hey there, Mr Invisible…You're in
          luck! - I'm feeling sort of cooperative
          today. But only because my other half
          has already raised this very topic.
          Otherwise, I would probably tell you to
          go and stick your head up a dead bea-

During this speech we've PANNED OFF HER AND TIGHTENED IN ON HIM emerging in a big hurry: FOLLOW him to 2-SHOT as he reaches her, clamping his hand over her mouth at exactly this point in the dialogue. She is momentarily outraged, before realising that he is heaving with silent laughter. The contagion spreads: she joins in.

FOLLOW THE 2S back in through the front door, clutching each other, tears running down their faces.

Poor Chic! - what must it have been like for him to be permanently allied with a woman of good breeding but such coarse utterance? Fortunately, he was almost always amused; but if I swore frightfully over any length of time, he would protest. And if I went on and on, he would become very grumpy indeed. It eventually filtered through my skull (large: hat size around sixty; takes stuff a while to make it inside) that gratuitous bad language was unwelcome in our house.

But he didn't raise any objections at all when I was genuinely angry or upset; and he could utter expletives with the best of 'em – even me! – if sufficiently riled. I do remember telling him once that as I didn't drink and didn't smoke, I should be entitled to this one peccadillo. Logic of a sort …

The point is that I didn't simply go along with everything Chic wanted, because I loved him. Nono! – I retained my behavioural traits, because they were mine and they comprised *me*, even if they were less than totally attractive or desirable as behavioural traits go. After all, it was me he loved – not a person made over to be some kind of paragon of the good behaviour and lovely manners that he might, on occasion, have preferred.

But as to whether I could have selected a less ... um ... contentious aspect of my personality to adhere to – well, they are not conscious decisions, these things.

WET STUFF

EXT.	DUPLEX GARDEN	EARLY

Still the Cammeray duplex.

DOLLY with his little 4WD as he stops outside, alights and lugs out of the back of it a very large package, which is obviously heavy and displays a certain lack of rigidity.

> <u>M.R.</u>
> (coming out of the flat; very curious indeed)
>
> What have you got there, Stringer?

> <u>C.S.</u>
> (puffing somewhat; it seems to have a mind of its own)
>
> Remember that little photographic session I did for the bloke who's just bought a boat sales yard? - well, this is the payment.
>
> And before you start getting indignant, it was my idea!

Having made all the 'who, me? - indignant?!' faces, she provides some fairly ineffectual help; but his oddly shaped package is eventually got in through the front gate and dumped onto the tiny lawn.

He removes the casing.

> <u>C.S.</u>
> (finding a knob on the end of a string, he yanks it, to the accompaniment of some mangled Shelley)
>
> Look on my works, ye mighty, and … um … behold!

There's a whooshing noise, and the package expands into a rubber…ahh…craft. It cannot be truthfully described as a boat, as it's absolutely tiny: in fact, it looks like a model of a surf rescue dinghy.

He gets another package out of the vehicle, which proves to be the inboard deck, for want of a better phrase: it drops neatly into the bottom of the minuscule craft.

A third and final package reveals itself as the outboard motor: at the sight of it, they both start laughing, for neither has ever seen as small an engine, of any kind; and it's hard to believe it can possibly work.

C.S.

(happily gazing upon it all)

There! – isn't it terrific?

We'll have great fun zooming around the Harbour in our boat.

She experiences one of her infrequent practical moments, and clears her throat hesitantly.

M.R.

Darling…do you not think that… perhaps…both of us getting into this…um…not frightfully big…vessel might…ahh…cause it to…

(having searched fruitlessly for a good word, adds lamely)

…sink?

C.S.

(has he heard right?!)

SINK? – no way!!! We are going to take this down to Tunks Park, launch it with a jeroboam, and then zip all over the bay!

Brief thoughtful pause.

Well, maybe not a jeroboam – there's no
keel to dash it onto. We'll get a really
good bottle of wine for dinner tonight,
instead.

He looks upon The Payment dotingly.

She is rendered temporarily speechless by the consummate
skill with which he makes every post a winner.

And he was right, dammit! – we put the parts back into the
Suzuki, drove down to Tunks Park and he assembled our
boat; and in the end, with everything kind of joined up, it
actually looked like one. The ability to more easily identify it
as something to get into for going upon the water didn't mean
that I was filled with confidence, however: my size/weight
didn't seem conducive to our messing about in this particular
boat.

But it was great! Admittedly, it didn't provide opportunity
to lie about sunbaking on the top deck while sipping
champers, but we both fitted in without developing cramp.
And we had *such* a time!

It was an extraordinary thing, being right at the waterline
and zipping about: all camera operators should have one
of these for low-angle water shots, we decided. There was
something amazingly daring about sitting down on the board
'deck' knowing that my bum was actually lower than the
waterline – for the only freeboard was where Chic sat on the
edge next to the teeny outboard.

A lot of our joy was derived from the expressions on the
faces of the other boating enthusiasts we passed: the Lower
North Shore's Long Bay had never previously been sailed
upon by any craft of that size, let alone one carrying two
people.

Yes indeedy: it satisfied the needs of we sometimes-idle
skint to grin and thumb our noses at the mostly-idle rich.

When non-working days were accompanied by calm weather (the amount of freeboard necessitated *total* calm), we were to be found whizzing about the waterways, enjoying ourselves mightily and having no care as to what the rest of the world was about.

Pity we never got 'round to having a naming ceremony for our little craft: we could have called it the SS *Metaphor*.

LOSING IT

At one time we lived in a really nice old Federation house in Kameruka Road, Northbridge: it must have been fairly soon after the Cammeray duplex, because we still had the tiny blue dinghy. I remember this very well indeed, for it was while we were living there that I launched myself upon that regimen of ill repute, the Dr Atkins' Diet Revolution (bear with me: there really is a connection to the boat).

Chic had taken a B&W shot when I'd gone down to the front gate to clear the mailbox: I turned around to see him aiming one of his many cameras at me, and so held my arms out wide, smiling hugely. After he'd processed a raft of negs and printed them*, including that photo – well, that was when I decided to Do Something About My Weight. Again. It was useless his protesting; the sight of myself in overalls, filling the gateway, was enough. Still, upon re-perusal of the photo, I suppose it was quite a NICE largeness: I'm smiling very happily indeed at someone who is utterly precious, so there could be seen a certain – pleasantness in me. But I was embarrassed for Chic: I didn't know any other bloke who had so capacious a woman, and I felt he was due something better (or, perhaps, less).

The first thing noticed about this no-carbohydrate-fat-only diet is the stage of ketosis, which makes the breath ... I believe 'unspeakable' is apt – and that's putting it mildly. Presumably, the ketones that manage to escape leave some repulsive deposit on the tongue's surface in proof of their passing; so that during the initial period, when adherents to the regimen are feeling delightfully high and utterly at peace with the world, those addressed at fairly close range must suffer hideously.

One day at the beginning of the DADR period we took the little boat out to the Lane Cove River for a bit of a change

---

* he always processed and printed his B&W shots, whether on crew or not

of launch site. I started to paddle, for we had decided not to use the outboard as the river was looking a bit murky, and we didn't want to stir up anything from the bottom – very much in our vicinity.

EXT.   LANE COVE RIVER   DAY

                    C.S.
          (slight frown)
        Darling, don't be quite so enthusiastic
        with your paddling, eh? – these mangroves
        are really low, and you could get swept
        away quite easily…

                    M.R.
          (laughs gaily)
        No worries; I –

She does a double take as C.S. rapidly turns head away.

                    M.R.
          (anxious)
        Did you see something? – a water snake,
        maybe?

This is difficult: he knows her very well, and can foresee
the reaction when he says:

                    C.S.
          (mumbling)
        It's your breath. It…well…ahh…

Takes the plunge, bravely.

<u>C.S.</u>
It'd kill a brown dog.

Silence.

He stiffens up the sinews, awaiting the killer blow.

Her next utterance is squeezed out through lips pressed
tightly together.

<u>M.R.</u>
(comprehended only with difficulty)

Then we're in the right place: there are
probably several already floating around.
If we come across any only half-dead,
I'll be able to give 'em the *coup de
grâce*.

We laughed for ages (although I had to keep my head turned): I remember being excessively pleased about my wit, for usually I can only think of clever responses several days after they're needed.

Chic wasn't wrong in thinking I'd give him curry over what I would inevitably see as a criticism; but happily for us both, the side effect of similarity to being on speed rendered me temporarily less sensitive. For my norm was – and still is, I regret to have to admit – to interpret virtually anything other than total approval as complete rejection; and this he had to learn to put up with and manage.

Somehow, he did; but he felt it only fair to make reference to it, every so often, e.g.:

INT./EXT.	ANYWHERE	ANYTIME

Having just uttered some pronouncement, she wears a
superior and righteous expression.

C.S.

(aghast)

No, I simply can't let you get away with
that: it's absolute rubbish, and you
know it.

Hastily:

C.S.

But just because I'm disagreeing with
you doesn't mean I'm REJECTING you!

But back to the mangroves ...

We paddled on, giggling as we claimed to see moribund canines here and there, until we actually did see a water snake – they used to be quite prolific in that filthy old waterway (probably still are, for it's London to a brick that it's still just as filthy).

Chic did his best to give it a wide berth, but it took a liking to us, and kept swimming in our direction no matter where we went. We were beginning to get a bit panicky: after all, we were right on the waterline, and this bloody great thing appeared to be not only at our level but intent on joining us in our toy boat. In a moment of madness, I huffed loudly at it, although it was about five metres away; and at that exact second an extremely slimy floating branch made brief contact with its tail. It did an instant U-turn and fell in love, happily for us, slithering off herding the branch.

That was the end of our outing: we paddled back a little nervously, but definitely hysterical, making references to the effectiveness of my breath as a marketable weapon. (Easy to discern the level of sophistication of our humour: we fell about for weeks on end, proclaiming to each other 'Smell *baaad*!', after we'd first watched *Labyrinth* and visited the Bog of Eternal Stench ...)

A really structural branch of the truth tree can be seen at reachable distance:

T³ *Something integral to us as a couple was that the funny side cut in before anything else.*

I think the ketone-breath must've worn off fairly shortly – that, or Chic was a bloody saint.

Fortunately for both of us, I went off the DADR after a couple of months: I'd become so sick of eating pork rinds, the only permissible snack food I could access without difficulty, and having to add cream to everything – we both *hated* cream: we hated even full-cream milk! – that I couldn't hack it any more. I would've been far happier drinking black tea with half a lemon squeezed into it and espresso just as it came from the machine (both of which virtuous liquids were imbibed during the courses of different diets). But most of all I missed my fruit: to have no apple, orange or mandarin pass my lips for months was torture, not to be borne! And anyway, Chic said it was unnatural having no mummified apple cores or bits of peel lying around, or sticky patches of orange juice attracting dust.

He was enormously proud of me for having got rid of all those stones and pounds, praising me in private and in company. But he was also totally uncritical when they reapplied themselves with enthusiasm at all points – not without assistance, it must be stated, from *moi*.

SORROW

There are times when I'm overcome with the utter joy of remembering him.

And then there are the other times.

For he is gone, who constituted every person in my life – my husband, my lover, my mentor, my guardian, my father, my brother, my carer and my best, closest, most beloved, most respected and most trusted friend. He is gone forever.

I don't know how to bear it.

I'm doing my best at this, for him. But I'm caught up ... enmeshed ... in sorrow deeper than I will ever be able to describe.

How can it be that Chic is no longer in the world? How is it possible that I shall never again hear that beautiful, loved voice ...?

I can't discover the sense in any of it – that he is not with me, caring for me, caring about me.

I never needed to ask anyone else anything: whatever I wanted to know, Chic was here to provide the answer. If ever I needed an opinion confirmed (or squashed), he was here to do it. Any comment I wanted to make, he would listen; any silly thing that occurred to me would be received and understood and readily discussed, regardless of the degree of intelligence. It was because I respected him totally that I was able to trust him to the same degree. And because of this, he had only to open his mouth to be believed: but then, he was never wrong. (Well, almost never: there was that time when he used bottled green peppercorns in a recipe – that was very wrong indeed, and we laughed about this sole culinary failure to the end of his days.)

A pivotal part of our relationship was the lack of need for dialogue. We would sit in our respective recliner chairs in complete and companionable silence, reading, for absolutely ages; and when one looked up to gaze with abstracted pleasure upon the other, s/he would already be doing just that.

Or when Chic had been working away at his PC and I would appear in the doorway beside him to ask if he felt like a cup of tea, he'd roll his chair back and grab me, laughingly accusing me of witchcraft.

§

During his last weeks, my second-eldest sister – who was also his friend, and oh, what a true and irreplaceable friend she was to us both! – came up to spend some days with us. He had been given back to me, in his hospital bed, to have and look after at home; for they wanted to empty the wards for a holiday period.

One evening he told her that nobody could understand our relationship. I thought he was referring to the fact that we spent our entire life in each other's company; but when I sought clarification, later, he was not strong enough to have a discussion about it, and disappointed that I couldn't grasp his meaning without needing one.

Could it be, I wondered later, that we never knew any other couples who lived as we did, and none as fundamentally happy? – no, that was a given ...

I've pondered at length over this; and I believe he may have meant he understood that

T³ *I, a highly intelligent woman of forceful personality, joyfully and with determination made myself entirely dependent upon him, readily accepting that I was fully functional only within the framework of his love for me.*

That total, surrendering joy has had a price levied that nobody should have to pay.

CRUST (DAILY)

We met, as you know, because we were in the film industry – about which there is a certain glamour ... that is to say, as seen by those who are not. In fact, I know beyond question that there are countless hordes out there who'd give their back teeth to have a job on a film crew. Dunno why: it isn't the be-all and end-all of employment, believe me.

Chic and I differed somewhat on this; but then, the crew slots into which we respectively fitted were likely to generate diverse reactions.

A stillsman led a life of total independence on crew: no one watched what he did, let alone offered gratuitous advice; no one told him how he should be doing it; no one chivvied him if he wasn't working faster than light or not quite ready for the next setup.

the Stillsman (as so often) waiteth – I *love* this shot!

He was responsible solely to the producer, and had only to ensure he didn't take up too much time having action restaged for stills purposes. But as Chic never in his career asked to have action restaged for the purpose of his shooting stills (he shot during rehearsals, and during the takes if no sound was being recorded), even that was something he didn't have to be careful with.

But there was the odd occasion ...

INT.	ON LOCATION #1	DAY

Everything has come to a stop: the entire crew is focused on the Stills Photographer, the Director and the actress.

Stills, one of his cameras in his hands, is looking polite.

The Director is looking embarrassed.

The actress, an American import, is looking outraged.

ACTRESS

(petulantly, to the Director)

Well?

Stills simply waits: he is not going to be drawn into a situation wherein the actress is spoiling for a scene of the non-camera variety.

DIRECTOR

(awkward)

Well ... Esther ... This IS only a rehearsal, which means it's the time when Chic is supposed to be able to shoot stills without causing the star any problems ...

Sadly, most directors are total wimps when it comes to difficult actresses – and that's not saying anything about the colour of their noses ...

                    ACTRESS
        And just how am I supposed to Act, with
        a damned photographer snapping off in my
        face all the time?!

This is so ludicrously unlike what has actually been
going on as to show her clearly for what she is.

The crew, unimpressed, start to chat quietly among
themselves.

                    ACTRESS
            (up a level)
        Is this how you Aussies make
        movies?-try to drive the star crazy?
        Well, it's not how we do things back
        home. I'm outta here.

She turns and stomps off to her caravan, gesturing
peremptorily to those in her way to get out of it.

Scattered applause from the crew, some of whom hold
up hastily scribbled scores on paper pinched from
Continuity: '2' seems popular-although, in the absence of
a benchmark, there is a '0' and also a '10'!

The stillsman puts the Hasselblad back into his camera
case and gets out his Nikon.

So Stills could occasionally be put under pressure, as you
see.

In contrast, however, Continuity was harassed and hassled
from opening setup to wrap:

She's just seated herself at her continuity desk to type up the completed setup when Boom Operator approaches. He has that look on his face.

She sighs, prepares herself.

> BOOM OP.
> (a word to the wise)
>
> Shouldn't Paul have still had his wellies on for that setup…?

> CONTINUITY
> (peaceably)
>
> Go away.

> BOOM OP.
>
> But –

> CONTINUITY
> (suddenly fraught)
>
> I know what…You boom the dialogue without getting the actors off-mic. or the windsock into the top of frame, and I'll watch what they're doing and saying and wearing. Good idea, you reckon?

She simply doesn't have time or energy to explain to him exactly why the actor didn't need to be wearing his wellington boots – it would involve so much DETAIL.

The Boom Op. gets the picture and exits frame sullenly.

Whereat she feels immediately guilty, as crew members actually do contribute, from time to time.

_____

Such gratuitous input was meant helpfully, and people never told me of continuity errors without firmly believing themselves right. This was genuinely well-meaning when it came from my colleagues, to give them their due.

But it caused me to wonder, sometimes, how they'd react if I offered them advice about their jobs:

| BRAIN | DREAM SEQUENCE | WHENEVER |

On crew, Lighting is setting up. Continuity walks over to where the First Assistant is discussing something in the schedule with the Director. Her visage is bright.

CONTINUITY

Hi, fellers!

Jim, about tomorrow's call sheet…

She has their attention.

CONTINUITY

Scene 119, which you've scheduled for the end of first location, would be much better shot before lunchbreak. We could finish with the actor a half-day earlier, and most of the extras.

The two men look at each other, expressionless.

CONTINUITY

(a bonus!)

Then you could shoot Scene 32 straight after, getting rid of the stunt double as well!

Smiles winningly.

CONTINUITY

Nice to be able to help…

Sun breaks out from behind cloudbank; magpies start up
in glorious warbling chorus from nearby grove of shade-
giving trees; Catering van's serving-hatch flies open
dispensing yummy smells throughout the location; Stills
(somehow now part of the group) smiles in support…

First Assistant punches her lights out.

In the '70s, Standby Props and Standby Wardrobe weren't
responsible for the actual continuity within their own areas:
the holder of the title was the source of all records, and
they came to her for guidance. Later, they became obliged
not only to keep their own records but to oversee their own
areas regarding continuity, and thus Continuity herself was
able to devote a lot more time to the myriad other demands
of her job – of which action continuity was easily the most
demanding, especially under the circumstances of working
with less-than-top-drawer directors …

EXT.	ON LOCATION #3	DAY

It's hot. Very hot. The crew is wearing an assortment of
things on their heads (including handkerchiefs tied at
each corner).

They are waiting in resigned fashion for the end of the
argument between the Director and Continuity.

                    CONTINUITY
          (urgent)
          Look. You didn't agree we'd crossed
          the line* *last* setup. Believe me, if we
          cross it again this is going to look
          like a Saturday matinee serial!

---

* e.g.: on screen a man is talking to two others – he is on the left, so he looks from
left to right of screen at them: in the subsequent close-ups of the other two, one
is ALSO looking left to right!; so the camera was moved to a wrong position,
crossing the 'line' between the characters that was established in the first shot

The Director is obviously considering whether or not to whack her in the mouth; in place of which satisfying activity he adopts the usual directorial fallback position:

                              DIRECTOR
                    (snappishly)
              Look, who's directing this?
              Next setup!-we've wasted enough time.

He turns away with finality.

She stamps off in a rage. The crew starts to come alive.

---

§

Chic and I adapted fine to life on crew – especially when on the same one, of course.

In truth he was better at it: that I had almost permanently to be on my feet didn't cause me to feel that life on crew was simply heavenly. And the demands made of Continuity were unendingly ceaseless, if that's grammatically possible: far more so than those made of a stillsman (as I remarked to him, pointedly, on more than one occasion). But like the rest of the freelance technicians, we became adept at working six-day weeks, usually of seventy-two hours, and at getting all the necessaries of life done on Sunday *if* pickups or reshoots hadn't had to be scheduled.

That what he did was something well outside my level of technical understanding while what I did was something of great interest to him, resulting in his providing me with lots of practical assistance, was just my great good fortune: whichever is the god of luck must have graced me, somewhere along the line, with one immeasurable, approving nod.

Later, when there were no directors left who hadn't heard on the grapevine how demanding I was, but Chic was still shooting stills, there was enjoyment to be derived from looking after him while he continued to put in all those hours.

Well … I called it 'looking after', even if he did have to still do the cooking. But he never saw that as a chore.

Speaking of the set, we went down to Melbourne late in the '70s to work on a movie being shot in various Victorian locations. The director had seen Chic's stills from Sandy Harbutt's iconic *Stone** and been knocked out by them; and he made no secret of the fact that he was intending to borrow *Stone*'s look and feel for his own feature. I was hired because I was with Chic; but also because the Lighting Cameraman, having worked with me, had given his seal of approval.

The original script was absolutely excellent, and the whole crew was looking forward to it. However, the director, whose first feature this was, decided after it had been issued to everyone that he needed to change it. I have no memory of him discussing his changes, but that's not surprising because I don't remember him ever discussing anything with anyone.

C.S. in background, stills cameras swapped for a 16mm Arri

---

* the first feature Chic worked on, and he also appears in it (briefly) as a photographer!

Chic enjoyed the shoot, as always – particularly as he got to do some operating on the really big setups, becoming one of several movie camera operators when there was complex action that involved lots of on-screen characters doing lots of things at once.

Unhappily, though, the movie brought us only grief.

He'd been paid a retainer as stillsman – nothing for the camera-operating, but he didn't mind – and the great part of his fee was to come when his stills came into their own during the movie's marketing, a common arrangement on Australian features back then. Eventually that time arrived, whereupon the producers came up with an excuse not to pay him – something about the word 'sales' as opposed to the word 'marketing' in his contract. His invoices were ignored and there were no responses to messages left. When he turned up in person the office was empty (the size of post-production was so minuscule that such evasion was easy).

The Stringer stills underpinned a totally successful marketing campaign: the producers were on a roll, their names bandied about admiringly. We saw the director frequently on TV, modestly agreeing that he had indeed directed the movie brilliantly, always seated or standing in front of one or other of Chic's wonderful stills for context. The then film industry union wouldn't touch us with a barge pole, the useless *pricks!*; and we couldn't possibly afford to go to law.

He realised he'd been hung out to dry and there wasn't a thing he could do about it, but Chic's only reaction to this chicanery was a deep frustration that he couldn't furnish our income: they owed (and never paid) him a quite large amount, and our living had been planned around it. We managed somehow or other until I found a job, and throughout this time we kept seeing his work as the movie was trumpeted hither and yon; but not a single still carried the by-line that should have been there – they might all have popped out of some camera in a kind of pictorial parthenogenesis.

Going totally against type, he never forgot this utter bastardry. It had been a horrible shock for him to find there were people completely without honour – or even common decency – in the industry he loved so greatly.

So negatively affected by it was he that, many years later, when a harmless bloke setting up something akin to a museum of the movie wanted to talk to him about the stills, Chic refused even to discuss it, then or ever.

§

In total contrast, the best thing that ever happened did so during that Melbourne sojourn: we got married. It was 18th February, 1978.

Reader, I married him

Our wedding was super: just us, Jo and her husband, and Sarah and Francis – four of the five people closest to us (Erica, by far the worst-harmed victim of Kit's behavioural implosion, was by then divorced and back in the UK). It was a civil ceremony, and held in a notable old building that had once been Victoria's Royal Mint: the room's real claim to fame was that the desk used for marriage ceremonies was that once used by the judge for the sentencing of Ned Kelly! Not much of a connection, eh? – in fact, a pretty strange bit of furniture for a marriage celebration room.

My brother-in-law brought home about a ton of champers and we all got stuck into it with great enthusiasm during the wedding lunch, thus rendering some of the shots for which Chic set the camera up somewhat less than level – not all of them, fortunately ...

Most of the film crew dropped around to have a jar with us afterwards, which was delightful: I was having such a good time that the Instamatic I took of the group was hopeless*.

And that is, in fact, probably all that needs to be told about the day.

§

The job I'd got was running the office of a legal and architectural management consultancy: my two lady employers gave us lovely wedding gifts, and sat back to enjoy listening to me answering the phone using my new name.

I never tired of it. I had looked forward so much to being Mrs Stringer, and was overjoyed to become her, so to speak ...

INT.   MANAGEMENT CONSULTANCY   DAY

                                M.R.
            (pompous)
        Balham and Associates – Mrs Stringer
        speaking...

Momentary frozen pause while the caller gets it together.

---

* doubt I took a decent Continuity shot in my career, to be truthful

                              CALLER
          (chaotically)

     Erhmm…Margaret Rose? Have you gone
     then…? Or is that you…? I mean – WHAT
     did you say when you answered?

                               M.R.
          (cheerful)

     Oh, hi, Frank! – I'm Mrs Stringer, now:
     we got married on Saturday.

                              FRANK
          (this hasn't helped)

     I see…

     But you're back at work on MONDAY?!

                               M.R.
     Whyever not? – we've been living together
     for over eighteen months! We're not
     likely to sail off on a honeymoon cruise
     or anything: after all, it's not as if
     we haven-

                              FRANK
          (in great haste)

     Nonono, of course! Well, congrats, and
     all that…

Whew! – just.

                              FRANK
     So; Mrs Stringer, eh? – and do we all
     have to call you 'Mrs Stringer' from now
     on?

She's thought of this.

                               108

(magnanimous)

Oh no – only people who don't already
know me …

And she reflects with immeasurable satisfaction upon a
lifetime of being Mrs Stringer stretching away in front
of her.

---

§

When the job offers on the movie had come through, I'd
persuaded Chic to make our going south an actual move.
He saw I was truly keen to go back to the city in which I'd
spent so interesting a decade, so had gone along with my idea
without a great deal of demurring.

I've been thinking about having been able to persuade
him so easily to take this step … He told me very often that he
loved me – but I can't remember what I thought that actually
meant, back then. I know that my love for him was fierce:
I was determined to protect him from anything that might
hurt him, physical or emotional. If he broke something I
denied its having any value or worth; if he forgot something
that impacted on us in any way I immediately said it had
not the slightest importance. His continued happiness was
paramount. Typically, I didn't comprehend that he felt
exactly the same. I suppose I didn't *expect* him to love me as
I did him.

Anyway … once settled in, I changed my mind, and
only partly on account of our having become financially
imprisoned.

To my own amazement, I could see that I had finally,
aged thirty-four!, realised where I really wanted to live, and
it definitely wasn't Melbourne. When the shoot was over
and ordinary life returned, I became desperate to go home
to Sydney; and Chic never castigated me for having pushed

us into an instance of foolhardiness now defined by a rental agreement.

We'd brought our cats with us, of course; but we lost The Captain to a fast car out the front of the house. So Chic took me out to the Cat Protection Society, and we chose not one replacement but two: a mostly tabby long-hair and a silver-grey short-hair, and we named them Arthur Sullivan and W.S. Gilbert.

The silver-grey ended up being called The Wooluf (a cartoon character). It turned out, after Chic did some research into his looks, that he was three-quarters Russian Blue; and it was he who set our feet on the path to Russian Blue fandom, which we trod throughout the years with joy. I can lay hands right now on a filing card covered in inky kitty tracks, labelled in Chic's writing 'WOOLUF prints' ...

Arthur was never given an affectionate soubriquet. Arthur was noticeably strange, and he loved only me*: he would sit on me in my beanbag and gaze lovingly into my face, and shortly he would start drooling! I didn't love him a lot; but he was a little animal, and really pretty, and I reckon it's hard to reject adoration from a pretty little animal, regardless of dampness of lap.

But we loved The Doctor greatly, and we loved The Wooluf greatly, and we put up with Arthur; and they all helped us through those seemingly endless months in Melbourne, when we felt as if someone had handed down a sentence that we must continue living there or go directly to jail (it's only honest to say that we sometimes felt as if we were already incarcerated).

Eventually we managed to track down the necessary moolah to go back: I'd applied for and got a job at the Film & TV School in Sydney so funds were in the offing; and the friend for whom we'd house-sat previously was good enough to take us in while we found somewhere to live.

If there was any real lesson to be learned from our

---

* hmm: maybe I could've written that better ...

southern confinement, it was for me – the underlining of the inescapable fact that you should never try to *go back*. Life is a river, flowing without pause; nothing stays the same, and revisiting past scenes of delight is out.

You can't dream the impossible dream.

But I was to discover that you can bear with unbearable sorrow.

TO THE ISLAND

Once back, we started thinking about getting a place of our own. It wasn't that the idea clutched us around the throat: we'd never been driven to 'possess the dream' so much as simply wanting tenure. We started looking in the paper for blocks of land, in a casual way; for Chic had decided he'd build a kit house if we could find an affordable block. I'd never heard of Dangar Island when I came across it in a Saturday *Sydney Morning Herald*: Chic knew of it by name. We decided to check it out.

Back in the late '70s the Island was quite delightful. It's hilly at one end and flat at the other, with the hilly part bushland and the flat part lawn and native trees – a totally lovely environment, with the mighty Hawkesbury all around. The solitary moving vehicle on it was the fire truck – an ancient topless Land Rover, used by the local volunteer bush fire brigade (which Chic joined promptly and with which he fought many bushfires throughout the region). Since the late '80s it's changed a lot, I believe: now it consists largely of houses to rent to holiday-makers, and there's been modernisation to keep them happy – always the way.

We fell in love with Dangar right away, and before very much longer were able to buy one of the bush blocks, halfway up the hill, with amazing vistas north across the river to the opposite bank, delightfully named 'The Icicles' for reasons we never ascertained, and an impossibility of being built out – not unless the council decided to allow skyscrapers along the foreshore.

Chic swung into action: he'd abandoned the idea of building a kit house, deciding he preferred to design one. He submitted his plans to the Hornsby Shire Council, which passed them without a single query: he project-managed the entire build, starting with quantity surveying everything needed, ordering it and arranging for it to be delivered by the only industrial-sized ferry on the Hawkesbury, and then he started to build.

like the truck's list? :-}

The Doctor loved it: he never let Chic go down to the site alone, and seemed to derive the greatest pleasure from climbing laboriously up the planks laid for access as the build rose from the surrounding bushland, so that he could be where Chic was working. He had also to climb a short but absolutely vertical ladder, once first floor level was reached, in order to get to the working platform! You can see him on the next page – at the near edge, just above the ramp...

Chic moved through footings, and flooring, and then onto the first of the two storeys. Before that was finished he installed an under-floor vacuum cleaner: my god, it was a memorable thing – everyone should have one! Just try to imagine the joy of not having to drag a machine behind you that gets obstinately stuck behind corners and chair legs as you heave it around ...

Then came the timber frame walls, and the second floor.

the foreman being active

By the time the second set of wall framings was up, it was already an impressive building, though not huge, by any means. It didn't need to be: it was just for us.

Of the two storeys, the top was set well back over the bottom so that there was a huge front deck upstairs. That storey contained our bedroom, a lav with a fabulous view if you left the door open, a bathroom, and a second bedroom, for visitors – of course, used as a study most of the time. The ground floor (actually quite high off it) was the laundry, the kitchen and the dining room along the back, with a most beautiful Chic-designed and -cut, J-shaped set of timber stairs leading from one floor to the other, its access between the dining room and a huge living room stretching across the front.

He did all the electrical and plumbing work. I have no idea how this came about; but as it had often to be inspected, it was certainly done in a manner that prevented any finger-wagging by Hornsby Council. Maybe he obtained a temporary licence? – I just don't know; but it all worked without a hitch.

There were verandahs front and back, the latter covered by the rear overhang – perfect for drying the washing as the sea breeze always came through, and he installed a flap-up rectangular washing line for me. Since doing the washing has always been my favourite domestic chore (the only one I actually enjoy), the laundry and this washing-line got used more than anything else.

Chic always reckoned that he couldn't afford to put down a single thing that could be described as an item of clothing because I'd instantly seize it and put it in the washing: he was prone to telling people that I tended to follow him about for this very purpose. Hyperbole of the worst kind, of course; but I was impervious to his insults and merely went about my business of making sure everything was perfectly clean, perfectly sensibly.

He made me so proud.

the foreman, more relaxed during glazing

§

Our block had a really severe inclination: I don't remember the degree, but the path ascended from Riverview Avenue to the house seemingly vertically, past a huge eucalypt with a beautiful cymbidium nestling in its heart; and even the super-fit Chic had to pause for breath. Then came the front stairs, to be negotiated through a hole in the verandah. The major benefit of this was the view, unassailable and wondrous. When we had parties at the house, the guests were almost invariably to be found on the two front verandahs, sitting swinging their legs over the edges (for there were no railings).

That enormous eucalypt – a blackbutt, I believe – caused us much grief, but also brought us financial relief.

I was off doing temp work at one of the big computer companies in North Sydney. On my way home I ran into a co–Island dweller at Hornsby Station, who grasped both my hands and gazed into my face with sympathy, crying, 'Oh, Margaret Rose, I'm so *sorry*!' – but I shan't go into how I had to drag her story out of her (it threw me into total panic: I was rigid with fear by the time I got home).

Chic had just finished the house's glazing: with two storeys of entirely glass frontage, there was an awful lot of it.

On this particular and memorable day, he'd stopped for a bite of lunch, taking the morning paper with him to the dining-room table while he ate. It was miserable weather – sweaty and overcast, with occasional rumbles of distant thunder.

Arthur and The Doctor were asleep, each in a beanbag in the living room, just around the corner from Chic, who was reading the paper in peace and contentment.

He told me later what transpired:

There is a tumbler firm in his grasp.

C.S.
(the amazement still with him)

First thing I knew was the cat flap on
the kitchen door swinging shut with a
bang: Arthur had left the lounge room
so fast that I didn't see him go past
me! And The Doctor went too - although
he couldn't move at Arthur's speed, of
course.

Another large glug of scotch (for shock: self-
prescribed).

C.S.

I was wondering what had freaked them,
and had got as far as deciding to get
up and go out the middle door onto the
verandah to see if someone was coming up
the hill, when it happened.

'It' was, the Islanders told us, ball lightning, seen in those parts from time to time, but not in the period we'd been on the Island. It came down Mullet Creek, crossed the Hawkesbury, and for reasons unknown zeroed in on our blackbutt.

It hit the tree as a fearsome amount of voltage and instantly – the adverb is chosen deliberately – INSTANTLY all the sap in that great tree boiled. It blew up like a bomb. Rather than being a huge, graceful, attractive native tree, it was suddenly a completely shattered stump; and there was a collection of enormous, killing shards flying towards our house – which they hit, without a lot of time's going by, in the middle of the bottom storey.

When the glass door in the middle of that glass wall was blasted in, its handle plate was driven across the living room with, I believe I can say absolutely accurately, the speed of summer lightning, and incredible force, and went right through the TV set against the opposite wall; from there it passed through both kitchen walls carrying TV glass, and bits were found lying on the back verandah, where they had fallen because of the plate's losing impetus when colliding with one of the steel poles supporting the top storey (the pole was very slightly dented).

Howzat ...?!

goodbye, cymbidium ...

Every picture on the living-room walls was damaged by flying debris – or if not by that, then by the branches themselves, which had ended up occupying most of the room. Well, there was nowhere else for them to go, really – not when they were being propelled by a force of unimaginable power and travelling in that direction.

I doubt much elucidation is needed regarding all those front walls of glazing that Chic had just finished.

hello, blackbutt!

If he had indeed walked across the living room to go out on the verandah and see if someone was coming, Chic would have been dead instead of telling me about it – an undeniable fact. It shook us to the core, as we had never considered for a second that such danger could exist: like, *inside your own house* you could be killed by forces of nature? – beyond the bounds of credibility, surely ...?!

We got over it, but. And every cloud, etc., etc.

The insurance company was appalled to think they had to pay not only for the timber and glass and fittings again, but also for a labourer to travel all the way up to Brooklyn, and then to and from the Island every day for a couple of weeks while redoing all the glazing. So when Chic suggested that he do it (again) and include the cost of his labour in the claim, they were rapt – and that was how we could suddenly afford to buy into the new marina that was under construction over at Brooklyn for Island residents. Back then, around 1980, the cost to each boat-owner was about a thousand bucks – no mean sum!; but we had become flush overnight, and buy in we did, with huge relief.

And the second glass pass was carried out *much* faster; for when you do something again – even if it isn't madly enjoyable – it always takes less time.

§

Here's one of the clear and glorious memories I have of our reglazed domicile: one morning I awoke – I slept on the window-wall side of our bed – to very small tapping noises, and lay there in a fairly muddled state wondering what on earth could be making them. Eventually my brain woke up too, and instructed me to turn over towards the source of them and look, which I did. There on the deck were about a dozen rainbow lorikeets standing in a row, tapping with their little beaks on the very bottom of our window wall (the only part they could reach) to say, *'Breakfast, please!'*

I could scarcely believe my eyes – lorikeets, clever enough to understand Pavlov ...?! Eventually, after what seemed like hours of selfish delight, I poked Chic through the duvet and hissed at him:

M.R.

(trying, quite unnecessarily!, not to
frighten the visitors)

Stringer… Stringer! - wake up! We have
breakfast guests!

C.S.

(comes to vaguely)

Hmnnhh…?

Turning in the direction of his beloved a bit grumpily,
his eyes widen in astonishment once he can see over her.

C.S.

What on earth??? What are they doing
there?! Have you ever…? How do they
even know we're *in* here?!

Having exhausted himself with this list of imponderable
questions, he sinks back into silence and some pillows.

The two of them stay there for a long time,
entranced, before the lorikeets realise that their
audience is awake: it percolates through their wee bird-
brains that tapping gently is not going to achieve their
aim, so they all begin to scream at once, *very loudly*…

Of course, we arose and fed the tiny creatures, with joy and
amazement, which led to uncountable repeat performances
in the succeeding years.

Lorikeets are utterly beautiful and irresistible, so the
suburban ones are very spoiled: anyone who lives in Sydney's
leafy parts will tell you so.

§

We were living on the Island when my sister Carole's life ended. She died in Ireland, where she was with her then husband, a dreadful man whom everyone else in the family loathed and feared: he sent her body back COD to our mother. It was an appalling time, and nobody could ascertain what had happened – in fact, we never did.

I knew I still wasn't emotionally stable enough to undertake the long flight that would culminate in another terrible family funeral in Perth; and my sister Jo and her husband weren't going to be able to get there because of their very young family. So Chic announced that he would go over for Carole's funeral: he said, simply, that my mother would need to have a man with her.

His arrival was welcomed with hysterical relief. She derived enormous help from having him there to partner her; and said she didn't know how she would have got through it without him.

On his return, I muttered something about the last line of Kipling's 'Gunga Din'; but he pretended not to understand the allusion, which I had meant sincerely.

§

We didn't ever lose our love of the house Chic built; but we did, in time, of the Island.

A maxim for you: never choose a place to live in that people come to for holidays.

Dangar Island was becoming more and more popular, even back then in the mid-to-late '80s, and its quaintness meant that families were buying up the little properties to use as holiday houses, either for them or for their friends and rellies. And, of course, as investments, curse of society.

This is not something to be happy about if you live there, I promise: it leads to constant influxes of strangers who care naught for their environment and want to do nothing but party endlessly. They scatter refuse, they have zero consideration for the inhabitants and they couldn't give a rat's about the wildlife – except for those visitors who briefly think it cute and feed it all the wrong food, thereby hastening its passing along the route to extinction.

But more than that: we realised we'd come to the Island too late in our lives – we should have done it when we were younger. For as the years passed, the block got steeper; and Chic's having to pull the boat in and out on its running line became more and more of a back-breaker; and dragging a full shopping trolley up the hill became more boring and less rewarding ... Basically, bracketing fifty by the odd couple of years on either side, we were getting too old for this caper; and we decided to sell up and buy somewhere on the mainland.

I sometimes think the people most upset about this decision of ours were the friends and acquaintances who used to come and visit us: the trip to Dangar by car or train, then the little ferry, followed by arrival at our lovely house with its wondrous views, an always delicious Stringer lunch and a bit of a walk about the Island was considered delightful – and so it was, of course! From our point of view, the fact that guests were obliged to catch the last ferry was A Good Thing, preventing lengthy lingering. Mind you, we did have house guests from time to time: Francis and Sarah, or Erica, arrived on the odd occasion; and various rellies.

walking the Island with Francis

We were remonstrated with for many years about having turned our backs on so beautiful a location. But what cannot be understood unless you've been there and done that is this: *beauty alone is not enough*. It cannot make up for the tiredness, and the lack of enthusiasm for the energy needed for most of what we did, as we got older and had less.

But there was another emotional factor that we didn't discuss for a long time. We preferred to be where things were happening, though we rarely took part in any. This may not seem to make sense ...

What we wanted was to be in the situation where we could pop into town at the drop of a hat without having to make any effort. We needed to have the *possibility*, and not be locked far away out of reach, on an island. We needed to be somewhere other than in a place where going anywhere at all involved walking down the hill, pulling the boat in, taking it to the jetty, loading me, crossing to the mainland, unloading me, mooring it, walking to the car and then driving for a very long way. Even if going out was a rarity, we still wanted the knowledge that we *could*.

So we bought a house in Annandale, in Sydney's Inner West, where we spent some really enjoyable years. Subsequently we moved to a little suburb right next to the CBD; and there we remained.

Slickers of the city, it would seem.

HAND TO MOUTH

Fairly early on I told you that Chic cooked like a god, yes? – nothing less than the truth. Well, as far as I know it: I mean, my relationship with the panoply of deities we humans have managed to dream up for ourselves is neither close nor binding...

There was a time when I thought about compiling and issuing *The C.S. Cookbook*. But then I realised that the way he cooked was to take a recipe that appealed to him and – well, change it, to suit whatever were his preferences. In other words, he was a true chef: he even invented some dishes that he also made changes to, later! It would never have been possible to commit this kind of innovative stuff to paper.

Guests coming to dine did so with eagerness.

EXT.	VERANDAH, ISLAND HOME	DAY

The small group of honoured invitees has struggled up from the ferry wharf, and the tops of their heads can now be seen as they toil up the block.

M.R. looks thoughtfully down from verandah's edge upon the slowly approaching file.

<u>M.R.</u>
(calls back into the house)

Stringer, were we actually expecting
FIVE people? I don't remember us asking
that bloke who hangs 'round with James
and Dot.

In the kitchen, C.S. mutters to himself something unintelligible about oven temperature, then shouts back:

C.S.

 <u>C.S.</u>

No, we didn't. But it's OK: I must've
guessed he'd turn up too, 'cause I've
made enough *spaghetti al forno* to feed
an army.

He joins her near the stair-hole through which the guests
must eventually make their appearance, making a move to
wipe his hands on his apron.

 <u>C.S.</u>
 (realises what he's doing)

Shit!–why am I still wearing this?!

 <u>M.R.</u>
 (meltingly–a C.S. meal is nigh)

Big horse. You're the *cuoco*, and
everyone knows that *cuochi* wear aprons!

He repels her untimely advances with hands still floury
from having put a *focaccina* into the oven, leaving a
messy handprint on her front.

That was pretty representative, that scene – we really did
have people turn up unexpectedly, claiming we'd reinvited
them after their last meal ('and it was such a lovely day for
a drive...'). It was never a problem, for Chic's cooking was of
the kind that didn't require a vast and ever-changing array
of sophisticated ingredients. Also, as we didn't have a large
number of friends, even the odd hanger-on was someone we
weren't displeased to see.

There in our house on Dangar Island Chic did more
çooking than ever, simply because more people wanted to
visit us so as to combine the huge pleasure of consuming his
cooking with the delights of wandering around the Island.

There were not all that many weekends we had to ourselves, it seems to me as I think back on it.

Though he didn't cook in any way formally, one of the things I've wondered about since having to learn to do it myself is how he was able to multi-task around the oven and stovetop without ever once losing his cool under the pressure of the differing timings. And then I've thought that maybe he did lose it, occasionally ... for although he loved our cats as much as I did, sometimes even Chic the mild-mannered could get terse and end up shouting a bit

Mr Walker? The Captain? – don't
remember and can't tell

§

Chic cooked – well, everything. Every 'cuisine', I mean (and I must put the word in quotes, for I've always considered it somewhat unfair that the French got the naming rights). His curries were sublime, his stir-fries too; he made a cassoulet that even Rick Stein would've really liked; and his *osso buco* was far and away the best of any. The bottom line is that he could turn his hand to anything – not only successfully but with panache. He claimed it was my enjoyment of his cooking that gave him his biggest thrill; so our culinary arrangement was totally satisfying to both of us.

But of all the cuisines over which he had mastery, it was the *cucina povera* of Italy that was the favourite of both of us. We ate it, I admit, most of the time. *La cucina povera* is largely pasta and vegetables – how unexciting that sounds, and how misleading! Those who, as we did, enjoy this kind of food, usually glom it down with greed and some wonderfully crusty *ciabatta*; because, as everyone knows, the gods invented Italian food with the specific purpose of its being accompanied by one or other of the many – and equally super – kinds of Italian bread.

Chic actually made our bread for a while, and it was terrific. But his joy in cooking sprang far more from inspiration and/or delivery than from careful, lengthy and repetitive preparation: before long, he found the stages of bread-making to be wearisome. In truth, this was part of his character: once initial enthusiasm had generated whatever it was, he would lose interest if it didn't retain some degree of challenge. It was sometimes unfortunate that if doing <X> became merely a matter of replicating things already mastered, he'd eventually wander vaguely away.

I've fairly recently been brought to the happy position of deciding that my remembering this tendency is what relieves me of guilt about having been the one who eventually raised the issue of leaving the Island, and who carried it, really. If I hadn't pushed the notion of selling up and buying a house in a place where we didn't need a bloody boat, I'm pretty certain we would've lived indefinitely in an almost totally unlined house. Mind you, that aspect didn't actually worry me at all; and it wasn't hard to understand the stultifyingly boring side to sticking up squillions of sheets of plasterboard. As I've said before, I wanted him to be happy at all times; and if this involved living in a house that was nigh on freezing in the winter and so hot in summer that all flat surfaces heated up, that was OK – no worries! But I'm fairly certain, now, that he went along unprotestingly with moving off the Island because it meant he would never have to finish that horrible job ...

From the photos below, you can also see that Chic had

Film School training group: nobody's missing the ceiling

their hosts: nobody's missing the wall linings

occasionally to cater for astonishingly large numbers; and this he did with pleasure and aplomb. Had it been me, I would've had a conniption fit as they started climbing the block, and had to be carried off foaming at the mouth. But he, having worked out how best to furnish a meal that didn't need to be cooked on the spot – well, not *all* of it – never turned a hair; not even if something got a bit overcooked on account of his being pestered for information by guests*when he was meant to be turning the gas off under it.

It was in our Island house that we had our only wall oven. No: it wasn't a wall oven ... but I don't know how to describe the kind that sits on a benchtop. A benchtop oven? – never heard the term ... Oh, forget it! – you know what I mean. We derived so much joy from this appliance that we were sometimes to be found just standing in front of it admiringly, considering what next wondrous Stringer meal to consign to its innards. Well, that's what *I* was doing, anyway: he tended more to bewailing all the years of not having had one; and it certainly did contribute to his doing so much cooking in the Island house. You want pizza with a thin, crisp crust? – here's a *quattro formaggi* to die for. You want roast pork? – here you go: whaddya think of that crackling? You want meatloaf? – ever eaten one so moist yet so firm, and so full of flavour as this one? And so on ... I could rave for pages about Stringer's meals, as you can tell: it's been suggested by more than one person that our marriage was so successful on account of them.

But, you know ... whether accepting being gourmands or gourmets – and both were correct – I always fall back with joy upon his firm belief that he only cooked as well as he did because of my enjoyment of it.

I mean, think about that: how often do you come across a bloke who attributes to his gluttonous wife the credit for his great skill as a chef?!

---

* he so often was: Chic had to spend a lot of time (perfectly happily) giving people answers to questions

Chic and I were alike in our somewhat cavalier attitude to our families. But I did eventually start to wonder about his siblings and their families: I conceived a longing to meet and claim Brothers, not having any of my own, and circumstances duly conspired to grant my wish.

The next brother up, Bruce, invited us to the wedding of his only daughter Anne Marie, in Canberra. Most of the clan was to be there: Mum and Dad weren't fit enough, though, and Chic's eldest brother wasn't going to make it. (In fact, I never met Doug, not once: his wife wasn't strong, and this fact kept them in a kind of social limbo. Doug was the first of the four Stringer boys to die: Chic went to visit him in hospital several times and was *deeply* upset to lose him, especially so soon after their relationship had been re-established.)

I don't remember many details of the wedding of Anne Marie to her Alex. I do remember standing there between the pews at some point during the church service and looking at Bruce, so obviously Chic's brother it was almost funny; I was wondering if he was even remotely as nice. He must have felt my thoughts: he looked up and caught my eye, saw who I was with and grinned, lowering one eyelid in a slow wink. I grinned back, and we were friends. It gave Chic the greatest pleasure thereafter to see how well the two of us got on – though as Bruce not only looked like but also had the same sense of humour as his younger brother, it was all that could possibly have occurred. He was a lovely man, Bru: and we were both desolate when his lungs gave out after a lifetime of smoking and he died, not all that many years later.

And as for Reg, number two of the four Stringer boys, he remains with us, I am very happy to say. Chic and I used to visit Reg and his wife Jill in the various houses they built for themselves (one after the other – not all at once!) down in Victoria, whenever we could get to them, for they always built down on the Peninsula. Not long after I'd started meeting Stringers, we were staying with Francis and Sarah during a Melbourne trip, and our hosts offered to drive us down to see Reg and Jill, visit friends of their own a little further on, then collect us on the way back. When we reached the house Reg was there to meet us, and invited them in for a quick jar, and a look at his latest build.

| INT. | REG & JILL'S HOUSE | DAY |

The four visitors have been wandering about and making many admiring comments, with the younger Mrs Stringer being her usual wordy self.

C.S. has already squeezed her hand sharply a couple of times, but it seems her ebullience cannot be tempered.

                         FRANCIS
                 (interestedly, to Reg)

        You've got some nice big pieces…Did
        you have to disassemble any of your
        furniture for your move?

Reg opens his mouth to respond, but is forestalled.

                          M.R.
                 (sweeping gesture upwards)

        But look at the height of the ceilings,
        my dear!-you could get the Eiffel Tower
        in here!

                          REG
            (looks benignly upon his sister-in-law)

        Will you stop trying to dominate the
        conversation?!

Her husband and their friends roar with laughter at such instant recognition.

She grins: no problem with admitting to one of her major character flaws.

Reg and I were mates from that moment: call my bluff and I'm your fan forever.

§

All the boys spoke at one time or another, and always with pride, of Dad's younger days when he was a comedian – and I mean that literally: he would take to the stage and perform any one of a range of comedic routines, and they said he was really funny. Reg speaks about Dad as having been, also, 'a thespian'; and he sent me some old newspaper cuttings bearing that out with a vengeance. It seems my father-in-law was someone of stature in local repertory, down there in Melbourne, before either Chic or I was born ... There isn't any of that kind of innocent enjoyment, not any more: we have 'moved on'.

Even when he was doing drama Dad couldn't keep humour out of it: Reg has a delightful story of the time Dad took on the additional responsibility of general backup, so that as well as having a rôle it was his job to save things by fair means or foul if any of the actors lost the plot. And when they eventually did, one night – it was always going to happen – Dad rushed onstage with a shotgun and fired it into the flies, from which fell a prearranged large rubber fish! Ho yes, and he was a man of great humour still when I was introduced to him – although by then he was already extremely ill.

my famous father-in-law

§

My four sisters were all met at various times, but it was my second-eldest sister with whom Chic formed a real friendship: she was the closest to me, so that was bound to occur. Jo was my surrogate mother from that time I'd arrived in Sydney under her care; and she remained so, regardless of our respective locations. I continued to love her second-most in the world; and, true to family type, we often fought furiously.

All four claimed that Chic strongly resembled our father, but the only similarity I acknowledged between the two men was that their hair receded in the same way as they aged. Still, I must confess that on the day Chic reached his sixty-fifth birthday I was deeply relieved.

How fortunate that prescience was not amongst my attributes.

§

Chic was happy the sisters lived interstate, for it meant no frequent family visiting in either direction: he had no wish that I be distracted by repeated incursions of either family or friends. Fine by me, that was: couldn't be better!

Throughout the thirty-one years of our life we never discussed our turning in on each other, because it simply didn't occur to us that we were doing it. We didn't feel a lack when couples we knew broke up and were not seen again, even though we had enjoyed their company; when others left Oz's shores we were similarly unbereft.

A quite good analogy is the time we looked thoughtfully upon the science fiction part of our ever-growing book collection, and decided it was no longer wanted. We pulled all the SF books out of the shelves, packing them for St Vinnies, and reworked the others to close the gaps; *et voilà!* – it was as if that part of our library had never been there. We had really enjoyed reading the SF over the years, but we didn't miss it when it was gone.

It was even thus that we proceeded on our merry way, slowly cutting from our life almost everyone – without, really, a moment's thought.

OLD HABITS

It is absolutely impossible for many and many a daughter to prevent herself from becoming just like her mother, ecco ...

–Q.E.D.

I found it hard to love my mother, as I have already related. I truly admired her excellent brain and her various abilities; but loving her was, for me, an almost insuperable challenge. And this in itself was passing strange; for in every other case, admiring someone meant that I also loved that person.

But unintentionally, with a kind of horrid perverseness, I could and did store all the things I *didn't* admire about her in my hindbrain, which would trot them out with depressing predictability. So Chic had to learn to deal with behaviour learned, all too lastingly, at Mama's knee.

In my own defence, I did recognise my failings, but only ever after the event: I seemed unable to warn myself, 'Uh-oh, another bad trait looming ...'. Rather, I embraced each one enthusiastically at the time, and was ashamed of them all, afterwards.

Had it not been for his steadfastness in the face of every example of my headstrong behaviour, I would have become a mirror image of my mama, rather than merely the pale shadow of her that I am. Why this should be, when she was not high on my list of favourite people, can only be explained by the theorem – with no diagrams or workings – at the beginning of this chapter.

Everything I did impacted on Chic, yes; but that held in reverse, too. Perhaps the strangest aspect of this is that our totally different personalities and behaviours, regardless of failing or eccentricity, were in fact what created the unbreakable bond between us.

And here I am again in front of that beautiful tree:

T³ *Neither was complete, but each able to supply the other with what was lacking; and thus did we make each other whole.*

See that? – it springs directly from the taproot.

KINDNESS

When Chic saw that <X> was needed, or simply that I could do with something, he would provide it. Often, to my great joy, this meant his actually creating it; from designing me a pattern to incorporate the word 'opera' in a beautiful font within the back of a cardigan I was knitting, to – well, anything my little heart fancied!

In our early days together, when we were still both working in the film industry, he watched me doing my schtick as Continuity over a couple of projects – having to find a space for my typewriter during breaks, or taking the easy way out and writing as neatly as possible (easy for *some*!) – and decided that what would really be of help would be a portable desk.

So he made me one.

It was sensational: its leathered desktop consisted of a built-in little typewriter with a flat space next to it to put the annotated originals from which I copied; and it had drawers to contain my custom-produced, self-carboning paperwork and everything I needed to work with (pens, pencils, erasers, white-out, etc.). Its legs folded against its bottom to turn it into something to be carried. It came with a small but solid fold-up stool (which was kept in the Stringer household forever, and which I still have and use). It was made of thinnish particle board, with camera-case reinforcing on all edges. And on top of this, it was painted bright yellow – easily my favourite colour, as he knew well. My desk was the envy of all who saw it: many was the time that someone offered to carry it for me so as to be able to study its construction.

On projects we both worked on, it was taken for granted that Chic had made it for me (it was known he could produce anything); and on projects where I was without him as stillsman, it gave me joy to tell those who asked me how it had come into being.

§

We had a really super dark blue 4Runner, second version (well ... I'd say v1.1 rather than v2.0) of the name: we were absolutely crazy for it. Some *fucking bastard* stole it.

While we were living on Dangar Island, we had to park our vehicle on the mainland, at Brooklyn: everyone who lived on the Island was similarly obliged.

There was zero security, but we'd never heard of any car being stolen, so we parked there without a second thought. Of course, we had one of those steering-wheel clamps – that's what everyone used, back in the '80s.

But one morning, after we'd moored the boat at the marina, got out with all our stuff and were making our way to where we'd left the 4Runner, it had vanished.

I had trouble taking it in.

EXT. PARKING AREA, BROOKLYN DAY

                    M.R.
          (mindlessly)
      The car's gone ...

                    C.S.
          (with restraint)
      I see that.

                    M.R.
          (utter confusion)
      Where is it?

                    C.S.
          (distracted)
      It's been stolen. We'll have to go to
      the police station and report it. Come
      on, we—

      What are you doing?!

She's started wandering about as if looking for the large, absent vehicle.

<u>C.S.</u>

>(loses it)

>For god's sake!—the bloody thing's been stolen, and that's it, OK?!

>(as he walks off)

>Pull yourself together!—we have to get the fucking 'processes' started!

For this was an event he had trouble dealing with: he was the one who did the looking after, and that covered being responsible for *everything*. It was the part he'd chosen because he wanted it; but it meant that something like the theft of our adored vehicle caused him suffering and guilt beyond the norm: he was rendered totally out of sorts. Happily, though, once due police process had been set in motion – a total waste of time, of course – he reverted to his normal sunny self.

Before long I was obliged to take issue with the leasing finance company, which sent us a letter of demand based on the Rule of 78 for what was still owed on the 4Runner. I responded by providing them with my own version of the remaining debt, pointing out that they had sneaked an extra month in. I took the month out again, and sent an ungentle letter of refutation of their workings together with provision of my own, and they were obliged to capitulate. Chic would often indicate that he didn't like my being a stroppy consumer, and was not happy with me Taking Issue so often; but on occasions like this he was delighted. This difference between us arose often, for I was (and remain) an unrelenting defender of what I believed right in the face of anyone's telling me otherwise, whereas he wanted a quiet life. To which he had every right, of course! But I found it impossible to roll over and play dead when I felt we were being rooked in any way.

Later, just to balance things up, it turned out that I'd stuffed up on the insurance. When the first renewal notice arrived, I hadn't perused it sufficiently carefully, and simply assumed that because the premium was higher we were paying to insure an up-to-date value. Not so, of course: it was a higher premium for the same value: the 4Runner was insured only for the $23,000 of its purchase price. Since the vehicle had proved so popular with the market, it was now selling for close to $30,000, and we were thus priced out of any possibility of leasing another.

Chic didn't remonstrate with me, or criticise my dickheadedness. He never showed any sign of wanting to beat me over the head for this or any of the mistakes I made (and I *think* there was more than one): he took the insurance money and bought a second-hand car. We went to the sales yard to collect it, and it turned out to be a yellow Falcon sedan. He watched my face as the salesman drove it up to us, and was gratified by my delighted reaction; he'd chosen it carefully from those he found technically acceptable. And we drove happily home, my hand in his pocket – remarkably comforting! – while I reflected upon my good fortune.

§

He became himself a protestor, briefly but totally effectively, on the day that the NRMA, our insurer, phoned to say that the 4Runner had been found. Till that moment, the vehicle had been finally acknowledged as having disappeared for good – probably completely repainted and engine markings altered, etc., etc. In fact, two days previously, the NRMA had called us to say that they would be drawing a cheque for the agreed amount (including the overcharged month's lease) and posting it at the end of the week.

The call to advise of the discovery came on the Thursday: the 4Runner was on its roof somewhere in Barrington Tops, nothing but a shell. The NRMA told me that they would not be posting the cheque, and that we should go and fetch the vehicle: how, they didn't touch upon. Chic took the receiver from me and spoke briefly and quietly, but with intensity. The cheque was posted that day – my guess is less than five minutes after Chic's short but pithy speech – and arrived on the Monday. I told him that he was better at this kind of thing than I was, but he waived any interest in pursuing the kind of consumer stroppiness that kept me on my toes so often.

It gives me joy even now to be able to say with complete honesty that I derived the most gratified pride and pleasure from his being able to improve on anything I did.

In fact, I *needed* things to be that way.

THE WAY WE WERE

To his dismay, frustration and impotent rage, Chic had shown how normal he was by becoming long-sighted when he was some years into his forties. That's what put a stop to his being a stillsman: there were no multifocal spectacles lenses back then, and he couldn't hang a range of specs around his neck – along with the cameras, meters, etc. – that would enable him to view at a moment's notice all the necessary tools of his trade.

So he moved into the organisational side of film production. But eventually we both grew weary of having to kowtow to mediocre employers, deciding (doesn't everyone?) to form our own company. CMR Films became an entity, trading first as Northbridge Films and then, having included digital, as ProVision Film & Video: we were its co-directors. We formed it specifically to produce training material, and from day one did our best to persuade clients to let us make them comedies, for research indicated that the John Cleese model was absolutely successful – and, of course, we enjoyed it enormously.

Chic was the originator and I was the organiser, and we worked together without problem. Well, that's not strictly true: I do recall the odd stand-up fight, here and there – all of which had to do with marketing, for which neither of us showed any aptitude whatsoever … we both lacked that necessary hard outer casing that enables one to be successful at selling.

We'd started with a bang, with contacts made when we were working at Film Australia – people from various government departments whom we'd met on various productions. And from there it was word of mouth for a good long while, which meant we could operate for many years without the need for marketing. This shielded us from harsh reality, alas!; while all along, but unknown to us, the Oz economy was slowing.

We were depressed to discover that even when one is one's own boss, there are still awful people to have to deal with. We had thought, naïvely, that not having to bow to employers who paid our wages would be the bee's knees; but we found that an obligation to agree with difficult clients was quite often worse – people who held the purse-strings and who wanted you to do something different from that which you knew, beyond a shadow of doubt!, would provide the best result. The ones who drove Chic to the point of absolute distraction, not to say screaming rage (that was my area), were the clients who belonged to the 'I accept advice from everyone who offers it' category: they could be relied upon to have changed their minds every time they turned up. When we had clients like this, unable to take responsibility for their own decisions, I simply kept away from them: Chic would not allow himself to become angry, but I wasn't any good at that*.

On the other hand, those clients we really respected and liked were not too thin on the ground: they understood that we knew what we were doing, and put their affairs into our hands trustingly. We never let them down and we never ripped them off. But then, we didn't rip off even the awful ones: our budgeting comprised costing the product and adding a standard margin for producing it. If the requirement for corporate film/video had continued, we could have got by very well indefinitely.

Keating's recession-we-had-to-have killed us off; and it did the same for all the small video production companies. It was only the large ones with major equipment that could ride out the choppy financial seas when corporations decided that the jury rudder to be affixed was represented by their ceasing to spend any money on marketing.

Afterwards we struggled on for far too long, thinking things would improve. Chic was less hopeful than I, for once: unhappily, this was the one time I should have been the pessimist I usually was about work coming in. By the time

---

* did I say that already ...?

he'd managed to persuade me that there was zero hope of our ever being able to get back to where we'd been, and that we absolutely had to think of some other way of earning a crust, we were well and truly in the financial doldrums, with interest rates running at *eighteen per cent!*

He started experimenting with computers: I went back to temping, using my office skills.

Chic took to PCs with a vengeance: the Windows environment provided him with a nonstop challenge (something you could label 'a universal truth', I think). Before long, he not only knew of and understood all PC software even remotely relevant to our needs, but would buy the parts and assemble a computer whenever his current one was no longer delivering what he needed.

But we had to sell our house in Annandale, with its beautifully refurbished office-that-had-been-a-cellar, and its truly marvellously refurbished bathroom and loo, and its stunning new interior stairs from the lounge room down to the office. We were both terribly cast down by having to

it begins   it progresses

leave all that work of Chic's, whose concept, design, deconstruction and complete rebuild had turned out even better than we'd thought it would.

He'd enjoyed it from the outset – somewhat more than did his generously proportioned wife: I found the cramped temporary shower setup really difficult when he'd had to remove the shower cabinet because of needing the space to install a glorious corner bath (but I wouldn't have whinged, would I?!).

Yes; that move made us more unhappy than we were when we farewelled the house he'd built on Dangar Island, for the latter relocation had been of our own choosing.

Eventually I found a contract as operations manager for a company in the CBD that came under the auspices of the Australian Vice-Chancellors' Committee in Canberra, where I had a large CEO for my boss, and he had a small CEO for his wife. I met her after a bit – a terrific woman. Then, not all that much later, it transpired that Chic went to work as a contractor for her. There we were, two married couples, one CEOs and the other their contractors. Chic and his were absolutely suited, and they never exchanged a heated word, not ever. Mine and I did, from time to time[*] and it was to our mutual credit that we were able to fight but not be enemies.

Chic installed and maintained a nine- or ten-workstation peer-to-peer network for Geraldine, and created and maintained her quango's website. These were his official responsibilities. However, as was ever the case with him, he also provided help of a general nature; meaning that when any of his women (for they all were, with the exception of a part-time male accountant) had a question pertaining to anything of any nature whatsoever, she would put it to Chic, and he would answer it. He absolutely loved it all: he was a man to whom practical helping, without its ever being gratuitous, was intensely enjoyable. I laughingly accused him of running a harem, and he just smiled. I was actually

---

[*] as you do, when you have me working for you

146

thrilled that he had found so delightful a niche: this, the last of his contracts, suited everyone down to the ground.

In a glorious little town we visited during a trip we made, we went shopping for something by way of gifts for Chic's women. It gave him enormous pleasure wandering about, searching for the right things to take back. He did politely ask my opinion on his choices; but he selected them off his own bat, after much cogitation. I hoped very greatly that his ladies would appreciate these delightful offerings, which had given him so much happiness in their choosing.

And at the end, his beautiful little CEO, during the gathering his brother and I held for him, talked about those very things with remembered joy.

ALLONS-Y!*

Among the literally – and I mean that literally! – countless things never to be forgotten about him is the time my husband conned me into travelling; and this one's pin-sharp because it changed our life.

It was while we were living in our Annandale house. All freelance activity long since over, we were running our own small corporate video company, very successfully.

In strolled Chic one sunny morning, to where I was sitting reading in the living room. I'd come up from the office below, giving myself some time off because I was pleased with having completed a complex video budget and sent off the quote to a potential client.

INT.   LIVING ROOM   DAY

                         C.S.
              (wandering over to the CD rack)
          Um – darling?

He idly takes a CD from their burgeoning Domingo opera
collection; then looks at it as if surprised to find it in
his hand.

                         C.S.
          I was thinking…

She, being an obsessive compulsive, inserts a bookmark
into her book and closes it; then pats the couch
invitingly.

---

* this very apposite chapter title is an iconic quote from *Doctor Who* (the David Tennant one); Chic was *tickled pink* when Russell T. Davies resurrected The Doctor in 2005

C.S.
        (sits down next to her)
    About Domingo...

Now, in order to comprehend his plan of attack, you must know that we were both huge Plácido Domingo fans. I was – and still am – truly one-eyed and passionate about this fabulous tenor: we had on CD every opera he'd recorded, and we had all the laser discs of his performances we could get, as well as a fair few tapes; for, as we're talking about the late '80s, there were not yet any DVDs. Chic, however, also appreciated other tenors: it had been one of his major triumphs to get *L'Amico Fritz*, in which Pavarotti sings the tenor lead, into our collection. But I wouldn't have a bar of anyone else.

There was a large number of female voices of which we both greatly approved: Cotrubaş, Freni, Ricciarelli, Scotto, etc. – whose names might help you place the operatic period – and an equally large assortment of baritones and basses. But when it came to tenors, the Stringer household had agreed to have all flags flying for Domingo.

(cont'd)

                    M.R.
        (looking at the CD in his hand)
    OK: Domingo. So – there's another opera
    out on CD?

                    C.S.
    No. Better than that.

He pauses.

                              <u>C.S.</u>
        I've been thinking that, really, seeing
        as how we're such fans of his, we should
        be putting our minds to-well…getting
        to see him.

He speeds up his delivery as her mouth starts to fall
open, to forestall anything too negative.

                              <u>C.S.</u>
               (standing up again)

        What I mean is…Unless we go to Europe,
        we will never be able to lay eyes on
        him. After all, he's scarcely likely to
        come to Australia!

She is gobsmacked. Europe?-Domingo? What on earth is
happening to the world?

He wanders about a bit, replaces the CD in the
collection, looking at her out of the corner of his eye.

                              <u>C.S.</u>
               (gently: this is all pretty radical
               stuff)

        We could do it, you know. And it would
        be something to remember for the rest of
        our life.

I was utterly terrified of flying. This had not always
been the case, but a bad landing in Melbourne many years
previously had put into me a fear that I thought could
never, ever be overcome. And before that, the farthest I'd
ever flown was between Perth and Melbourne. Chic had
been to Bougainville to shoot documentary stills, many
years previously; but, between us, we wouldn't've racked
up more than about three-quarters of a frequent flyer point.
Travelling was simply something that had never entered

my thinking: in fact, when I once read that Cancerians are supposed to be great travellers, I was mightily amused by how wrong was whoever had written that.

So – to go away, to see and hear Domingo? Could life actually encompass something as extraordinary?

(cont'd)

> ### M.R.
> (collecting jaw from fully lowered
> position)
>
> Are you serious?

He doesn't clout her over the head for being irritating:
he merely sits down again in preparation for a
discussion.

> ### C.S.
> Yes. Why not?
>
> I think you'd love it! – and I know that
> I would…

That's what it was all about, of course; Chic wanted to go to Europe. Having pondered long, he'd worked out a hook that would quickly yank me across onto his side. And why not? – no harm in a bit of manipulation, when no harm (and in all likelihood a positive good) can befall via its application.

(cont'd)

> ### C.S.
> (into his stride)
>
> I know your first reaction is about our actually GETTING there; but I have a solution!

Now, Chic's solutions to anything at all were unfailingly effective, and also fascinating: I never once knew him to say that he had one, for any situation, without delivering, and in spades. So just to hear him say that was … well, much more than merely interesting – it was *exciting*!

(cont'd)

> ### M.R.
> (the idea now has appeal!)
>
> Zo, chenius: vot iss dis zolution? – and it'd better not be rendering me unconscious by tapping on my head for several hours with a ballpein hammer, either!

> ### C.S.
> (ignores silliness)
>
> I did a bit of research, and found a group called Fear of Flying, here in Sydney, that gives courses for getting people to where they can … ahh … stop having any.
>
> I don't have all the details yet; but …

A wave of his hand dismisses all that for later as he smiles happily and expectantly at her.

At which point, all reservations were banished to kingdom come even before their formulation: Chic's plan was suddenly fully-fledged and ready to fly, as I duly became. I had had no idea that so wondrous an organisation could possibly exist; but was prepared, instantly, to accept the fact that it did, and that it would work. Because his summarising the enticing concept of getting us into the presence of the most amazing musical talent in the world, to lay our very own eyes on him, and, not only that, but to hear him sing, with our own ears! – well, if he was ever going to be able to persuade me to get onto an aeroplane, that was the way to do it.

He did it. After a lot of preparation, we undertook the trip: and from that time onwards were Europhiles without equal. Our main drive at home here in Oz became the accumulation of funds, in every way we could think of – including gradually selling off our few valuables – in order to return to Europe.

We got to make five trips. We became travelling fools!

Here's a load-bearing branch:

T^3 *I know myself hardly at all; but my husband understood me totally.*

VOICE FOLLOWING

I won't deprive myself of singing opera as long as my voice follows.
— Plácido Domingo

A flashback – but only to before the previous chapter.

It was not until my real life had begun that I was exposed to the wonders of opera. I'd grown up in a household passionate about European classical music; but opera didn't feature, so my knowledge of it was virtually zero.

Well. There were Chic and I, sitting watching the telly one Saturday afternoon because he was waiting to get some news of the practice session for the next day's F1 race. He was an inveterate channel-hopper, and eventually we found ourselves looking at SBS, which was showing a dramatised performance – filmed for TV, not performed on stage – of Puccini's *Madama Butterfly*.

Our life changed forever on that afternoon somewhere in the mid-'80s, because we caught that telecast early enough to see the riveting opening sequence. It was a flashforward of astounding dramatic power. Domingo was singing Lieutenant Pinkerton with his whole heart and his whole soul and his deep-pile velvet voice and his stunning beauty and his amazing acting ability ... and I was lost – or, rather, won.

INT.	LIVING ROOM	DAY

The telecast has just finished.

                              M.R.
                    (not quite there)
            Stringer...Have you been watching this,
            or just letting it slide over your head?

He sees immediately that Something has happened. Knowing
her as he does, he is instantly aware of what.

                          C.S.
          (truly happy)
          I have, I have! You liked it, eh? - you
          REALLY liked it!

                          M.R.
          (turns to him, overwhelmed)
          It was … it was … Oh, Stringer! - it was
          unbelievable!!!

                          C.S.
          That bloke singing Pinkerton was pretty
          special, eh?
          What's his name …?

He locates the TV programme, picks up a pencil and
circles the par. about the opera.

                          C.S.
          Plácido Domingo. Nice name. Says it
          translates as 'quiet Sunday'.

Folds the programme carefully and places it on the
mantelpiece, then sits down again.

                          C.S.
          Next week we might pop in to Rowe
          Street* and ask George for something
          Domingo's recorded, in case we don't get
          to hear him again - whaddya reckon?

---

* Sydney's Rowe Street Records: certainly by then no longer in Rowe Street, but
somewhere in that area … wonderful shop! - we spent lots of time and money
with George Cooks

And with these words so signally lacking in foresight, Domingo enters their world.

Chic knew quite a lot about opera; but back then Domingo, while already a huge star in those countries operatically oriented, was a virtual unknown in Oz. We began collecting him on CD, and I started to learn what I could about this amazing new (to me) art.

My overall feeling was one of having been cheated out of something glorious for a large part of my life, and I roundly upbraided my mother telephonically about the total dearth of opera at home. Her unworthy excuse was that as no operatic performers ever came to Perth, she had had to confine herself to attending symphony concerts; but this didn't explain that I clearly remember classical music on the radio all the time, but never opera. Eventually, persistent brain-cudgelling elicited the facts: Dadda was a great fan of Gilbert & Sullivan's operatic spoofs, and raised us not only to love G&S but also to mock the real thing!

As time passed, Chic and I realised that it was not all opera that we loved, but the passionate, emotional works of all the Italian and some of the French composers. Wagner we would walk over burning coals to avoid, not counting the instrumental-only parts of his operas (the overture to *Tannhäuser*, e.g., or the *Siegfried Idyll*, both almost indescribably beautiful!; but once voices cut in they'd be switched off): and I have to tell you that we were not moved at all by Mozartian opera. Yes, you may laugh and point, but I'm just being honest: when it came to opera, we could only love what was *emotionally* melodic and heart-stirring.

Thus did I slowly develop a genuine love and admiration of the music itself, as well as of its best and greatest protagonist, while Chic happily extended his horizons. He bought us a laser-disc player and we started collecting Domingo in that medium, too; as well as on tape (VHS back then, as opera on Betamax was not available in Oz; so their shelf life was very limited).

We were mesmerised by Plácido's ability to portray operatic characters such as to make you believe in them: I can only illustrate this by saying that it made no difference how often we watched, for example, *Carmen*, we were deeply moved by Don José's tragedy *every time*.

§

You know from the previous chapter that Domingo was the way Chic managed to get me onto a flight to Europe.

Well, before we left home, we'd managed to organise tickets to only one opera he was performing in Europe that season – in Barcelona, at its famous Gran Teatre del Liceu (one version thereof: it burned down a couple of years after we were there, and that one hadn't been the original – not by a very long shot!). It was Cilea's *Adriana Lecouvreur*, not so well known and with possibly only two famous arias: but it was an Italian opera – and, I feel fairly sure, we would actually have gone to watch the Ring Cycle, if that'd been all we could get.

We didn't have the tickets in our hands: we'd made telex arrangements with the concierge of Barcelona's extremely famous (and concomitantly priced) Ritz Hotel to get them on arrival. If you ever find yourself wishing you knew how to get tickets to some terrific performance in a European city, search out the head concierge of one of its big hotels: it's an unfailingly successful method.

So off we went to Europe, filled with enormous excitement and anticipation at the thought of seeing and hearing Domingo in an opera.

The Ritz was eventually gained: we'd thought it practical to book in for a few nights, on the off-chance of offending the concierge if we stayed anywhere else. I shan't reveal the tariff – you'd probably pass out. We'd already done that weeks before, when we'd received the concierge's telex and immediately made reservations there to keep him on-side; but that was past, and by now we were carelessly profligate.

It was absolutely super, the room they put us in – complete, of course, with champers and an unending supply of fruit and chocolates – part of the suite that Franco used occasionally as a stopover, so that it had quick-response steel shutters that could cover all windows in less than a second, they told us. Alas! – we didn't get to see 'em do their thing: that certainly would've been something to write home about.

It also had, much more interestingly to me, a bathroom with a sunken bath the size of a small swimming pool; and there's a photo of me in it, having a whale of a time down there amongst the bubbles and laughing a great deal. Chic told everyone he had to lasso me and drag me out, or we would never've got to the opera. Pfuh!

We organised via the front desk to meet our benefactor as soon as he had the time:

| INT. | THE RITZ FOYER | DAY |

They are standing with the Concierge, having just been given The Tickets, at which she is staring spellbound.

The Concierge has no English, they have no Spanish (let alone Catalan!), so it's an impasse.

<u>C.S.</u>
(out of the side of his mouth to her)

I forgot to find out what's the going rate for this kinda thing…Any ideas?

Her expression of delirious joy turns suddenly to alarm: she's as ignorant on this as he.

The Concierge casts an eye upwards, calmly studying the ornate ceiling.

They start to sweat.

C.S.

Well, I can't keep him here all day
while you rush off and ask someone. I'm
just gonna have to go for it. Make a
guess. Take the plunge.

Cross yer fingers…

He takes out his wallet. The Concierge's eyes travel down
from the ceiling.

He takes out some notes, looks at them; the Concierge
also looks at them, thoughtfully.

Some more notes: he sneaks a glance at the Concierge, to
no avail.

Doubling the number of notes, he takes a deep breath and
hands them over with a feeling of helplessness.

The Concierge is looking down at his hand without
expression.

C.S.

(beaten)

I give up. I really don't think we can
afford any more. Let's just smile and
make a run for it!

They force polite grimaces and walk casually off.
Reaching a corner of the hallway they speed up markedly.
She looks back.

M.R.

(gasping)

It's OK, he's not following.

They slow down with relief and return to their room,
where they hide the tickets behind a picture on the wall:
you can't be too careful…

We had our tickets, we figured: come hell or high water we'd be seeing Domingo the next night, which duly arrived; and Chic and I togged ourselves up in our Really Good Clothes, unused to being so formally attired but quite pleased with how we'd scrubbed up. We went down to the foyer. There, lined up on both sides of the Ritz's front door like soldiers at a wedding (but for the arched swords), were the concierge and what gave every appearance of being a large proportion of the hotel's staff. Their faces, bearing some signs of anxiety, cleared to show beaming smiles: the laboriously packed and transported evening wear had been worth it; for we were, unmistakably, passed as entirely suitable to attend Barça's Gran Teatre.

As we made our way through the honour guard, they all shook our hands and made it obvious they wished us much joy; several of them came out to help us find a taxi, and when we indicated that we would prefer to walk to Las Ramblas we had some difficulty in dissuading them from making the little journey with us.

It didn't take a whole lot of effort to work out that we'd inadvertently created an *après nous le déluge* precedent. Although unable to ascertain the precise amount of silver actually expected to cross the concierge's palm, our hindsight-benefited guess was that roughly a quarter of what we gave him would've done it.

§

The Performance was truly indescribable: I couldn't *possibly* do it justice. You'll just have to accept the following:

- the theatre was gorgeous;
- the seats the concierge had got for us were incredible – third row in the Circle!;
- Plácido was everything and more that we'd been building him up to be for ... oh, it would've been three to four years by then.

He has a presence on stage that no one else does: he has only to walk on, even in the background, for every eye in the audience to swivel in his direction. And it's not just while waiting for his mouth to open and that incredible voice to come out of it: it's a kind of magnetism, that comes with the complete and absolute confidence in one's ability to do what one's there to do and excel in the doing.

We were utterly gobsmacked. And if it had all finished there – if that had been the first and last time we ever set eyes on Domingo – we would have still been grateful for the rest of our lives.

But it wasn't ... not by a long shot!

§

The previous day we'd staggered back into our stunning room after a particularly terrifying taxi ride around Barça (we never did get up the courage to take a bus anywhere – zero language to do it by – and the downside of that was Barça's taxidrivers, all quite *insane*!) and collapsed with large strong drinks, when to our astonishment there was a phonecall for us. Turned out to be the bloke who ran the translation service in Sydney that we'd used while preparing for our trip and trying to get opera tickets. A very nice person indeed, Christian Büchner, who'd asked for our itinerary – we thought just out of curiosity. We were wrong: for this lovely man had liaised after our departure with a friend of his in Germany, and the friend had obtained for us tickets to Domingo in *Tosca*, in Hamburg.

Another opera?! – je-*sus*! We looked at each other in incredulous joy: we were going to get to do it twice! And we did. We instantly completely reworked our travel plans so as to include northern Germany, in a few days' time. And that, too, was a bit of a giggle ...

From the Ritz we'd booked ourselves into a hotel in Hamburg, giving the woman on the phone there some details of the reason for our very late and very urgent reservation.

They've just come from a horribly early-arriving
overnight train, after very little sleep.

As they enter the hotel foyer, a woman approaches them:

                        WOMAN
          (in accented but totally comprehensible
          English)

          You are Australians who have come to see
          Domingo.

The identifiable Aussies drop their suitcase handles in
unison and lean on each other for support, for there's
something about her that's really worrying.

                        WOMAN
          I own hotel. I take your booking on
          telephone. You say you have tickets for
          Tosca. But there is problem.

They knew it! All this way, all these trip changes, all
the bookings and unbookings of the last day…for nothing.
They're not going to see Plácido again after all.

Their shoulders slump further.

                        HOTEL OWNER
          (starting to stammer with anxiety,
           tries to get her act together)

          W-when he goes to Staatsoper he does not
          like staging. Not at all. He w-will not
          perform.

They exchange glances of misery. They're so tired, and
these are such awful tidings.

HOTEL OWNER
(clasping hands for punchline)
So they all agree…

Her face is by now a picture of misery.

HOTEL OWNER
He w-will sing *La Bohème* instead…

Their eyes snap open. They stare at her quite rudely: CAN
THIS BE TRUE?!

M.R.
(gabbling in her joy)
But that's…that's…FANTASTIC,
Madame! – *Bohème* is my husband's VERY
FAVOURITE opera!

And they hug each other in joy, then hug her too for
being the bearer of such terrific news[*].

Our meeting with our Sydney translator's friend was
indicative of the pleasure we derived from all the Germans
we met: Peter Drüge was – and could indeed still be, for all I
know – the owner and CEO of a corporation manufacturing
really big recycling machinery. He turned up at our hotel in
a cashmere overcoat that looked like it was off the cover of
a men's fashion magazine (and so did he). Absolutely lovely
man. Handed over the tickets, accepted their face value
and wouldn't accept another pfennig, having queued like
any ordinary person for god knows how long to get them.
He spent an hour or so with us, chatting in impeccable
English, looking super-cool and being utterly charming. We

---

[*] *Tosca* was amongst our all-time favourites, but we'd been nervous to the point
of anxiety about the directorial setting of this production in *Nazi Germany* …

wondered if there might've been a couple of other things he had to do with his time ...

So another opening night – although this one was actually a gala performance for some charity or other, so it was in fact The Only night.

In the Hamburg Staatsoper the ninth row was as acoustically impressive as the entire theatre – quite wonderful although pretty new. It was a second thrilling evening of watching and hearing Plácido doing his schtick in his inimitable way, and us weeping at the end for Rodolfo's misery. How joyful to weep at beautiful music, how amazing that it be Chic's favourite!

As we walked back to the hotel we told each other how incredibly lucky we were to have actually laid eyes on Plácido Domingo performing live on stage – not once, but twice! But it must be added that, really, luck didn't have much to do with it; for Chic's determination to get me to Europe and see the man had been the cause of it all. Without his drive throughout the lead-up time it would never have come about.

And, would you believe? – that *still* wasn't the end of it!

In fact, the best was yet to come.

first ever!   wrong opera ...

GETTING PERSONAL

It was about ... oh, I'd say two months after our return from Europe that my eye fell upon a smallish item in *The Sydney Morning Herald* as we worked our way through breakfast one Saturday morning.

'Plácido Domingo to tour Australia'! – he was going to be *here*, on our doorstep!

What would we do about this amazing fact? – well, everything we could, as you will understand without difficulty. We got in touch with the *SMH* to see if there was anything more available, and there was, and they faxed it to us; thus we ascertained that the body responsible for bringing him out was the Victoria State Opera (long since declared financially nonviable and subsumed, but oh, what a body in its heyday!), and we obtained from them a schedule of his performances throughout the country. I must explain that Plácido wasn't going to perform an opera Down Under, but simply give recitals – if they could be called that in the enormous auditoria in which he found himself singing: he was absolutely delighted to be performing for the first time to audiences of something like 14,000.

I wrote heart-rendingly to the VSO general manager with a plea for advance bookings, explaining in my inchoate fashion why we were so keen; and he wrote back *personally*! In fact, we all struck up quite a friendship – a delightful man, Ken Mackenzie-Forbes, and he helped us greatly in our quest.

The tickets were far from cheap, but as we were not planning on undertaking any more international jaunts there was nothing preventing us from splurging; so we booked for Melbourne and for Sydney (needing to become subscribers to the VSO we also went down to two of their performances*). Because of our liaising at so high a level with the organisation, we got tickets in *the front row* in Melbourne, and in the sixth row in Sydney! At the Rod Laver Arena I had a small bunch

---

* the *Faust* was superb and the *Norma* unspeakable: make what you will of that ...

of red and gold roses a florist arranged beautifully and I gave them to Plácido at the end of the performance; and that was so thrilling, and Chic so proud of me, that it was just ... glorious.

And in Sydney Chic took many photos, one of which you see: at the time we thought having Plácido looking directly into his lens and smiling was about as good a thing in life as one could possibly expect.

I *mean* ...!

After that performance I queued to get Domingo's autograph on my copy of his ghosted autobiography, *My First Forty Years*, just released. Clutching the duly signed book to my bosom, I said, '*Muchas gracias, Señor Domingo,*' and he smiled at me and replied (they tell me), '*Encantado; gracias por venir.*'

Chic and I were like a couple of kids, gleefully recalling the exchange a thousand times while admiring the autograph as we made our way back to our hire car.

So you're asking: that's it, yes? – the end of your Domingo adventures?

Nup.

More like the beginning.

§

Another bit of flashback, to a time shortly before we discovered that Plácido was going to brighten our lives locally.

When we bought *My First Forty Years*, we'd read therein that a great friend of Plácido's had been living in Australia for many years. In Perth, in fact – town of my birth and all that.

That was one coincidence; but another and much stronger was that this bloke, an Italian, was married to a Mauritian woman over there. I had strong links with Perth's Mauritian community: one of my sisters had been married to a Mauritian, and I'd had a Mauritian boyfriend for a couple of years before being sent off to the other side of our continent. And I knew my mother was still in touch with some of this group via church attendance[*].

Chic and I agreed that it would be A Very Good Thing to have someone to talk to/correspond with on the particularly delightful topic of the world's greatest tenor – that is, *someone who knew him* – so we decided it was time Mother finally came good with her responsibilities.

INT.	LOUNGE ROOM	NIGHT

A telephone conversation is underway between M.R. and her distant mama, who has been speaking of herself for quite a while.

M.R. is feeling virtuous for having allowed this to go on for so long without doing more than rolling her eyes at C.S., seated nearby and doing a fair bit of eye-rolling on his own account at the lengthy silence, Sydney end.

But enough is enough…

---

[*] *chacune son goût*

                          M.R.
                  (brutally stemming the flow)

          Do you know Josée Bertinazzo,
          Mither?-she's one of the Mauritians,
          and she's married to an Italian tenor…

Her mother is used to being interrupted.

                          MAMA
                  (seamlessly)

          Oh, yes!-I see her at mass, quite
          often. Last time we spoke she admired my
          new jacket, and asked me whe-

                          M.R.
                  (brisk)

          Yesyes, I'm sure she did.

Crosses eyes at C.S. before continuing, hectoringly:

                          M.R.

          So you know her quite well?-I mean,
          well enough to discuss something I'd
          like you to talk about?

Mama's interest is piqued sufficiently to make the topic
of herself *almost* secondary.

                          MAMA
                  (curious)

          I would imagine so…

          But what in heaven's name could you
          possibly want me to discuss with her?

Cards on the table time.

M.R.

                    M.R.
         Her husband is a close friend of Plácido
         Domingo's. We want to be able to find out
         everything possible from him, via her,
         about Plácido.

Adding, longingly:

                    M.R.
         We'd like to be able to…you
         know…just…talk about him…

Drifts off into a reverie.

C.S. makes urgent 'STICK TO THE POINT!' signs.

                    M.R.
              (snaps out of it)
         So we need you to set it up…

And set it up she did: we reckoned it more or less cleared her slate in terms of all the stayings over. Josée Bertinazzo and I struck up a most satisfactory correspondence regarding our mutual hero, punctuated by the occasional phonecall. We became friends; and also with their daughter Marie-Chantal, then living in Sydney.

So the Stringers and the Bertinazzos had much to talk about regarding Plácido's arrival in Oz; and it was decided that we would meet by travelling to Adelaide for the Domingo performance in that city. They were to fly from Perth, the Stringers to drive from Sydney, and everyone would come back in our car so that they could visit Marie-Chantal.

I booked us all into a not-too-expensive hotel in Adelaide, ensuring the two couples were in adjoining rooms so that they couldn't get far without our knowing about it; and by sheer good luck it turned out that the hotel was virtually across the road from the Hyatt, where Plácido was quartered. We arrived first, checked in and went out to the airport to collect *i Bertinazzo*, keeping them under our watchful eye from then on, the poor bastards! We were hoping for a glimpse firsthand, I suppose – I don't recall any other motive in shadowing them thus.

Time wore on during that first day, and we were sitting in their room having a drink, early afternoon, when the phone rang. The Stringers stiffened like bloodhounds.

INT.	HOTEL ROOM	DAY

                    GIUSEPPE
            (picking up the receiver nonchalantly)
        Pronto…

A pleased smile lights up his face.

                    GIUSEPPE
        Ciao Plácido! – come stai bello?

The Man speaks…!

After a while, Giuseppe looks idly out the window and buffs the nails of his left hand on his shirt-front: he appears to have lost concentration.

Her anxious grip on C.S.' arm tightens and he winces slightly.

                    GIUSEPPE
            (in fact listening with all due
            attention)

        *Ah sì sì – nessun problema… Stasera
        allora: alle otto mi dici?*

The guests in the room are as statues, their eyes fixed on him, their greedy ears trained in his direction as they attempt without success to translate the dialogue – which continues for a few moments, until Giuseppe puts down the receiver.

And then, saying something to Josée in Italian, he excuses himself and GOES INTO THE BATHROOM!

We were stressed out. What had that phonecall meant? Was Domingo going to drop in to visit the Bertinazzos? Were we going to lay eyes on him again? – maybe even *be introduced to him* in passing? Or could we shadow them and watch them meeting him somewhere?

When Giuseppe returned from his ablutions, there was light chat as he poured drinks and took his seat. It was fairly one-sided chat: the two of us were on tenterhooks and out of conversation.

But finally they took mercy on us.

(cont'd)

JOSÉE

(casual)

Beppe tells me Plácido has invited us over to his hotel for dinner tonight.

The visiting pair exchanges a not terribly subtle glance of jealous rage.

JOSÉE

(sip of her drink)

I think I've brought something that'll be OK to wear…

She looks down at her skirt and smooths it as if considering it, too.

JOSÉE

Hmm … Anyway …

Looks up and grins:

JOSÉE

What are *you* going to wear?

Momentary frozen pause.

What were we going … You mean …?????

She meant. Giuseppe had made us part of the invitation. We were going to have dinner with Plácido Domingo.

§

I don't know what I can say about this occasion that would do it justice. It was … it was all you would expect *and far more.*

Plácido was everything we had dreamed he'd be – big, beautiful, gentle, enormously intelligent, friendly, interesting.

We had our meal in a small private room within the hotel's dining area; the meal itself was actually, I regret to say, fairly forgettable, but nobody cared. There were seven of us in total; the other two were a couple of Australian businesswomen based overseas, in Adelaide at the same time as each other specifically to see Plácido, whom they'd met in London some years previously. Our host was in excellent form, and it took absolutely no time for us to respond to him as if he were one of us. Who teaches these huge stars how to charm birds out of trees …?

I have a very clear memory of looking across at Chic as I sat next to Domingo, upon whose forearm my hand was resting as I talked about – oh, something or other. Chic was grinning at me: he was gaining easily as much pleasure from all this as I was, and partly because I was so happy.

Some dialogue I can remember is when Plácido told us about watching during the afternoon, from his hotel penthouse window, the cricket being played down on the Adelaide Oval (Oz v. Sri Lanka?): he'd found it completely mystifying. We all chipped in to try to explain the rules of cricket to him; but when I leaped to my feet to demonstrate how the LBW rule works*, Chic was absolutely delighted (he described it to everyone he came across on our return).

When several hours had passed, Plácido rose to his feet and said goodbye to the two women, who went off to their rooms; he was going to see us out of the building. And as we all went down in the lift I had hold of his arm again ... He walked with us all the way out and down the carriageway, as far as the footpath, and watched us walk across the road to our hotel. We, in turn, stopped to look back at him: by now he had his hands in his pockets and was wandering slowly about the forecourt, looking up at the starry night sky with very evident enjoyment.

We realised that it was only down here in the Antipodes, among our largely unaware populace, that Plácido Domingo could walk about with his hands in his pockets and take a breath of night air, untroubled by a single soul.

§

The next night was his Adelaide performance. It was quite brilliant! – I could only repeat myself endlessly in trying to describe it – and there was a VSO party afterwards at which we met up with the delightful Ken Mackenzie-Forbes, who'd been so kind to us. Chic and I enjoyed ourselves mightily. By that time, of course, we felt as if this was our circle, to which we had permanent *entrée*; and there had to be a fairly rapid and severe coming down to earth, afterwards.

---

* with the help of the back of a dining-room chair and a rolled double damask dinner napkin

But in spite of the fast descent back to reality and being relegated once more to listening to (and seeing) Plácido on CD and laser disc, we remained deeply happy. Domingo was the zenith of our cultural pleasure, and, thanks to the Bertinazzos, we had actually *spent time in his company*!

I put it to you, somewhat rhetorically: how many people in this world get to have an experience like that?!

JOY

There were many, many other noteworthy things about our amazing first European foray, life-changing experience that it was – especially for me, till then a person who'd clung determinedly to all things known and safe. One of them was that I found I could curse Chic viciously for behaving like a tour guide in charge of a wayward group member, wishing him to the devil with passion, then forget all about it within five minutes – often less. It was an eye-opener, this discovery; it showed me I was less like my mother than I feared: she was not good at forgiving.

On a more practical level, the joy we derived from eating during our travels increased with each trip. Impossible to overestimate how important a part food played during our time in Europe: we often identified places from fondly remembered meals consumed there!

§

Well then. I was got cleverly onto a 'plane by himself and taken away to that extraordinary European winter of '89–'90, so unusual that the author Peter Mayle wrote of its wonder in his first and by far best book, *A Year in Provence*; and the photos we brought back show almost nothing but blue skies (upon reflection, maybe that should have been an early inkling of climate change!).

How recent seems to be that time, all those years ago – us flying smoothly along at a bit over 40,000 feet and the glories of Europe ahead ...

We didn't get there through the happiest of gateways. Our landing at Heathrow was cancelled and replaced with Manchester because fog had fallen – or whatever Pommy fog does: sinks? inveigles itself? – upon the intended destination; and back then Qantas 747s weren't fitted with ground-based radar. One of the many benefits of business class then emerged, for we got a shuttle flight* back down to Heathrow in a 757, long and narrow; utterly dissimilar to the model only ten digits behind and infinitely superior in being fitted with the aforementioned radar. (I name our aircraft where I'm able, btw, because Chic adored flying and the vessels that carried us about: he found all that stuff almost as enjoyable as reaching our destinations.)

But of course we'd missed the Madrid connection, and there wasn't another flight for something like nine hours. So Chic worked some magic on the extremely reluctant BA desk staff, who coughed up a free day-room at one of their hotels (ghastly) and vouchers for a meal (inedible). Though by then somnolent, I wasn't too gaga to enjoy watching their expressions change from rude and uncooperative to amused and helpful as The Stringer Factor had its way.

Our flight did eventually take off that night, though several other European flights didn't, and we set foot in Madrid – *in Europe!* – somewhere before midnight: exhausted, ravenous, and breathless with anticipation.

§

I'd like to be able to explain with confidence the impression made upon us, but I can do no more than try ...

Imagine two almost middle-aged people who had lived girt by sea all their lives (not counting Chic's three-day photographic business excursion to Bougainville, many years previously), but with a sufficient amount of English-Irish-Scottish-French-German blood in their veins to have had Europe dinned into them throughout their childhoods ... And that's the key: for both, Europe was a fairytale place we'd spent our early years reading about and hearing grown-ups talk about. Our childhoods, only imprecisely remembered, were now far beyond reach – as we had once, without fuss, thought of Europe as being. Chic had reached the point,

---

* cattle class had to wait for buses, poor bastards

however, where he was no longer content to be unfussed: he had determined that part of his childhood dreaming was to become reality; and, as the other half of him, mine.

Our preparations for the trip began somewhere around May, and we flew out of Sydney near the end of November; and throughout we kept telling each other how ordinary all this kind of thing is to most people. I mean, making bookings for hotels in European cities is scarcely anything to get excited about, is it?

WHAT?!

We were beside ourselves for the whole of our lead-up time: Europe? – all those thousands of years of history and tradition? – all those fabulous cities of which we'd read so much throughout our lives? – all that beauty around, so different from that to be found in our own (much-loved!) country? – all those *skies*?

We were kids again. I can't remember how many times we plotted and planned where we'd go – depending upon Domingo's itinerary, of course. Nor can I recall how often we fretted over what we'd pack (nor how often, close to departure, we packed, unpacked and repacked – and still we took far too much stuff).

As the trip got closer, our faith in actually getting there grew tenuous; we felt that it might all turn out to be a dream, and we would never find ourselves on The Mighty Continent. But of course it came about; and there we were, on European soil.

No matter that we'd never been out of Oz, not really, and that I'd just flown for more than twenty-four hours (in spite of what seemed a lifetime of terror of aeroplanes), we felt as if we'd returned – as if we'd come home.

§

Madrid wasn't kind to us with regard to eating, it must be admitted right away, but it wasn't the city's fault. We knew absolutely nothing about Spanish food, and we had basically to vamp it, without success. For that first trip we'd not thought to research eating places, and we had nothing of the local language. But in spite of failing to find glorious meals, we did find the delicious *bocadillo* – Spanish equivalent of the *panino* and just as yummy – which we consumed with great enjoyment. And we did find Madrid impressive, though the collections in the Prado were very depressing ... We didn't know if this was an aspect of our nationality, with its lack of bloodshed-depicted-in-art, but the fact is that we were cast temporarily into the depths of gloom by the endless galleries of dark and extremely gory paintings of myth, religion and warfare.

Fortunately, there were many, many other things to see in Madrid that lifted our spirits back up to their normal level – like, for example, the Templo de Debod, seen through some of Chic's nifty remote camerawork (you'll find this and all the shots in colour among the plates grouped together, on pages 233 to 248 ...).

And as to why so beautiful but so very *un*-Spanish a thing is to be found in Madrid, the fact is that when the new Aswan Dam threatened the temple, the Egyptian government decided to give it to Spain in gratitude for Spanish help in having saved another fabulous ruin, Abu Simbel. In 1970, the temple was carefully dismantled, then put on a ship to Valencia, followed by a train to Madrid. Whereas pretty soon thereafter we did the exact reverse, taking from Madrid a train to Valencia.

That city seemed almost in another country. Of course, Madrid is right in the middle of Spain, and Valencia in the south-east on the coast; but there's more to the difference than that. One seemed impressive and formal and the other light-filled and casual. It's possible that our opinions were at least partly affected by our hotel rooms' outlooks: in Madrid our window gave onto an ugly light-shaft comprised of the backsides of all the other buildings that created it; whereas in

Valencia we looked out on the Plaza del Ayuntamiento – light-filled ... plant-filled ... glittering fountain–filled ...

We found that the trains in Spain, indeed largely upon the plain, are very, very good, and their stations: we had thought Madrid's Atocha super, but it was as nothing compared with the Estació del Nord in Valencia. Preventing myself from inserting another travel photo only because neither of us was sufficiently on the ball to take one, I can only say that we had never seen – nor did subsequently – anything as beautiful as the timber and mosaic work that decorate this railway station. Why? – *¿quién sabe?*: that an engineer with a soul once made a sensitive decision was enough explanation for us.

And so good is the famous Catalan Talgo we took from Barça up into France that we made the hideous error of thinking all European trains would be this good, and their food. This led to our having a midday meal on a train from Milan to Arezzo, and from that disgustingly and unbelievably expensive experience we learned not to extrapolate from travel already under our belts when assessing a new situation, for it was often not germane.

I believe we could have been forgiven for noticing nothing at all about Barcelona, because we were about to experience the most exciting event of our life: but Barça had its way with us, in spite of the imminent, wondrous distraction of *Señor* Domingo. We walked the whole of Las Ramblas, sought and found Gaudi buildings, shopped in El Corte Inglés (as we had in Madrid, where I bought a long black German overcoat that I still wear!), admired Columbus on his plinth, realised this meant we'd been walking through the red light district and giggled, gazed wonderingly upon the methodology of Barça's parking police, and generally enjoyed ourselves greatly. This is a very good-looking city, and entirely suitable to be a Site of Momentous Occasion.

In summary: to us instant Europhiles, Madrid was most notable for being our very first port of call in Europe, with concomitant thrill; Valencia for being beautiful and having the fabulous Torres de Quart that introduced us to the glory of mediaeval ruins; and Barça for being where we first saw and heard Domingo. Not to put too fine a point on it, we'd journeyed about Spain in a fog of wonderment.

§

It was when we reached France that our hearts were taken from us – a surgical removal that left in our Aussie bodies only vestigial signs of where they'd once been. We never got them back but spent the rest of our life working towards returning and then doing so.

We disembarked from the Catalan Talgo at Valence, in the *département* of Drôme in the *région* of Rhône-Alpes, found our way to the little hotel booked from Barça when we were rearranging our entire itinerary to accommodate the second opera, and joyfully explored to the extent we could. But soon we wanted to get much further afield; so we hired a car from a local bloke, put our room on hold – we'd established good relations with the hotel owners – and sallied forth for a few days to check out Drôme and, although unidentified at the beginning, Vaucluse.

That was when those *départements* insinuated themselves into our deepest recesses: and with the exception of our 2002 trip to Italy, we returned there on every other journey. This is a heavenly part of France, and although contained within Provence – that frightfully over-touristed and lavender-choked part of the Rhône-Alpes region – there's lots to it. Trust me on this!

In Drôme we first experienced mountains. Happily, they are also in a lot more countries we visited, but of all Earth's offspring that we discovered, these were the first, in all their majesty, and we never forgot them. We found something totally magical in this evidence of the forces of Nature; after all, there are no huge mountain ranges in Oz other than in Tasmania (and we never went there) – so the Montagne de la Lance and the Montagne de Couspeau, and all those other glorious mountains that fill the eye as they stride away magnificently to the horizon ... they filled our hearts, as well.

Something that very rapidly became as important were the ruined castles liberally dotting the countryside, especially where they coincided with mountains – which they very often did, to our delight. There's a heavenly photo among the plates, taken during that first foray into the south of France: the Photographer at work in the incredible setting of the ruins of Le Château d'Aix-en-Diois.

On a day that will live in my heart for as long as it beats, the two of us sat on the grass in the utter peace and beauty of those glorious ruins, eating our delicious baguettes of *saucissons et cornichons*, a blue enamel sky stretching above us and the only sound the call of the kites as they hovered and swooped in the sun.

We were alone in the world, one in bliss.

§

Our first TGV journey took us out of Valence, that late amendment to our itinerary – through Switzerland up to Hamburg in the far north-west of Germany. There were timetable-related and very lengthy stops at both Geneva and Basel, stations we found impossible to differentiate between in terms of their utter ghastliness.

Train travel has one problem: it introduces you to towns and cities via their worst bits. We discussed this, deciding that as soon as it became obvious the train was getting near a town, we should shut our eyes and keep them shut until the train stopped: but we never did it, of course. So we got to see an awful lot of industrial areas and slums and stuff – far more than when we were driving (the sole method of transport for all our subsequent travels) – as well as the nice parts. Which was possibly just as well, because otherwise we would've believed that the whole of Europe was like a beautiful dream, whereas it's only partly like that, and the rest is reality.

Night trains in Europe mean you miss a lot, and the beds are longways rather than across, making for *extremely* bumpy sleeping. Well, that's how we found it; but at least it meant we missed some of the sleazy areas while we were lying there snoring and drooling, and snarling when awoken for the umpteenth time.

And thus did we arrive, definitely the worse for wear, in Hamburg. Although sleep-deprived, we could immediately see that it is an absolutely terrific town. And we also found that it's not only really good-looking, but has restaurants that serve seriously delicious tucker. I was reminded strongly of Sydney because of that part of it sited on the Big Alster*; but it is an essentially foreign city, of enormous charm. That most of it was completely rebuilt after the firestorm rained down on it by the Allies tells you all you need to know about German creativity, German engineering, German *will*.

Our brief stay in that country was actually noteworthy for involving us almost directly in history in the making, for just before we arrived, the Berlin Wall came down. As I wrote on our travel site, later, it's the norm for Australians to be far from almost everything that turns up in history books. But we were in Germany very shortly after that momentous event, and made very much aware of it – even though all we actually saw, or heard being discussed by the locals, was an influx of East Germans driving their awful little Trabants, from which they leaped with relief and walked away, never to return.

We felt as if the fall of The Wall carried more weight with us than it did with Hamburghers: Europeans are used, after all, to things of enormous significance happening around them. But of course we were quite wrong, and simply seeing things through very unsophisticated eyes.

---

* Hamburg looks over the Big and the Little Alster, a pair of adjoining lakes

And again a train, back down through Germany with a stop at München to change to another for our last leg, to Venice; and that would be it for our long-distance Eurail pass.

Italy. Crumbs. Yep, Italy – Venice, in fact. Venice of almost fabulous history; of quite extraordinary beauty; of booths selling carnevale masks all year long; of confusing little alleys and amazingly familiar vistas; of boats of most kinds, on … water. Everywhere. Nor any drop to drink, for sure. Didn't matter though, for in Venice I was introduced to the most wonderful wine I'd ever tasted, so not a lot of water needed to pass my lips thereafter.

For Chic, it was a case of more of the same only better: he was a drinker of Italian wines at home, whereas I scarcely touched a drop – but only because I never found wine (even Italian) in Oz that I really liked. He'd long since explained to me that it's a commodity that simply doesn't travel well, which meant I was highly unlikely to ever find anything at home that appealed. But in Venice he indicated the likelihood of local plonk's being worth a burl, and the result was our discovery of a fabulous local wine, a *merlot del Veneto* which we quaffed at whatever hour we thought wine-drinking wouldn't be frowned upon – happy for us that we were in Italy … Sometimes I think it might even be worth living under the likes of Berlusconi for the sake of wine like that.

The other discovery made in Venice was equally momentous, but much more surprising:

INT.   VENETIAN *RISTORANTE*   NIGHT

They have just dealt with their unappealing second courses in desultory fashion, and are considering whether or not to fill up the gaps with dessert.

<u>M.R.</u>

(grumpy)

Bugger it, Stringer: does every
ristorante in the world have *tiramisù* on
the menu? How about we have some cheese,
eh?

<u>C.S.</u>

(shrugs a bit disinterestedly)

OK, might as well. Wonder what kinds are
on offer?

He manages to catch the eye of a distantly lurking
Waiter, who approaches at glacial speed.

She addresses this unfortunate bloke in very uncolloquial
Italian; having, before they left, paid a fair bit of
cash to a university Continuing Education course for
travelling purposes. The Waiter is man enough not to
flinch.

<u>M.R.</u>

C'è del formaggio per piacere?

The Waiter bows his head silently in acknowledgement of
the fact that there is indeed cheese to be had.

<u>M.R.</u>

(flushed with success)

E di quali tipi?

adding, in quite unnecessary* verbal parentheses:

---

* Chic was never taught a second language, but the Stringer brain furnished
generalised translations for the majority of occasions upon which Italian or
French was spoken – and often when *I* hadn't understood!: he reckoned it was
just logic :-\

184

                         M.R.
       I asked him what kinds of cheese they
       have…

The *cameriere* throws his eyes to the ceiling, reciting
from memory and with an indifference bordering on
loathing a very long list.

She is lost almost immediately, and her expression
becomes more and more frantic until she hears a single
word she recognises:

                         M.R.
           (grabs Waiter's arm urgently)

       Gorgonzola! *Lei ha detto 'gorgonzola',
       sì?*

       Stringer, you like gorgonzola, don't
       you? Yesyes, of course you do.

Without waiting for a response, as she feels the need to
order before they lose the Waiter's interest forever,
she demands some gorgonzola and adds in her schoolgirl
Italian that he can bring whatever other cheeses he…
chooses.

Confusion crosses his otherwise expressionless
countenance: they suspect it means he hasn't understood
her. But what he brings shows the confusion to have been
due to the fact that ordering any specific cheese means
you get just the one.

C.S. looks down at the entrée-sized plate in front of him
covered almost from edge to edge with a single, thick
slab of softish white cheese, marked here and there with
enticing little rivulets of mould.

                         C.S.
           (bends down to sniff it)

       Crikey! This is gorgonzola? - it smells
       TERRIFIC! I thought gorgonzola was
       supposed to pong…?

And, after briefly surveying the large, careless assortment of unmatched cutlery provided, he picks up a knife and fork and gets stuck in.

She's somewhat taken aback by the unexpected result of her order, and a little hesitant.

M.R.

> Erhmm…so…what's it like?

His expression has become glazed; and it takes her a very short time to understand that from beneath the glazing ecstasy will shortly burst.

She checks out his cutlery choice and copies it.

There is complete silence for quite a while, broken only by sounds of knives and forks on plates. And finally of the cutlery's being put down and chairs being pushed back.

C.S.

> (dreamily)

> So. Gorgonzola, eh?

He sighs, away with the fairies for a bit…then returns to normality.

Indignation settles upon him.

C.S.

> Wonder what the stuff we get at home
> that they call 'gorgonzola' really is?!
> But more importantly, where are we going
> to find some of THIS
>
> > (gesturing dramatically towards where
> > the cheese once was)
>
> when we get back?!

The Waiter has materialised, astoundingly enough, and does a nice (Italian) double take; for they've run their fingers around their plates seeking out remaining vestiges, thus leaving for him what appear to be virginal objects.

C.S. appears to have thought ahead in terms of avoiding the ghastly rhyme that the subject attracts:

> ### C.S.
> (addressing him politely while indicating)
>
> What company manufactures this, please?

To her amazement the Waiter obviously grasps what he wants to know: within a minute or two he's back with a very large chunk of gorgonzola still in its foil wrapping.

GALBANI, the printing says, and *Dolcelatte*-words ne'er to be forgotten.

As for the other aspects of Venice, they were appreciated far more by my husband than by me: the glories of *la Serenissima* were not actually lost on me, they were merely pushed into the background by her less appealing parts. For Chic, there were no parts of less appeal: he was in love with her; and you'll find among the plates a shot that clearly shows as much.

What was wrong with me? – I didn't like the filthy bits. Or the countless starving cats. Or the rats to be seen in seemingly every little *calle*. Or those buildings that had been allowed (encouraged, probably) to run down, and looked to be on the point of imminent collapse into their canals ... although I must admit that never once did I see one that had actually done so. Or the undeniable rudeness of the Venetians, the poor sods permanently and totally overrun by tourists. Still, it was their lot, after all – they'd chosen it.

Being our first time in Italy, I had not yet reached any level of comprehension of the country's mastery of being able to present simultaneously two diametrically opposing stances on almost everything. Consider: only in Italy will you find dazzling beauty and frightening ugliness; hideous cruelty and great kindness; brute force and loving gentleness; monstrous evil and selfless good*. Only in Italy do great opera and mindless TeknoRap vie for popularity. Only in Italian towns and cities do you see stunning buildings of obvious historical importance next-door to falling-down hovels. Only in the Italian countryside are there glorious vistas to bring tears to the eye, interrupted here and there by half-built dwellings with rusty reinforcing rods sticking out of their ground floor walls and people living there in perfect equanimity.

It is a nation so dual in character that its professed and hysterically defended religion, Catholicism (headed until recently by a man who once belonged to Hitler's youth movement), sits perfectly happily with its unmatched production of porn and its seriously lower than zero population growth.

But note this: I recently discovered it wasn't until 1979 that for the first time internal polling showed 'Italian' – i.e., the Tuscan dialect – *to be that spoken at home by more than fifty per cent of Italians*. So don't think I'm getting stuck into them: I'm really just commenting on the fracturing.

Because we came to love it: Chic from Day One, because there was no intolerance in his nature. But I needed my unwillingness to accept the strange and the unfamiliar to be broken down – which it was, with his help, before too much longer. And then you found in the Stringers a pair of passionate Italophiles and proud of it. I still am. But not of the politics, not of the religion! – I must clarify that.

Still, I can't reflect on *any* politics or religion with other than rage.

§

---

* if I were trying to be amusing, I'd add 'and that's just amongst the politicians!'

We took a local train down to Bologna. This not terribly thrilling fact remains in my memory because as we sat opposite each other looking at the passing scenery, I found I had tears rolling down my cheeks. I was appalled, but unable to stop their flow.

INT.	ITALIAN SUBURBAN TRAIN	DAY

He reaches over to take one of her hands.

C.S.

(gently)
You're missing Mr Walker, aren't you?

She nods silently.
C.S. sits back, grins at her.

C.S.

Reckon he's thinking about us and crying?

She bursts out laughing and blows her nose trumpetingly.

It was deeply comforting being reminded how well my husband knew me.

In Bologna we collected a reserved hire car, in which Chic drove us right down through the country to 'the ball of the foot' and back up to Rome – not all at once, of course! – with ease and confidence. Alas that I couldn't share it: I found driving on the *autostrade* so terrifying that we actually had to stop doing it to prevent my having some kind of nervous collapse. I can remember the day I first arrived in Sydney from Perth, when I was so appalled by the freneticism of the traffic that I thought I would never recover; but Sydney traffic is as a family of ducks waddling across the road in comparison with what goes on upon the Italian *autostrade*.

Very early into our first venture upon one (suitably enough, it was the A1) we came upon a work-gang, and fairly soon came to understand that the gangs were dotted all along these hugely used, gigantic roadways – so often at heights as to engender terror in the sternest breast – to keep them in good repair. The problem for me was that the *autostrade* do not run straight. They often curve savagely, so that you can't see what's ahead and never know when you might sweep at high speed around such a curve to find one of the work-gangs under your wheels, thus needing to change lanes at high speed while a Bimmer and an Audi are bearing down upon you at something like 180ks ... It was a fear of fear, really – a residue from my emotional problems, coupled with having only in theory completely overcome my fear of flying, that created such paranoid anxiety – felt by me alone of all those thrumming along at huge speed.

I'm told there are actually people who go to Europe expressly for the thrill of driving at these unimaginable (to me) speeds. Hideous thought.

But my heartfelt plea to abandon these horrible tollways meant our discovering the more pleasant red roads and infinitely more delightful yellow ones – the whites we found on the following trip – and we were then able to actually enjoy the driving, rather than looking on it merely as the way of getting us from A to B with me spending most of the time cowering below the dashboard.

That driving included our only experience of having in our hands a completely relevant, detailed road map but being totally unable to reach our destination. After the fourth or fifth circumnavigation, we decided that whatever the secret was, it was known only to locals, or possibly nationals. Certainly, it defied us *stranieri* entirely. So we gave up trying to reach Benevento and drove away, which turned out to be a really good thing as it meant changing our itinerary; and that led to our— that is, *his* finding an unexpectedly lovely place. Trani. Puglia. Adriatic coast. GLORIOUS.

Driving off the main road into Trani brings you almost immediately into a big open piazza, unsurprisingly called the *piazza* Duomo on account of its heart being a lovely, uncluttered cathedral; and to one side some impressive oldish buildings, all looking out onto the Adriatic a hop, skip and jump away. And when, as we wandered about, we found one of these oldish buildings to be a hotel, delight settled upon us. I used my all-too-slowly-improving Italian on the elderly *padrona*, and we obtained a room – oh, what a room! It was on the first floor, accessed by a wondrous wide and shallow stone stairway; it was huge; it had under-floor heating. Being on the corner of the building, it had windows looking in all directions that filled it with light. And it was cheap, because we weren't in the tourist season. (In fact, in all our European peregrinations, we never travelled then; this first occasion was in winter, but all the others in either the spring or autumn shoulders – and thus could we afford to fly business class, hooray!)

We went for a walk out to the end of the groyne and admired (1) the Adriatic, (2) Bari, a faint presence on the far horizon[*] to the south and (3) the *duomo* and our hotel behind us. Everything was peaceful and beautiful: we took a photo and it's a beauty. Then, somewhat bored with admiring, we strolled back along the groyne and wandered up to our room to refresh ourselves with a shower after all the driving, and in readiness for dinner. As we came down the stairs of the old, thick-walled building, we heard bells – was it a carillon? – seemingly fairly close by.

---

[*] I understand this to be the kind of distance from which Bari is best admired

<u>C.S.</u>
(stops momentarily on the stairs)
Wonder where that's coming from?

A rather strange expression crosses his face…but, shaking his head as if to dismiss a thought, he says nothing further.

<u>M.R.</u>
(hunger has her)
Oh, who cares?! – come ON, darling…

And into the dining room they go.

    We had a truly delicious meal, at the start of which we were introduced to that appetiser so common, nowadays, *bruschetta*. We didn't order it, they just brought us some as a kind of *amuse-gueule*, I suppose – the first time we'd ever eaten out and been offered something gratis as part of the eating experience. The menu was almost entirely of fish, of course, and we had zero problems with that; Chic loved fish, and I was always happy to eat it if I could be positive it were the fresh kind. And it was, so I was, and so was he. And they were, too, to see us glomming everything down with such obvious enthusiasm and laughter.

    Then, as we ascended the lovely stairs after that yummy meal, its memory lighting our way to bed, we heard the sound anew: 'Ding-dong-dong … dong-dong-ding-ding … DONG-DING-*DING-DONG-DING*!' with a kind of self-satisfied crescendo at the end.

That expression is back on his face as they stop on the stairs.

She puts a hand on his arm.

                         M.R.
            (the penny is up: it's spinning…)
        Stringer…
            (it drops)
        Oh jesus…

Her beloved is looking both alarmed and resigned.

He sighs.

Then puts an arm around her shoulders in faint hope of her accepting such encouragement as sufficient unto the hour.

Yes … a (recorded) carillon within the *duomo* that someone had decided should commence at sunset and continue *all night*. And that's not the worst part: the carillon rang out *every quarter-hour*!

Oh, what a night we had … or didn't have, if you equate 'night' with 'sleep'. Never experienced anything like it (and never have again, I'm happy to say). It was horrible, truly; nothing about it took our thoughts heavenwards. We arose tousle-haired and baggy-eyed, feeling greatly the worse for wear and looking for trouble. Which we found: there was no hot water in the bathroom. Not a good morning, in spite of the glorious view and the luverly warm floor.

The restoration of the *duomo* had been fairly recently completed, with some cretin installing the carillon as his idea of a crowning glory because he didn't live anywhere near it, whereas our hotel's north wall was common with the cathedral's south. Chic reckoned he ought to have known as soon as I told him they wanted 60,000 lire for a room like that – had me in stitches miming how his head should've been swivelling around, seeking an explanation for so tiny a tariff.

It wasn't till we had left Trani behind and were on our way to the rest of Italy that we could laugh thus: and then we did, uproariously. Because it had actually been like something P.G. Wodehouse would write, greatly amusing his readers. And it did us, too – afterwards.

§

I was thrown into fear and trembling when we came across another Aussie while wandering through Pompeii.

Those with good Italian geography will quickly work out that I've skipped a lot of country; well, *we* had to skip Sicily, very unwillingly, because of the nationwide strike that was about to paralyse the Italian transport system, including the ferries. At the time we moaned and whinged to each other about our luck, timing, etc., before coming to understand that transport strikes are part of the Italian (and French!) way of life.

We'd already been cast into gloom (easily discernible in the colour plate) by the township of Pompeii – it's a summation of everything truly naff in today's Italy. Meeting this bloke the day before we were due to drive up to and arrive in Rome for a five-day stay really was bad timing.

Chic was a huge fan of the Romans all his adult life: there was little about that almost incredible Empire he didn't know, and most of it raised in him admiration and enthusiasm. He'd been looking forward to our Rome stay for the whole time we'd been *in viaggio*, and had got me pretty excited about it, too. The Aussie we ran into couldn't have been much more different, both in knowledge of and attitude to it; and he didn't hesitate to share his opinions, volubly and aggressively.

He told us that Rome was filthy, and full of garbage, and rats, and con merchants, and *lousy food*! He said the weather was terrible most of the time. According to him, there was no public transport, and walking meant having to struggle up and down hills of fearful gradient. By the time he'd finished his rant there wasn't a thing left standing in favour of this so old and so great city.

To say I was dismayed is an understatement: I was actually quite frightened. Fortunately for me, however, my travelling companion was made of far sterner stuff. He cross-examined the man for a bit, eventually ascertaining that he'd been lodging with an unloved sister, far out of the city on one of its seven hills, in a suburb no one has ever heard of and apparently without either *trattoria* or even *bar*. I think the bloke was telling us porkies in his keenness to get across his heartfelt loathing of Rome.

| EXT. | RUINS OF POMPEII | DAY |

Having farewelled their compatriot without reluctance, they are walking slowly back towards the *scavi*'s gates.

                    M.R.
          (bit of hand-wringing)
        Shit a brick, Stringer! -what're we
        going to do?

He's been expecting this.

                    C.S.
          (calm)
        About what?

                              M.R.

          (stops)

       Whaddya mean?-about ROME, of course!
       We're there for five days!

He stops, turns, grasps her shoulders and gives her a
little shake.

                              C.S.

       Darling…Do you actually mean to tell
       me that because one miserable, unwashed
       and on-the-nose denizen of our shores
       proffers his opinion on one of the
       world's great cities, and it's not a
       favourable one, we should give Rome a
       miss?!

Drops his hands, wags his head.

                              C.S.

       Did you not discern amongst his negative
       ramblings some reason for 'em?-the
       place he was staying in sounded to
       me like the camp in *Brutti, Sporchi e
       Cattivi*!

At this she can't help but laugh.

   Anyone who's seen that Carlo Ponti movie will
understand why; and anyone who hasn't can check out just
about any publicity still from it amongst the many to be
found on the Web (you will be entertained, I promise!).

> M.R.
> (stops laughing as she makes the
> association)
> But that WAS Rome, Stringer…

He turns to continue walking.

> C.S.
> (firmly: there is no arguing to be done)
> That was a person we wouldn't spend the
> time of day with if we were at home, and
> you know it. Why fer crissake are you
> so ready to be convinced by him and his
> very subjective opinions HERE?

There being no (possible) response, he continues:

> C.S.
> We are going to Rome, as we planned; and
> we are going to have a *really good* time
> there, also as planned – OK?

and he pinches her a bit, for emphasis…

Do I need to tell you that it was even as he said? And had that Aussie been living in the ghetto of the movie, we were still unable to work out how he'd arrived at the description he gave us of the city itself: Rome was *gorgeous*. Still is. It became his favourite city, and was at that time mine (but Milan lay ahead).

There is so much to see in Rome that you could spend a year there and still not cover it. Oh, sure it's dirty: who's been in a major city that isn't? There isn't garbage everywhere, nor rats: dunno where he got those from. And its food is perfectly fine!; of course, being a major tourist destination, the *ristoranti* are grossly overpriced; but their menus are more than merely acceptable, and if you have funds to scatter, they're excellent. If you don't, you should do what we did and travel there in winter, so that you can spend very small numbers of lire – of course, it's euros now – on utterly delicious things like *porchetta* rolls in the *piazza* Navona. Sighh ... Or slab pizza in any of the dozens of stalls nearby. Oh, that slab pizza! Gosh, even in retrospect all that stuff makes me drool.

And of all the places we got to see, in all our travels, it was only in Rome that we found the amazing, extraordinary bird balloons: flocks of *passeri*, little birds that no one seems to be able to identify positively, that swoop and swirl into extraordinary formations, so unexpectedly and so astoundingly and so gloriously, over those ancient rooftops – one of our favourite things in the Eternal City.

§

We finished with the car hire in Rome and took a train northwards, where I fell madly in love with Milan. Chic was bemused, as the city did not include anything thus far established as an M.R. criterion for liking places: no views; no quick access to adorable little villages; no made-on-the-premises bread shops. Its only (semi-)ruin is the *castello* Sforzesco, and it has very little greenery.

I have never been able to pinpoint the reason for my affection for this large and fairly impersonal city but from the moment we first set foot in its centre, I was to be overwhelmed with a sensation of its being the place where I wanted to be; and if it were not for the fact that my life is now changed forever, such would still be the case. Apart from having to spend almost an entire morning collecting the tickets from/for La Scala that had been reserved for us from Sydney by our much-loved friend Ercole Perego, we spent a lot of time in Milan eating – which, being all really enjoyable, does at least something to explain my approval. Ercole, by the way, we knew well from enjoying a very large number of meal-times at his little pizza-&-pasta *ristorante* in Willoughby; and I had become friends, also, with his amazingly beautiful wife, Ivana. Like most Italians, *i Perego* were generous and kind to a fault; and also like most Italians, Ercole derived great pleasure from being able to use influence to help others.

We had another brush with history there, too: we sat breakfasting in a very upmarket *bar* and read, in *Il Corriere della Sera*, about the end of Ceauşescu – not to overlook the lovely Mrs C., of course! – in Romania. It was extraordinary to be in Europe with amazing things happening around us: by then I believe the Stringers were feeling very *du monde*, whereas we were in fact as unfashionable as can be imagined. You don't set or follow trends when you are careless of everyone else.

Ercole and Ivana, by now themselves in Italy on holiday, took us to see that acme of all places tourist, San Marino, but neither of us fell in love with it. It was definitely worth seeing... but going into? – nup. Chic did his best to be enthusiastic about it on account of its giving its name to an F1 race, actually run at nearby Imola; but even his passion for F1 couldn't bring him to wax lyrical about San Marino. (The tragic death of our hero Ayrton Senna on that very course, four and a half years later, caused us to come to associate San Marino with bad things – fairly silly, but it was a deeply emotive issue.) However, we were delighted to be with the Peregos: they took us to lunch in some *ristorante* in San Marino, but what we ate was so totally forgettable that I have totally forgotten it.

That was more or less it for Italy, after which we went back to France for two or three days in Paris, which would go up there amongst Chic's very favourites. What wasn't included on that list, though, was couscous. Our little hotel turned out to be in the Moroccan Quarter ... or perhaps it was the Algerian or Tunisian ... whichever, the eating places around served virtually nothing but. The first couple of times were fine: we'd not eaten couscous before, and found it interestingly different; but thereafter the interest waned rapidly, and we had soon to stop ourselves from screaming at the sight of piles of tiny beads of semolina, regardless of what they were served with. We wandered far in search of anything *else*, which led to bad temper when having to walk for hours without coming across anywhere at all to eat: it was as if there was an area you ate in and then ... you didn't! – not for miles and miles (but if it hadn't been for my refusal to use the *métro* we wouldn't have got so hungry; a hangover from my insecurities, alas – it took another trip to get rid of that fear).

We also traipsed off into the unknown to find both the old Paris Opera and the new. The latter turned out to be a most uninspiring setting for glorious music; although it did provide many useful corners for the homeless, and we enjoyed ourselves mightily developing an opera story along those lines. On the way back to our hotel, we were rapt when approached by some Japanese tourists seeking directions to somewhere or other, and we were able to tell them! This made us proprietorial about Paris, as if we knew it all intimately; and over the course of more trips, during which we spent longer there, we did grow familiar with a fair bit of it, lovely city that it is.

Back to England – a couple of planned stays this time, with people I've written about: Erica, now in Reading, and Francis and Sarah, holidaying in a friend's flat in Knightsbridge. The latter pair took us to concerts and the theatre, and we found and ate at several vegetarian restaurants because our friends were already long established as non–animal eaters (only took me another twenty-odd years). Erica had us, *inter alia*, wandering and wondering amongst Oxford's dreaming spires.

There's something special about that university, even though France and Italy have older ones: probably that there are so many of the great English writers who studied there – and at Cambridge, of course ... And we even got to see my loved nephew, then flying for a UK-based freight company.

But we weren't frightfully thrilled by London; probably because it was the only place in the whole trip where people were rude to us. I think Londoners have had their fill of Aussies – there are so very many of us lodging there. As well, the weather was very ... English.

If we'd travelled about within that country, so liberally studded with Roman and mediaeval ruins and history, our view would have been different: imagine if we'd been able to get up to Yorkshire and see what remains of Middleham Castle*! – but venturing down to Bath by train was as far as we journeyed: due, largely, to that short journey's having consumed the remains of our money. Struth! – British Rail ...

With so many familiar faces around it was a bit like being home; and this made us aware that we'd been too long away.

So home we went, dazed by so many different experiences and places.

And, of course, *meals* ...

---

* the favourite residence of my all-time historical hero, Richard III of England

LEARNING

Once home from stalking Plácido and joyfully discovering mountains and ruins, and with no more possibility of getting to any really good opera, Chic decided it was time to widen my classical music horizons.

He introduced me to a whole group of composers, hitherto aliens in my world: Holst, Ravel, Mussorgsky, Dvorak, Prokofiev, Rimsky-Korsakov, and on and on. None had been part of my early years. Moderns like Satie and Gottschalk – even Aaron Copland – all these he gave to me. And Gershwin: how he loved 'Rhapsody in Blue'; it was his favourite piece of music. He was invariably right on the money: this I found incomprehensible when I reflected upon his upbringing and its lack of music for listening. Where did his love of it arise? How? Under what circumstances? When? And even, perhaps, why?

But the biggest 'why' is that of my never having asked him any of these questions. There was no deliberation in it but now I regret incalculably my failure to have done so.

Still, let it not remain unstated that I brought some music into his life, too! Before we were together he knew nothing of Italian pop – now referred to as *la musica leggera** – or its performers; but after a not very long time we were enjoying equally the music of all the major *cantautori* of our time (I'm talking the '80s and '90s, of course). And the list grew as the years went by and so did our enjoyment of them all; and the only point of difference between us was which ones we enjoyed most.

Writing of that brings back those wondrous days of the early '90s, when we had Galaxy TV piped directly to our flat-block, and could thus watch Italian television to our hearts' content – which was most of the time. I particularly remember a day when on our favourite pop show from Rai

---

* as opposed to opera, which is described by Italians as *la musica lirica*

TV a bloke sang a most beautiful song that we wanted to be able to identify (truth to tell, a large part of what was said on Italian telly went over our heads). The method we chose was to telephone Rai in Rome! – as you do ...

And there was a most gratifying phone conversation with the show's host, who was tickled to be called from Oz, and had no trouble comprehending my dubious Italian (!). He was able to tell us all about Enzo Gragnaniello – a personal friend of his – who was, totally coincidentally, in the studio for a rehearsal at that time. He called over the studio intercom to Enzo that he had some Aussie fans on the phone, and relayed back that Enzo was very pleased, and sent his regards!

Oh, such fun we used to have!

§

Another and very different aspect of creativity that Chic brought into my life – he was a natural teacher and I was ever ready to be taught by him – was web-authoring. He had taken me into the world of PCs years before, once he'd mastered them, and we ended up having one each, at which we would sit side-by-side in absolute companionship and pleasure, doing whatever we did.

I evinced a wish to learn how to make my own site when I developed a passion for an Italian footballer, some time early in 1990, in the days when SBS used to telecast a summary of the previous weekend's fixtures from the Italian *Lega Calcio*. He was (and still is, of course) Roberto Baggio, *il divin codino*, playing like a little god; and we derived huge pleasure not only from his game but *the* game, becoming aficionados of the worst kind and able to boringly quote statistics at the drop of a hat. In my usual fashion I became a hero-worshipper of this beautiful and talented bloke, and my own beautiful and talented bloke became a willing accomplice in helping me turn the hero-worship into something potentially useful.

Chic searched out web-authoring software I could use without screaming and tearing my hair. He had to get me into the web-authoring mindset; to nurse me through the most basic learning curves; to progress me on to more sophisticated areas; to teach me to *think first* and actually plan what I wanted to do (so as to prevent yells of frustration when I realised what I'd left out, completely stuffing everything that followed); to do his best to ensure that I never forgot to save as I was working. I created with this inexhaustible assistance *The Roberto Baggio Italian–English Website*; and it was hugely popular amongst the Web's Baggio fans as it provided Italian articles about Roby, together with full translations and photo galleries, thus keeping lots of people happy.

Even though I found some software learning challenging to the point of difficult to the point of impossible, with concomitant ire, Chic was rarely angry with me. He would often leave his TV viewing and wander casually into the office when he heard me swearing, and look calmly over my shoulder, ascertaining the problem without difficulty. If I was incandescent with rage he'd make me laugh by pretending to be trembling with fear, then sit down next to me at his PC and show me how to fix whatever balls-up I'd just created.

He'd taught himself web-authoring, and had gone rapidly from beginner to webmaster. He created several commercial sites, for a range of clients, but I believe he found the most enjoyment in constructing the portal for our travels, together with a site for one of the trips. This was totally non-lucrative, of course, and not in the least challenging to him; but I'd made the sites that documented the first three of our European journeys – to which he'd contributed enormously – and by helping me he'd discovered how much fun it was. And it is, too: it's a bit like redoing the journey, making a travel site.

He'd moved up through various versions of his software until that current when he was doing his last work, Dreamweaver 8. He liked to work in tables, which involves all manner of amazingly complicated things, and I couldn't do anything remotely like it. He tried to show me how to use Dreamweaver, but had to admit defeat when it became obvious that I was not going to assimilate its complexities (my face's becoming contorted with frustrated rage may have provided some indication). So he dropped that, and left me to potter around with what he'd first found for me – a programme with drag-and-drop ease of operation.

But he did manage to din into my bonce the basics of a professional graphic design software he used. Having seen me downloading all manner of gumph – dividers, background, buttons and so on – from the Web, he showed me how I could use it to make my own! As well, even though they may not be the most technically brilliant photos you've ever seen, those within this book, scanned many years ago at dpi of 72 or 96, have been rendered at least recognisable by enhancing them with it: Corel Photo-Paint 10*, roughly as old as I am ... I was amazed that I managed to take it in, and absolutely delighted; and I reckon he probably felt the same on both counts.

Having Chic teach me is one of the things I miss most of all.

---

* I may now be the only person in the world who *doesn't* use Photoshop

TOWNHOUSING

INT.	KITCHEN	DAY

A small townhouse in Pyrmont.

A little galley kitchen opens straight onto the tiny backyard, wherein are some not terribly thrilling plants and lots of brick in the form of chin-high walls on all three sides.

She is looking in the fridge, without success, for any already-thawed cat's meat.

> M.R.
>
> How come The Captain hasn't been chewing my foot off for this, already?

He is seated at the PC in their office (originally the living-room) that opens out directly from the kitchen.

> C.S.
>
> (only half-attending)
>
> He's sitting out there on the fence, admiring the view we won't have for much longer* …

She has ended up, as so often, with a small packet of meat from the freezer, which she puts into the microwave.

She washes her hands at the sink and walks out into the yard.

A few seconds later, she's back:

---

* reference to the imminent destruction of the old Pyrmont Power Station, to be replaced by the hideous, unspeakable and *unceasingly expanding* casino

<u>M.R.</u>
(not yet worried)

No, darling – he's not out there: he
must've come back in without your
knowing.

Cut from 2S to single as he stands up INTO FRAME: *he*'s
worried.

<u>C.S.</u>
(hurrying through kitchen and exiting)

No, he didn't! – I'm talking two minutes
ago!

The Captain was sitting on the wall; I
walked from the espresso machine out
here; you came down the stairs and went
to the fridge.

I can say quite definitely that he has
not come back inside the house.

Nor had he. He'd finally decided to venture down to the
end of the common wall at the back of the row of eight
townhouses (of which ours was the third), and had then got
up the courage to take The Leap into the car park behind us
all. It was a *looong* way down.

From there he'd made his way via some route or other
up onto the top deck of a building that faced onto the street
running at right-angles to ours: the deck was the top storey,
rear, of this building, and it was very, *very* high. And up there
he was, wandering about forlornly and calling us; he had
forgotten how he got there, he told us plaintively: he had no
way of getting back. Would we call the fire brigade, please?

We dithered for a while: would we? – or what ...?

Fortunately, Chic had ported most of his house-building
infrastructure during every move we'd made since leaving
Dangar Island, and this included an extremely long
ladder – so long that it frightened me when he mounted it.

It was closed and stored ... somewhere. Dunno. I can only remember that he got it out from wherever that was with a fair bit of difficulty, as it had been there for a couple of years.

First problem was how the devil to get this monstrous piece of equipment from the townhouse yard and down into the car park. That was solved fairly soon by Chic's practicality: he heaved it, somehow or other, to the top of the brick fence behind the townhouse and pushed it over – *et voilà!*: it was, noisily, in the car park.

Second and more serious problem: after he had dragged it sweatily all the way across the asphalt, no matter how enormous it was, it wasn't quite tall enough to enable him – once having put it up against the wall of the building with the deck and heaved upon by its various ropes to extend it fully – to actually reach our Russian. Who had been for some time prowling anxiously and yowling very loudly, thus adding great emotional pressure to an already fraught situation. But try as he might, Chic could not get any closer, his arms at full reach and himself a very, very long way up in the air, than a metre or so shy of the deck being prowled.

The Captain was watching all these carryings-on and had become noticeably calmer the closer his beloved father came; I was languishing several fathoms below, crying surreptitiously, but only for fear of the long-unused ladder's ropes breaking – for I knew perfectly well that whatever Chic did would be OK.

Then The Captain, having assessed the likelihood of being actually picked up as ... well, not too hot, to put it mildly, solved this major dilemma himself: he oozled down the wall onto Chic's upstretched hand and continued down to his left shoulder, where he sat himself with perfect confidence, awaiting transport outta there. And thus did they come back down to earth together, at ease and looking smug – although it is to be noted that even Chic had been momentarily startled by The Captain's total confidence.

> <u>M.R.</u>
> (hastily dries her tears for fear of
> their being misinterpreted)
>
> Oh! - you clever things!

She is rewarded with a gracious smile from her beloved,
and a brief whiskery glance from the silver furry one.

This one was as imprinted on Chic as all our other cats had been. Every single one of them seemed to fall with a huge sigh of relief into his caring and reliable arms – much as I did, come to think of it.

§

That carpark was the source of immense irritation, every now and then. It wasn't the noise made by cars coming and going, because we were never aware of that; no, it was that, every so often, some moronic imbecile would decide to turn on his car alarm.

As everyone knows, car alarms are not to warn off would-be car thieves; they are manufactured for the purpose of giving maximum grief to all those poor unfortunates who, for their sins, are situated within the environs of the car that some cretin has decided to fit with one – and leave turned on, of course.

Mostly, the problem would be solved within a tolerable period of time, as the car owner would emerge wrathfully from the multi-business-occupied 100 Harris Street, stride masterfully towards his vehicle, and find – nothing, of course (I forgot to remind you that the other purpose of car alarms is to ensure that they can be set off by a bee's flying too close, or a bit of spider web floating past on a breeze).

But sometimes, the dastardly car-owner would decide to leave his car parked over the entire weekend, and would, with totally subjective logic, turn on its alarm. Just who was expected to save it if a thief tried to steal his precious bloody car we could never work out: suffice it to say that the weekend park-over was always that which caused us problems.

| INT. | DINING ROOM | MORNING |

M.R.
(starting to clear the breakfast table)

Stringer, don't forget it's council elections today, eh? - you'll have to have a shower and get dressed soon, if we're going in to Town Hall to vote.

He moves into the living area to start a promising game of something or other on the PC.

C.S.
(somewhat inattentively)

Yeah yeah: much and all as I'd LIKE to forget we have to go and make our mark for a pack of drongos, I haven't actually done so.

No mad rush but.

M.R.
Agreed; but I was reminding you now becau—

A ghastly din interrupts: it sounds like someone trying to murder a rhinoceros to dance music.

C.S.
(rolls eyes wearily; mutters to
himself)

Vandalised yet again by dickheads.

The din continues, with variations.

They, being fairly inured, do their best to ignore it:
this kind of thing has happened so often that there is
no longer even any amusement in trying to guess which
horrible noise will follow which.

But it was another of the *unending* alarms; some total prick had left his car parked for the weekend, armed by what was probably the latest in that technology field, and left us to suffer. Suffer we did, believe me! – the noise just went on, and on, and on, and on – and there was absolutely nothing that anyone would or could do about it.

Before very much more time had passed, Chic had had it: this must've been about the fourth or fifth time that a weekend had been ruined in such fashion. He went to the fridge and removed the five eggs he found therein, putting them in one of his caps (and thus making himself look like an Edwardian watercolour of a naughty schoolboy who's just raided a bird's nest). Then he sallied forth purposefully into our wee backyard, and stepped up onto The Thing we kept there for peering over the fence, surveying the carpark.

EXT.	REAR OF TOWNHOUSE	DAY

C.S.
(perplexed, shouts)

Come and see if you can tell which car
it is that's making the row.

She emerges and heaves herself up onto the very small remaining space on The Thing, teetering uncertainly.

                    M.R.
          (always eager to be useful, yells back)

     Could be that red thinggy over there.

Points uncertainly, being no revhead.

                    M.R.
               (continuing to shout)

     Doesn't it look as if there's some
     movement about it? - and there'd bloody
     have to be, for all the row it's giving
     off.

The alarm stops for one of its breathers just as she's finishing, and her bellowing at close range into his ear nearly makes him fall off The Thing: he has to do a quick bit of juggling with the capful of eggs…

I can't remember the make of the red car that we worked out was the culprit; but our decision was shortly stamped *CONFIRMED* by the fact that the owners of the few other cars still there of a Saturday morning drove off (to vote, one righteously hoped) – we had the guilty party, all right. Chic scoured the area with his eyes; looked right, looked left, looked right again … checked the battery of windows in 100 Harris Street. Not a soul to be seen on this already hot Saturday morning.

And then he let fly.

SPLAT! – missed.

SPLAT! – missed again. He was infuriated: he was usually very good at throwing – him with that accurate left hand.

SPLAT! – yaaaaayyyy!!! Got the bastard! Right on its bonnet! The alarm, now giving a rendition of a duet between Arnie as The Terminator and a bull seal on heat, gave an uncertain hiccup, paused, thought about it, and then recommenced its song in a somewhat lower key.

SPLATSPLAT!!! – both onto the roof! – that's the stuff to give the troops!

Wiping fence-top dust from his hands he returned to the house, and forgot it immediately, going dutifully into the shower. I stayed there for a while, looking at the smashed eggs turning hard in the hot sun, and gloating (men might be from Mars, but women are from Revengeland).

It must be admitted that in spite of the success of our activity, the alarm continued its unspeakable caterwauling. We went out to do our civic duty – forced out, in fact; and it was still going when we came back (having found various other things to keep us away) after tea. Fortunately a battery or something died and it petered out just in time to save us from total insanity, before we went to bed – although not before maddening us to the point of having a row over some meaningless thing.

I reflected upon the fact that it was the first time I'd ever seen Chic take a stand: his normal response to trying situations was to remain laid-back and wave a tolerant hand. But he'd behaved just like me! Thinking about it, I hoped I wasn't starting to influence him too much: I needed him to remain the Chic I knew and loved ...

Happily, my anxiety was unfounded; for, in all the years we were together, there was only that and one other time when he reared up on his hind legs, baring his teeth.

PAIN

The little townhouse was our first experience of this suburb: we'd moved there early in the '90s, burdened with a sense of failure after our company activity had wound down and then stopped, and a feeling that we were being punished for it. Well, let me be honest: that's what *I* felt. Chic did experience the former, but he would never, ever indulge himself in the latter: he had not been raised a Mick, and was thus refreshingly free from guilt. We lived in the townhouse for four years.

It was very brick, that small residence; and its separating walls were very *hollow* brick, alas! – many was the time we lay awake wondering how long our neighbours on the right were going to sit up playing their CDs, when we made our bedroom in the front room, upstairs. And when we moved the bedroom to the back room, we would wonder how long our neighbours on the left were going to argue hysterically. You might think that the latter would be a salutary lesson to us but it was in this very location that Chic and I experienced our only – what word to use? Perhaps best to say simply that here we experienced the only period during which our marriage was not completely stable and utterly happy: in fact, it was a dark, confused and confusing time – but at least it didn't last for long.

For background, suffice it to say that Chic was extremely worried about our financial situation, as our business was not making enough on a regular basis to live on. Before long, I found a job that was very well paid, but which I almost instantly detested; and he was afraid that I would walk out on it, for I had a history of behaving like that with jobs I didn't like. In such a boiler situation, Ebb & Kander were omnipresent: their musical statement from *Cabaret* regarding love's flying out the door when hunger (or penury) taps on the window – well, Fred Ebb had the right idea. Unhappily.

I know, I know, you who are familiar with the song: we weren't within cooee of freezing; and certainly, I wasn't even close to normal weight, let alone thirty pounds under. My reference to the song 'Money, Money' is meant to give dimension to the undercurrent of tension that was brought on by our lack of financial security. I truly hated the fact that Chic expected me to stay in that hideous, loathed, mindbogglingly awful job indefinitely; and, of course, the spectre of Authority was lurking. However, my deepest problem was that, as I saw it, *he was not looking after me* – a frightful thing for a person who has existed for years in the sure and certain knowledge that the person she loves most in the world will always care for her – and I'm not talking financially.

In fact, I think that was just my excuse. The bottom line was that I was not capable of accepting the responsibility he was putting on me. But Chic himself suspected that he wasn't looking after me; and this upset all his *modi operandi* just as much as it did mine. The period after our company went from boom to bust had brought all the problems you might expect: it was only afterwards I came to understand that there were more for him than for me.

In a kind of childish rebellion, I suppose, I would spend hours of an evening in what was one of the very few Internet chat rooms, known simply as 'MSN'* and made available to those who, as we, were beta-testing Win95, while Chic watched TV in the living room; and therein I struck up a friendship with a man from the Suisse Romande. It offered a temporary solution to a horrible situation: I had not the maturity to deal with the strangeness of whatever it was that was happening between us, so I escaped into this man's life on the other side of the world. He was not a happy man – in fact, seriously depressed – having more than his share of very real problems, in which I became interested. Perhaps I preferred them to ours. I persuaded myself of the romance of it all.

He was a policeman, and the only reason I tell you is because I often worried about his taking out his gun and shooting himself. Did you know that many policemen do that

* not even *remotely* similar to today's version

215

when things get tough? – well, it's true. They have guns, so they have The Means, when most of us don't. Which is a good thing, our not having them: the fact that policemen have them is definitely a bad thing! When deep in misery for whatever reason and seeing no way out, we have to do something long-term about it, like find someone to talk to, whereas they just haul out their shooters. The statistics are appalling, but you'll never read about them.

While I worried about my Swiss mate on many an occasion, I suspect Chic wished he would indeed shoot himself, and the sooner the better!

INT.	OFFICE	NIGHT

C.S.
(tight-lipped)

You might just as well be going out with someone else every night for all the value you're placing on our marriage!

M.R.
(flashing back irrelevantly)

And I might also just as well be working at McDonald's every day for all the value you're placing on my career!

And *still*, in spite of the fact that Chic saw the man as some kind of threat, he would help me with any chat room technical problems! I talked about Jean-Claude to him a lot of the time: it was with no intention of hurting him, but because I wanted him to become part of the friendship. Chic had no wish to become part of it: he just wanted it to go away.

We hadn't the wisdom for handling this situation: we had zero experience of rifts from which to draw, so everything was completely out of the norm for both of us. To say that we were out of our comfort zone is grossly understating things:

we were lost, totally adrift. Maybe there's something about having no children that means you don't develop the ability to be responsible, and you just wing everything; and when living by winging, you're awfully lucky if things work out OK after bad times.

Because this was our bad time, this completely unreal business of my having interest in the life of an unknown man on the other side of the world, which went on for about ... oh, I'd say five to six months. At no time, it must be clarified, did it enter the head of either of us that this shift out of our normal relationship might entail a split. But there I was, behaving exactly as my mother had on so many occasions, with selfish immaturity.

What will be difficult to believe is this: *I don't remember how we sorted it*. True as I sit here. I can only say that I've always been able to forget anything if I put my mind to it – which means, of course, that I've wrapped up that episode, covered any cracks with gaffer tape and plastered over the lot. I would write about it if I could, I can say only that: after all, it's not as if I've spared you much regarding myself so far.

The fact is that I have absolutely zero memory of any discussion that Chic and I must have had in restoring the balance and harmony of our life. For restored it was: I left the ghastly job and listed with a temp agency: through it I found immediately a good and sound job that saw me go from temp to contractor in a matter of weeks, and I stayed there for five years with my large CEO. This couldn't have happened unless agreement had been reached; and how it is I can't remember discussing it is pretty bloody amazing – in a depressing kind of way.

No cloud had floated till then nor ever would again over the horizon encircling our marriage. Half a year after it all began, it was as if there had never been a problem: Chic no longer saw or felt there to be any threat to our relationship, and I no longer saw him as being threateningly authoritarian. The friendship with Jean-Claude did extend to include my husband: he and Chic were useful to each other technically on many an occasion via the Internet, and each would have me transmit messages to the other.

We eventually got to meet him when we were in France (and wife number two, on one occasion – after which we were easily able to understand his tendency to depression).

In Annecy, J-C took the photo of Chic that's the best of all – see plates. It's my personal second-favourite, but it's definitely *the best*. And that could be because J-C was very fond of Chic; and, as well, he wanted to take a really good photo of a really good photographer.

It shows a man who, although he knows his life will not last for very much longer, is determined that the other half of him will not grasp this fact – at least, not until there is absolutely nothing he is able to do about it.

FEAR

I seem to have lost my muse: she has abandoned me and I'm not sure why. Maybe it's because of remembering having caused pain to he who never did a mean thing to me in our life.

But maybe it's because the writing is leading me inexorably towards the end of our story.

My brush with death when I lost my father threatened to shut down the world as I knew it, but soon afterwards I met the man who took me into a new and far better world, wiping out all the grief and emotional anarchy with which my head and heart were filled.

Now I am in a terror-filled place: I have lost *everything*.

All that exists is the memory of happiness that once was mine ... and it's only intellectual, remembering.

§

The bald fact is this: as I saw it, my husband might as well have been god.

I put it to you: who is 'god' but someone who

loves deeply and truly,
protects,
cherishes,
listens,
supports,
encourages,
laughs with,
teaches,
challenges,
understands,
provides solace ...?

– and those are just the aspects of Chic that come immediately to mind (I can scarcely include 'stirs the blood' in a list likening him to a deity).

As well, he was the person whom I respected above all, in whom I had total and absolute confidence.

I loved him beyond measure, beyond description.

Such was he whom I have lost. And I shall never see him again.

CARING

Prior to my having accumulated a large number of years on this earth, sickness was something I knew nothing about. But during the time I was contracted to the small company in the CBD with my large CEO, my gut decided to claim centre stage. I should tell you right away that the problem was never satisfactorily diagnosed: it was certainly treated – and how! – but various medicos of differing specialist areas were unable to reach any conclusions regarding it. Well, none that were ever passed on to us, anyway.

I developed Symptoms. To begin with, I started losing weight. While this was not something that caused me any grief whatsoever, it was nevertheless strange. And the next symptom was abdominal pain. Not constant, mind; but I did go about clutching my belly and complaining, eventually falling onto bed and complaining *loudly*. However, these spells were brief.

One night I was chatting to J-C on MSN and Chic was watching telly and occasionally shouting to me about it, when I became aware that pain was creeping up on me: I cut the chat short pretty brusquely and stepped uncertainly into the living room. He looked up, saw my face and leaped to his feet; putting an arm around me he led me gently into our bedroom and helped me lie down, starting to take off my shoes and socks. Before he'd got one lace undone, I was back on my feet, screaming with pain and fear. I was so filled with agony and panic that I just stood there beating his chest and ululating.

INT.	BEDROOM	NIGHT

<u>M.R.</u>
(shouting at him)
What's HAPPENING??? What IS this???!!!

She gasps in terrified pain, trying to suck in breath.

He holds her very tightly.

> C.S.
> It's all right, Margie…it's all right,
> darling…It will pass, I promise
> you – I've got you…

And as it does indeed pass, she is brought gradually to a
degree of calm.

Its duration was around a minute, but it seemed like
hours. Chic put me down on the bed again and sat next to
me, holding my hands and talking quietly until my panic
subsided. Several more attacks ensued, and he nursed me
through each one – the first bout's having come to an end
as he had promised enabled me to get through those that
followed (although not without the screaming, I must admit).

Next morning I was very far from well, and we drove the
very long way to the GP we'd had since being on the Island.
I remember sitting next to Chic, shivering unceasingly and
uncontrollably during this lengthy journey, even though it
was early summer. It transpired that the shivering indicated
infection, and our GP wanted it all looked into really quickly.
So we drove all the way back and checked me in to Emergency
at Royal Prince Alfred, our local hospital, and the saga of the
gut commenced in earnest.

My bad luck was to have found on call that day a surgeon
who was addicted to keyhole surgery on gall bladders.
There's a simple phrase for this – I'll google it … laparoscopic
cholecystectomy – there you go: heaven knows I should
remember it. So this bloke was absolutely rapt to have another
victim turn up, and I doubt that an enormous amount of time
was spent arguing with himself about a diagnosis while tests
were being carried out. Once I was ensconced in a ward
bed, he and his acolytes came to tell us about The Plan: it

was pretty straightforward. They were going to have a look inside me to see if they could find – who knows? And if they found whatever it was they thought might be there, they'd remove the bit containing it, the gall bladder: did I have any problems with that...? If this bloke had suggested going in there with an angle-grinder I wouldn't have minded, not if it meant there would be no more of that pain.

And it came to pass that I woke up in the post-op. room with a feeling very like indigestion in the troublesome gut. Not the pain, something else. But unhappily it got worse and worse, until I was crying with it. I told them I wanted my husband, and they got him without further ado; and I cried at him, too, about the 'indigestion'. He was fairly amazed about it all, and asked the nurses to get a surgeon's acolyte, immediately please. One of the young blokes turned up comparatively smartly and, having been told of this different pain, started to smile.

INT.	POST-OP	DAY

He is glaring in disbelief at the intern:

                          C.S.
                (unrestrainedly angry)
              And just what is it about the pain my
              wife is in that causes you to smile?!

Have you read of someone's 'having the smile wiped from his face'? – that's what happened to this bloke. He explained, gabbling with anxiety to get it said: all that was wrong with me was that in order to get at the various parts the surgeon had needed to see, my gut had had to be pumped full of (some kind of) gas. It was done all the time. Everyone had gas pumped in. There was no problem, no problem whatsoever. Just gas. It would be gone in no time. Minutes, possibly. He rushed away in a very big hurry, mad to be gone from under Chic's furious gaze.

But it didn't go away in no time. In fact, it stayed with me until around four the next morning: I spent most of that night wandering the hospital corridor, clutching my front and groaning, and giving no thought at all to the fact that my hospital gown was hanging open down the back (there wasn't really an alternative, taking into account the size of my arse and that of the standard hospital gowns issued).

When Chic turned up at sparrow's he was appalled to hear about the duration of the gas bloat, his face darkening. But as it had by that time dissipated I was carefree, even blithe!, and looking forward to learning from the surgeon about the removal of the offending organ.

You may be ahead of me.

They hadn't taken out my gall bladder at all. They'd looked around in the appropriate spots, found what the surgeon referred to as 'some sludge' and cleaned that out. His story was that they couldn't remove the gall bladder because of all the gas! – and he wasn't in the least embarrassed at having *created* this paradoxical situation. I was to return in another week and it'd all happen again.

The next time, before allowing the nurse to put a cannula into my hand, Chic extracted from the sorcerer's apprentices – a different pair – a promise that they would *not* pump in the gas the way it had been done last time, and that they would take every step they possibly could to ensure I didn't end up with the same bloat problem. They swore. And they lied. There was no way they could make that promise; but they didn't tell him that. It was only sheer bloody luck that the terrible bloat didn't occur again.

So finally I was without a gall badder, and happily without gut pain. All the gods were thanked, votive offerings made and consideration given to human sacrifice (the surgeon was definitely our number one choice).

§

Peace reigned for two years and then the whole shooting match started again! – I began to lose weight, and suddenly I was experiencing exactly the same pain I'd had before. Different surgeon in Emergency; had to go through the whole story again, Chic there holding a hand, as always.

The procedure this time was an ERCP – endoscopic retrograde cholangiopancreatography: as I was being wheeled in to surgery, they asked me all those strange test questions you get asked on your way to being cut into, and the extension of the acronym was one of them! It's an investigation of the bile duct.

No one offered any explanation as to how I could be having that same pain in the absence of a gall bladder, ostensibly the cause of it on the previous occasion. No one seemed surprised by anything – we never got any information that linked my previous attack to this one. It was as if I'd turned up for the first time, and we were not happy about that. Chic told me afterwards that he really loathed the feeling of having no control over the doctors' continuing to cut me up – bit of an overstatement, but he was truly distressed.

Throughout all this pain/hospitalisation/procedural time, he was there and loving me and, indeed, doing what he did so indescribably well – caring for me. I was never once nervous, let alone afraid, of what was being done to me; for Chic was there, watching over me. No anodyne soothing: just the deep, reliable comfort of practicality sprung from wisdom.

I entrusted my life to him; and it is with remorse that will never diminish that he could not, nine years on, do the same with me.

§

Another aspect – more fundamental and far more impor-tant – of his caring for me was the fact that from the outset of our relationship he knew I was suffering from a problem in my head that I didn't understand, and he willingly took on sharing the burden with me.

We got to where we understood that I was terrified of being away from the familiar unless I knew I could get back to it in a very short time – I *had to be* in control of my environment. And there occurred still, occasionally, that inability to breathe.

These days such symptoms are as comprehended as is the ABC: they are those of a person suffering from agoraphobia who is having a panic attack. But back then there was very little known about it, and it wasn't something you picked up info on when leafing through a magazine in your dentist's waiting room (or wherever you read magazines).

Chic took a proactive rôle in helping me: he didn't just hold my hand and say 'There, there...' when I fell to bits. Happily for me, he understood that the thing I needed most of all was his presence – although I suppose this was a given, really. There was even a period when he was reluctant to go anywhere without me, in case an attack seized me during his absence. But with experience we came to realise that I had these panic attacks only when unable to control my environment: and it was our coming to understand this that gave him a direction to move in.

He slowly and carefully extended my environment from the known one, driving a little further on outings, always ready to turn back. And sometimes he had to do that. But eventually we made our first triumphant trip down to Melbourne, and none of our friends or family had any idea of our secret mutual glow of success.

Even local environments could be threatening, and the day I got the whole way through a movie in the Broadway cinema was a red-letter one.

It was thus, knowing Chic would always be there for me, that with his inimitable assistance the agoraphobia was defeated.

We discovered its origins, hearing by sheer and immensely fortunate coincidence a radio broadcast on the subject; and I followed up, finding the book recommended. I wept hysterically when I understood what had caused all this terrible business; but the tears were also of joy: I wasn't mad! To learn that all that ... *stuff* that went on in my head was experienced by others, and many!, was relief beyond description.

The little knowledge gained, far from being dangerous, was a wondrous thing: if the end of 'Into this house we're born' hasn't already told you more than it did me at the time, I can only add that what a child interprets, all unaware, as parental rejection is wont to fundamentally damage her psyche. All it had taken was my father's sending me away: poor man, if he'd realised ...

One day, on an outing to the beach at The Entrance, I'd found that upon alighting from the Land Cruiser and walking down to the sand, things started to go a bit haywire for me. But as I sat there and watched him setting up the camera's timer, the panic left me; and you can see this in the photo. He was so ... *capable.*

The couple you see comprises two people inextricably bound together; she by her total dependence on him and he by his joy in being thus depended on.

And, of course!, by love.

we were a fairly good-looking pair, she said modestly ...

TURNING INTO TRAVELLERS

Our second foray OS didn't happen until ten years after the first. During that nice round decade between 1990 and 2000, our thoughts often went back to those fantastic six weeks; but we'd thought ourselves never financially capable of travelling again. However, as the somewhat momentous end of both century and millennium loomed, there I was, contracted as Operations Manager for my CEO, happy to be doing it and bringing in what was for us a sound income.

For goodness knows how much lead-up time, it was all the Olympics in 'Sidder-knee!' – you couldn't get away from them. But as we'd never been athletics fans, it was our dearest wish to do exactly that. And one of the venues was around the corner from our flat! – we simply had to escape ... All that was necessary in advance of doing so was to organise a friend's family to cat-sit – very easy, as they *wanted* to be in Olympicsville.

We went, of course, back to Europe; this time restricting the travel to Italy and France.

§

In Italy we fell in love with Lunigiana – that almost wild, mountainous, northern extremity of Tuscany, where not many tourists go (or hadn't at that stage, but who knows what's changed since then?).

And then over the mountain pass into France, where we found Grignan, a truly pretty town clustered below its *château* on a hill. Here we became smitten forever with love of another place discovered on-line by Chic – Le Clair de la Plume, a B&B that is so much more – owned and run by a man called Jean Luc Valadeau; and as well as his fascinating and entertaining presence it has great beauty, history, delightfully good taste, peace and tranquillity, luxurious comfort, nearby places to explore and a gorgeous garden for taking tea in.

Chic wrote something lovely in the guest-book: if you knew how atypical that was, you'd understand how much he'd come to love it. For anyone planning to travel in France, I offer clairplume.com – consider it a gift from me to you.

The final, Parisian leg of the trip saw us actually visiting the places all the tourists go to: Erica had come from the UK to join us for a weekend, and, as she hadn't been in that city since she was in her teens, she was desirous of Seeing Paris. We took her to do this – something we ourselves had not thus far done because of wandering in unplanned and delightful idleness, avoiding the famous spots (because We Didn't Want To Be Tourists). Well, mostly Chic took her, as I rapidly discovered how much physical output is required. I was at somewhere near my fattest in those days, and physical effort something not dear to my heart – although heaven knows it should've been! So while I was happy to be amongst the little party travelling in a *bâteau-mouche* down the Seine, and even walking about the Bois de Vincennes, positively outrageous activities like climbing the interior of Sacré-Coeur had little appeal, and I left them to it – and to several other, similarly demanding jaunts. Always available for meals, though. :-)

Paris had wormed its way right into my heart; and this made Chic happy, for he loved it greatly. Because we were us, it was vital that no situation arose wherein one of us really liked something but the other didn't (and so far outside our ken was such an occurrence that we wouldn't have known what to do about it).

The trip had been amazing, extraordinary – confirming every reaction to Europe drawn from us during our initial foray. Once back home, the title for its website sprang entirely unbidden into my head: I set about making a site I called *Heaven and Other Places*.

§

Then, about eighteen months after the Heaven trip, I left the small company in the CBD when my CEO took early retirement and the board went bananas and replaced him with an absolutely *frightful* man. Chic's response to our huge row and my departure was a sigh of resignation: it'd been just a matter of time, he said, once having met the bloke and knowing me as he did.

It seemed perfectly logical to us to return to Europe – especially because there followed an intervening period that gave rise to our deciding on a specific destination: I obtained qualifications to teach English as a second language, because I wanted to do it in Italy. Chic the Italophile was hardly averse to the idea. So I used the Web to set up appointments at some Italian English-teaching colleges, and off we went …

We flew in to Malpensa, and after a few fantastic days in Milan took a train down to Arezzo (this being the trip mentioned briefly, earlier). It's a town I could rave on about for pages! We were enamoured, coming to the conclusion that if we had to choose a favourite Italian town, Arezzo would be it. I am obliged to add, however, that as days passed such a choice became far more difficult.

It was the first Site of Interview: a delightful college, run by an intelligent and appealing young woman, whose own English was impressive. A very positive meeting, they were all very keen to have me; but the college had to contact the relevant government department for permission to employ me, as they'd found I didn't have an EU passport. It had never been pointed out by the college I graduated from that this was a necessity: I'd fondly* imagined that we mother-tongue English speakers would be clutched to the generic European bosom with relief and gratitude.

For the rest of the interviews I'd organised, most of the colleges turned out to be either awful or in awful places, so I didn't follow through on them. But on reaching Rieti we found ourselves in another situation just like that in Arezzo: we fell madly in love with Rieti and its environs; and the college and its Principal were both super. He mentioned the negative

---

* and stupidly

aspects of how things were in Italy since the EU in terms of *stranieri* – of which I was indubitably one, being (I believe) third-generation Aussie whose peat bog Irish peasant blood has become so diluted as to have become unidentifiable. Chic was even less useful, as his Oz antecedents went back further than mine – for at least four generations. The *professore* had thought I'd have a European grandparent, at least; because he'd imagined I'd have been sensible enough to check all this stuff out before I came. Um. However, as he was very keen to have me if it was at all possible, he approached that same government department. But just as he responded to the college in Arezzo, *Signor* Scajola and/or his minions rejected me as someone seeking to steal bread from Italian mouths. So our intended purpose didn't meet with the slightest degree of success – disaster, some will even say.

But we'd spent a month travelling around Italy; and you can't call that disaster, not in anybody's terms!

§

While we were in Rome, Sarah and Francis arrived to join us. We stayed in the same little hotel but each couple went their separate ways during the day – they to see Art and we to see Places. We ate together each night, and found this to be an excellent way for a small, close group of friends to share photos and talk of experiences.

One of ours was the discovery by chance, as we delightedly rode Rome's tiny tramlines, of the church that is her cathedral, San Giovanni in Laterano, and its incredible, breathtaking, coffered ceiling. After you've drunk in its glory for a while – and you can do this, too, for you'll find it in the colour plates – you start thinking about what it must've cost ... at least, the Stringers did. It had obviously been fairly recently refurbished, so whatever the sum, it was to be reckoned in contemporary terms; and our minds boggled to the point of cynicism (you could count on our attitude to religion and its artefacts emerging).

Chic was as far from being a man of faith as one can be, but in a totally laid-back way. It simply didn't bother him. He found belief in a god of any denomination to be ludicrous; but he never fulminated against it, or got worked up into a passion by the pronouncements of any church leader. His spouse, of course, was *positively* anti: just seeing anything in print about 'men of God' or the like would see me frothing at the mouth. To this day.

Well, he was raised in a household in which religion played no part, while my upbringing was one steeped in Catholicism, with priests and nuns for relatives at every turn. I can only imagine that this fundamental difference in the backgrounds of our early years was the reason for our totally disparate reactions.

But it might bring into the frame the huge difference in our characters: on the one hand, Chic with his wise head and placid nature, reasoned approach to everything, unwillingness to become angered.

And on the other ...

The Prado: this is the *anticipation* of cultural joy

Brobdingnagians at the Temple

Nyons, in Drôme: a *numéro un* for the Stringers

Le Château d'Aix-en-Diois – heaven: mountains, mediaeval castle ruins and Chic

Venice: Chic was understandably proud of this evening shot

Pompeii Town effect: this photo never fails to make me laugh

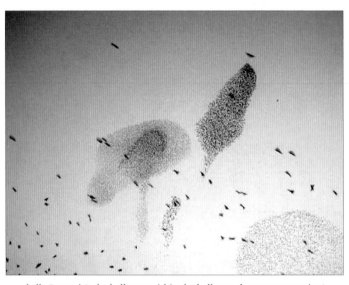

bella Roma: it's the balloons within the balloons that are so amazing!

Annecy: even Chic quite liked this one – the camera, I think

Lunigiana: *nelle Apuane*

approaching Rieti: behold!–the Gran Sasso

San Giovanni in Laterano: <gasp!>

Bonaguil: the last fortified castle

Les châteaux de Montrésor

Pyrmont Bay doing its erstwhile thing

la route du Château du Vieux Bostz

my beloved Chic – the most precious image

in the Writing Room

KNOWING

On our return it became evident that someone had to get a job. My choice was me, as I'd become addicted to having Chic look after me in the rôle reversal we'd long since established. So, to my amazement, I did exactly that – I don't know which of us was more tickled. He told me how proud he was of me, getting a job at fifty-nine.

A horrible thing happened as soon as I started this job. On my second day there, we lost The Captain to cancer. We loved him overmuch, as I have described, so his death affected us more than I could explain. Our Russian had been slowly becoming ill, and Chic had had to take him to our vet that day as he couldn't bear for The Captain to suffer. He didn't talk to me about the likelihood; he didn't call to tell me; he just took on the responsibility and did what he could to spare me. And it is only now, long after first writing about it, that I think I've come to understand ...

Years before, Mr Walker was dreadfully ill and we'd had to leave him in the care of the Sydney Uni Vet Hospital for further tests; and on the day they told us there was no hope left at all, I simply started to walk away. David Church, very special vet, asked

```
Don't you want to see him to say goodbye?
```

and I turned, shaking my head silently in horror and grief. I was incapable of dealing with it. Like everything else, Chic took that in and never forgot it.

I don't know if it's possible, but I think that our domestic tragedy of The Captain, causing so much deep grief, speeded up what was happening to him.

Because a few months after that, something happened that was so frightful, so ... indescribably appalling, that reality went out of our life, to be replaced by a kind of suspended animation.

The same sentence of death was passed on my husband.

Our GP had broken the news to him one afternoon, after he'd sent Chic off for a chest X-ray. Maahir is an excellent diagnostician: when Chic turned up talking of an irritating need to keep clearing his throat, Maahir was, it seems, immediately alert (and perhaps dismayed). The results of the X-rays confirmed his worst suspicions. I will never know what they said to each other that day – I don't want to know. Maahir suggested I be brought in the following day, so that I could be told.

But Chic went home and thought about that, and he conceived a plan. Knowing me as he did – and I can't think it possible for any husband to know his wife better than mine did me – he understood what it would mean to me to be told that he had lung cancer, with high probability of its being fatal, and in the short term. So, because he loved me as truly and as unselfishly as anyone has ever loved, he decided to keep it from me.

He woke me up in the middle of the night and gave me the ... the bare bones, I suppose you could call it: the word 'cancer' wasn't mentioned at first, not until he said that he'd be going in to the hospital for chemotherapy at some stage. I was puzzled: told him I thought that was something only given to people with cancer. And then he indicated that such was a possibility, in a dismissive kind of way.

As I got out of bed the next morning to get ready for work, I remember saying to him something like

    I don't *think* it's life-threatening, darling…

because that's what I needed to believe.

§

Two more terrible things happened after the diagnosis, one very soon and another quite a long time afterwards. The first was that after a special X-ray they told him there were no metastases: he was to be operated on for removal of his right lung, and he actually had a good chance of recovery if the operation went well. There was a period of something like ... I think about three weeks, it was; and after different X-rays were taken using a new machine, he was given the correct facts – given the truth.

His oncologist had made a mistake. He had not X-rayed Chic's head (I was present at the consultation during which he decided that it was not warranted); and in that amazing, *wonderful* brain they found a lung cancer metastasis. It was Chic's death sentence.

I didn't comprehend what the discovery meant; I knew only that there would now be no operation; and that seemed to me to be preferable to Chic's losing one of his lungs. The surgeon – visited for the second time so that he could tell us of this fact and, in theory, why – lived up to the reputation surgeons have created for themselves: he was utterly vile. It was hard for me to persuade myself I hadn't understood his casually cruel throwaway lines. I managed it, though.

In spite of all of this, Chic was not defeated: a programme of all the therapies available to those with lung cancer was undertaken. He had everything to live for, he said. Later, he told me that he didn't want to leave me – much later ... but even then I couldn't be honest about what was happening.

With the exception of those periods when he was having chemotherapy, you would not have been aware there was anything wrong with him. And, once he'd employed the Stringer charm on the chemo nurses, they slipped him after each treatment the really expensive anti-nausea drug instead of the standard one that gave him a blinding headache and didn't help the nausea *at all*; so he came to manage even the chemo with aplomb.

The radiotherapy course didn't affect him as much as the chemo; but the stereotactic radiosurgery recommended after that single metastasis had been located was a terrible thing, even though effective in the short term. I went from work one afternoon to meet him at Prince Henry's, where this procedure was to be carried out, and never can I forget the sight of him sitting in a waiting room with a thing like a double iron halo screwed around – screwed *into* – his head. I think my sanity drifted away. I don't know that it ever came back, not one hundred per cent.

Maybe this is not something I should write about: I've been instructed by experts that readers need to feel the author is 'all right': that you may worry I'm losing it when I start to tell of such terrible events.

But in writing of Chic's leaving I have to inform you of what I know happened, what he went through, to honour him.

§

And so the last part of our life began. He was diagnosed; reacted; took it in; made his decision about how he would deal with it; undertook various treatments; and then, as it were, dismissed the whole thing.

Reading that will give rise to scepticism, but it's what happened: when the therapies were finished and there were no more visits to the hospital, we went on as if nothing had changed. In the culture of denial I'd plunged myself into, nothing had.

That was exactly what he wanted.

BREATH

The medical team expressed enthusiasm about our pursuing previously laid plans for another European trip, which was this time to be only to France. I know now that oncology people always urge patients to travel and see the world, but I didn't understand it at the time: they gave me the impression that it would be positively good for him.

Far more importantly, Chic, having ensured the family dynamic was as he wanted, was *really* keen to go – especially because we were going to fly in a 777, which he was very excited about. There was no doubt in his mind: life was to be lived, and this trip to be one of its best bits. Thus do I write just something of it, in remembrance of the joy it brought us – the best trip of them all.

Everything was fine ...

§

Our 2004 travels began in the City of Light, on a Lauda flight that had brought us via its Vienna hub. Since the Heaven trip, when we'd stayed at a little place within spitting distance of a *métro*, I'd become an old hand at travelling via Paris' underground rail; so now I could hold Chic's hand and stride on board without a second thought. We crisscrossed Paris to an amazing degree, with him remembering all the stops and able to tell me where we were, surface-wise, at any time. The downside was that we met those denizens of Paris' bowels we would far rather not have – homeless vagrants pissing defiantly, or dragging along on strings pathetic dogs quite obviously starving. No country ever stops paying the price for the glories of Empire.

This being a trip we called our Magical History Tour, we spent time in Paris' Museum of the Middle Ages, which is full of marvellous and beautiful things. I was long a devoted fan of the period, and Chic became deeply interested in the

Hundred Years War – happily for me, as this meant he could explain stuff when I had questions.

We took a train south from Paris to pick up a car in Avignon. This time, we leased a car rather than renting one – a terrific car, a Renault Clio. We fell in love with our Clio; and near the end of our trip, when we dropped it off at Geneva before flying to Vienna, Chic was very unhappy to leave it. But that was later ...

Joyfully we returned to Jean Luc at Le Clair de la Plume and our Blue Room for some quality time, in the truest sense of the adjective. Our stay in Grignan included a visit to the Montirius winery whence had come a wine sent by our Swiss mate J-C to Chic for a birthday, and it proved even more delicious in situ. I have the clearest image of him, sitting next to the beautiful and hospitable Madame Saurel as she opened one bottle after another for our tasting – laughing, chatting, discussing knowledgeably. In his element! Such happiness, that memory.

Our next stopover had been planned for the express purpose of a noteworthy meal, as we'd read on-line about a much-touted hotel-restaurant there. Dinner was indeed excellent, but it was *nouvelle cuisine*, alas – teeny serves on gigantic plates, arranged to millimetric perfection and edged with creative designs in *jus*. The Stringers vastly preferred the portions large and no bloody decoration!; and, adding insult to injury, the waiter behind the cheese-trolley permitted me only three very small pieces of cheese[*]. That was possibly the only French meal we had after which I didn't need to try to dissuade Chic from having coffee. He never gave up hoping that the next *café* he ordered would be as good as it should be; and every *café* he ordered turned out to be total crap and quite undrinkable. We never worked out why the French are so hopeless at making coffee but we were enormously amused by the fact that they have no comprehension of this failing, seeing themselves as baristas *par excellence*!

---

[*] one each of cow, goat and sheep milk cheese – *one*, mind!: no gourmands served in Belcastel!

In Carennac we spent our first stay in a *gîte* unhappily, as it was stuffed to the gills with unusable and uncomfortable furniture, and our landlords lived next-door in grumpy overlordship, dropping in at will. Carennac itself was pretty, though being let run down, with empty windows in many buildings. But oh, le Château de Bonaguil! – the stuff of dreams ... Worth driving for hours to reach. Find the plate and see if you don't agree.

In Brantôme we found the *gîte* lovely, with a delightful landlady. I know Chic would not forgive me if I didn't mention that aspect of '*La Venise du Périgord*' that gave him huge pleasure: the incredibly fortuitous juxtaposition of its two top shops, the *boulangerie* and the – wait for it ... *boucherie charcuterie rotisserie-traiteur*, which face each other across a lovely little arcade off *rue* Gambetta, where we became *habitués* within a day. We spent a truly peaceful and beautiful week in Brantôme, not doing as much driving around as usual and eating shameful amounts of food. We read and read out in the garden, enjoying the glorious weather and surrounded by little birds in the bushes – exactly the kind of break needed.

And then a week in Montrésor, and another *gîte*-&-landlord set-up to die for. Here the *boulangerie* was across the road from our *gîte*! – far from unexpected, as Chic had come across it in the *Gîtes-de-France* listings, declaring firmly that we would stay there come hell or high water. He loved to buy our breakfast – in French! – every morning: one of his favourite things of our journeyings.

`Deux croissants et une baguette, s'il vous plaît ...`

Here in Montrésor our history hunt was based around Fulk Nerra, progenitor of the Plantagenets. I have been for more years than I can remember a passionate devotee of the last of that line, Richard III of England, so was deeply interested in the Black Falcon when Chic came across him during research and bought for me a wondrous biography (albeit a bit academic in places) that provided the source for some local research. We sought and found Nerra's castles all over his Angevin domain, and had a thoroughly satisfying time of it. *Le Faucon Noir* seems to have been a fascinatingly horrible kind of bloke, slaughtering people all over the place and then sailing off to Jerusalem to reclaim it for the faith, thus gaining forgiveness and making Chic laugh like anything.

§

I went back to work, of course, once we returned; while Chic made on his computer two huge, superb posters. He named them simply *Châteaux en France: Un* and *Châteaux en France: Deux*, and each comprises photographs of eight castles from that trip, identified by *département* and *région*. They are really beautiful posters, thoughtfully shot by Chic then creatively put together by him from go to whoa: idea, selection, design, assembly, artwork – everything. Once they'd been professionally printed up, he chose with care where to hang them; and there they still are.

He also made four lovely A4-sized colour prints of photos we had both taken: two were his and two mine. He chose plain black frames, and spent a lot of time mounting them in a particular place and in a particular way on the lounge-room wall, where they remain.

This time, he created the website for our journey, making it the portal for all our trip sites; and during this occupation his degree of interest, starting from being merely practical, moved through fascination to huge pleasure. I wrote the descriptive text and Chic wrote the by-lines for all the photos, and there are several instances of his humour that make me laugh every time I read them. His work was much better than anything I'd done, and as his joy in completing it grew stronger, so did mine. (If you go to stringertravelling.com.au and start reading the *Magical History Tour*, you'll soon be able to tell that either I'm ignorant of Chic's condition or I'm in a state of denial; and the fact is that both were true.)

He included on the site's last page a quote from Tennyson's 'Ulysses'. I thought it was evidence that he was feeling hopeful and positive. I even told him it brought tears to my eyes, for I could recognise that the words were to do with loss of strength (age-related, maybe?); but that was as much as my shutters allowed me to see:

> *Though much is taken, much abides; and though*
> *We are not now that strength which in old days*
> *Moved earth and heaven, that which we are, we are;*
> *One equal temper of heroic hearts,*
> *Made weak by time and fate, but strong in will*
> *To strive, to seek, to find, and not to yield.*

I genuinely had no understanding of what all this activity was – that he was assembling for me as many things as he could that would help me recapture, after he had gone, some of our glorious times. He wanted to leave me access to that happiness.

I can only explain my incredible ignorance by saying that I was already more than a little mad.

THE TINY SUBURB

My last job called for walking across Pyrmont Bridge into town each morning, admiring the city skyline while listening to the Sony Walkman Chic had bought me and dodging all those *bastard* cyclists.

This suburb has an … appeal? – is that the right word, I wonder?: maybe I mean it has a particularly strong pull on me … because it was Chic's last home. We lived in many places for varying amounts of time; we were tenants and we were house-owners; he was a builder and he was an improver … oh! – and I was a gardener! Thank heavens!; I've finally remembered something that shows I did pull my weight (but not literally). When we moved here at the beginning of the '90s, it was without any certainty that it would be our last suburb, but in the hope we wouldn't need to move again. We'd packed and unpacked too many times to remember, and on each occasion we'd settled ourselves in as if it were for the duration – for how else can you live?

In the tiny suburb we lived in the little townhouse in John Street for four years; then a year in a quite expensive and large flat with two bathrooms in Harris Street; and finally, long worked towards, this very small flat in Pyrmont Bridge Road. I say 'worked towards' for one reason: it would provide us with life tenure – for we'd reached the stage where that had become our only goal.

In our early Pyrmont stint (around twenty years ago) we could see, over the back fence of the townhouse, the CBD with the Centrepoint Tower stretching up to touch the sky and not a lot else in its vicinity. And looking out the other way from the front, across White Bay towards Balmain … well, that's what we saw! – Balmain, I mean. I clearly remember coming downstairs one weekend arvo from having had a bit of a kip; it was getting on for five, and sunset thinking about happening. As my gaze travelled through the living room towards the north-west, I observed with pleasure the superstructure of a nice big cargo ship, moving slowly past the end of Pyrmont Point to where it was going to dock in Johnstons Bay. I spent some time watching this truly lovely sight, in the peace and tranquillity of a Saturday evening in spring. That was then ...

Now, if you were to look over the back fence of any of those townhouses (for they're still there) you'd see nothing but the south-western facades, almost within spitting distance, of that group of buildings that comprise the ugliest erection in Sydney, our horrible casino. And if you came inside and went upstairs and looked north-west off the balcony, you'd see nothing but huge multi-residential buildings, starting with one immediately across the road, smack-bang in your face. And beyond that there are lots and lots more, in their serried ranks of unvaryingly ghastly architecture, between you and Pyrmont Point Park. The beautiful big cottonwood trees are long gone, of course.

Chic didn't live to see the completion of the huge corporate office building that they put up between this little flat and Pyrmont Bay, the view of which had afforded us almost indescribable pleasure over nine years. But they'd started on it before we left on our last trip, so he knew what was coming.

INT.	PYRMONT FLAT	EVENING

She's just got home from work, tired.

                              C.S.
                    (taking one of her hands)
                Darling, come over here...I want to
                introduce you to our new neighbour.

He is leading her towards the living-room windows as he speaks.

He indicates something outside, letting go her hand so that she can move in and see it.

C.S.

(beside her, looks out)

It started being put together not long
after you left for work this morning.

They finished assembling it awfully
quickly.

And there 'it' is: one of those monstrously huge gantry
cranes that requires its operator to climb about fifteen
storeys in order to reach his driving cabin – at the same
level as which is a forest of huge engines, certain to
generate appalling noise.

Right now it's not working: the builders have knocked off
for the day.

She stares at it dully.

C.S.

(stressed – she can hear it)

Please don't go off your head about
this – I'd REALLY like you not to do your
'nana, as usual…

That dialogue between us is burned into my memory
forever: I was deeply ashamed that my character was such as
to cause Chic to feel anxious. I think I made some laughing
protest of the 'who, me?' variety, and pretended it was of no
moment.

In fact, I was filled with sorrow and rage; later, I came to
think that the sight of that particular crane was a promise of
everything to come in this small, suffering suburb.

Not long after the crane was put up there to dominate
Pyrmont, they turned on at night an advertising sign – the
name of the construction company, stretching all along its
vertical length. At which point Chic decided enough was
enough!, and for the second time in our life took issue with
something he didn't like.

I wish I'd been around when he contacted the council; but all I can tell you is that one night I came home from work to find him with a pleased smile, pointing out the window at the crane (late autumn at this point; much earlier sunset) that bore not a trace of anything lit.

§

Among the plates I've included a photo that Chic took of what we so loved for the years they let us have it: from the roof of our building, you see Pyrmont Bay with the lower North Shore in the background and a ship coming away from The Hungry Mile, when Sydney's was a true working harbour. Oh, it was glorious!: those great ROROs came and went all the time, with their power and their might, and afforded us almost unbounded joy; for there are few things in this world as rivetingly, endlessly wondrous to watch as a working harbour. In fact, a big part of the joy we found in living here was the fact that we actually preferred being able to watch the working harbour than to gaze upon the peaceful views of the Hawkesbury, which were to be had from all points in our Dangar Island house.

And there were special times, like the one in this picture; it was the tenth anniversary of the Bicentennial, and a great excuse to arrange another fleet of tall ships in memory of that much bigger fleet of a decade earlier. You can see the kind of view we had for all that time, and thus perhaps some hint of what it meant to us to have an excrescence of a commercial building go up between us and it.

But Chic ... he had to live with the going up, with the unspeakable row of the excavation over months and months and *months*. So the introduction of the crane must have represented something positive to him, in terms of what he'd been living with for so long – the cessation of excavation (I wish that didn't sound so much like one of the 'stations of the cross'!).

Even though he knew that the building's going up would remove our wonderful view forever, the end of that godawful, mind-numbing row must have seemed like heaven to a man as ill as he, whose life was ebbing.

§

How terrible it was, that rushing by of the two and a half years between his being diagnosed with cancer and his death ... And yet some good times were still to come, because of his last and greatest kindness, to me, the only person he really loved.

I don't know why that last phrase should have been so difficult a thing to write, but it was ... Well, it's me writing this: I always had difficulty with openly believing that my husband loved me absolutely – I had to kind of come at it sideways ... He loved me but I couldn't believe it; yet, equally, I never doubted it. Whenever I thought about the fact that my husband loved me, my mind skated off the idea and slid about. It was something I just couldn't be sensible about.

Au fond, as the French say so succinctly, it was not natural for me to think that anyone at all loved me, let alone he who comprised the world and everything in it. Now, having written it, I want to shout it to the rooftops: my husband loved me above all others and all else in this world.

AGAIN BUT NEVER AGAIN

Our 2005 trip, for the second time travelling only within France, was the last we ever undertook – although we had no idea of this at the time, as it had been only weeks prior to departure that the second truly appalling thing happened to Chic ...

The trial drug he'd been on for a few months started to show positive results.

He phoned me at work one afternoon, after he'd been in for his monthly visit to check on the most recent X-rays, to tell me so. I'm happy to be able to write that when I picked up my phone and he said, without preamble, 'It's STOPPED!', I knew instantly what he meant.

You can only guess at the effect this news had: Chic was in remission – life had been given back to him. It was as if he were reborn.

We were both utterly and completely joy-filled.

I honestly believed with my conscious brain, and I wanted to convince him of it, that if I seemed to be making almost light of this *wonderful* fact, it was only because I had never believed he was going to die.

§

I can't know how long it was before he knew. He didn't let me in on it when he realised the truth: that the Tarceva had stopped saving him and, instead, had started to kill him. Even this he spared me.

I do know that at the time of getting ready for our fifth European journey he was truly happy. But some time between preparation and implementation, he knew. Certainly, by the time we arrived at our first stopover, he knew.

I'd like to be able to say it was the flight that did it, for any explanation is preferable to none. Just before we went to France in 2004 I'd been warned by a widowed colleague that those with cancer ought not fly, but she'd qualified the statement casually with an addendum to the effect that it varies with the type of cancer.

And Chic had shown no bad effects of any kind from the flights involved in our History tour, comprising not only the long-haul flights to and from Europe but also a couple of short ones between France and Austria.

His oncology team hadn't uttered a word on the topic – neither that time nor before this, our final trip.

But it is a fact that the flying, this time, put paid to whatever vestiges he may have retained of hope.

§

That trip did bring some more enjoyable times to be added to the Stringer memory bank – truly, it was not so different from the others. You will not be amazed to learn that I originally wrote of it in detail, the memories of the joyous parts filling my heart, but advice regarding that early draft was curtailment – no travel diary, this! (Still, if you're interested, you can read much more about it on the website.)

But Chic had become unwell, so I cut the trip short by a week, pretending that my back was playing up – not a problem I'd needed to invent, as the state of my lumbar region* had necessitated his making a back support to enable me to lie in bed, which we'd packed and taken with us. I was concerned at his seeming weak, and I wanted him to be at home – where, I told him laughingly, he could be grumpy, for thus he had been during the few times in our life when he'd been sick.

Quite early during the trip he'd developed a cough, and decided to use the pills his oncologist had provided in case of chest infection: as they were very strong antibiotics they brought on severe diarrhoea. He managed to fix this (of course!) with an over-the-counter pharmaceutical solution,

---

* since recognised as osteoarthritis, but then just another medical mystery

but the episode reduced him. Not that he complained ... He must have seen the pattern emerging, but he stayed true to his plan.

What would we have gained, either of us, from talking about his death?

How could we have dealt with the unspeakable pain ...?

He could be himself because it was not spoken of, and he needed to maintain his rôle.

I stand again before that tree of truth; and see one of its branches, developed only recently, now great ... strong ... reaching out beyond many of the others:

T[3] *Chic's main drive, in the almost incomprehensible goodness of his character, was to prevent me from thinking about what was coming – to keep me ignorant of the future.*

I don't think I ever completely understood the generosity of his spirit when he was alive.

§

There is a colour photograph from that trip that brought him happiness: it's of an avenue leading away from the Château du Vieux Bostz.

It's what he'd been trying for since our very first time in France in 1989: a country road over which the trees arch unbroken in beauty, creating a tunnel of green and silver, with gold and red in the leaves on the ground.

It is absolutely beautiful and absolutely meaningful, and I think he intended and hoped for both.

SHINING

The beauty of the soul shines out when a man bears with composure one heavy mischance after another – not because he does not feel them, but because he is a man of high and heroic temper.

– Aristotle

The flight back was very bad for Chic, and it completely exhausted him: he could scarcely drag himself into the building when the hire car delivered us – the last time he ever came home as anything other than an invalid. It was the end of October 2005, and a few days before, in Paris, he had turned sixty-eight.

§

Something significant we'd done while away was to send an email of resignation when we were in Moulins, in the Auvergne, to my Sydney employer; so on our return I was a free agent, and able to – I was about to write 'look after him', but that would be exaggerating my rôle: I was simply there, all the time.

November saw him pottering around the flat, spending most of his time at his computer; starting to set up what we intended to be a website that would combine all our previous travel sites and include the trip just taken. We'd planned this as a super thing for our retirement at the time he was finishing the History portal, so his inactivity didn't alarm me. He continued to do the cooking; he read; he watched television and commented scathingly on most of it, as ever. But he never left home again, except for a single X-ray appointment.

He was eating less each day, and gradually growing weaker. Unknown to me, the tumour on his right lung was taking over, but the tumour in his brain – or the oedema surrounding it – was not yet in play. That came later. In the meantime, he started having some difficulty with normal breathing, so oxygen arrived, with a very long tube winding about the flat. I found some way of explaining this away to myself.

Near the end of that month I discovered two frightful things: he had three smallish sores on his body that were so horrifying I can't describe them; and his ankles and feet swelled up in a way I am equally unable to put into words. As to how I could have missed these things earlier – it's simply that he took great care to prevent me from seeing them. The crab was tightening its pincers: it had never intended to let him go.

I had to fight him to make him let me take him to the oncologist: he kept saying that his next appointment wasn't for a week or so, that there were other patients in line before him. I phoned the woman who was his liaison at the cancer clinic and told her what was going on, and she made an appointment for the following morning. I organised a wheelchair to meet the taxi we would arrive in.

He and I had a great deal of trouble trying to get shoes onto him. In the end we not only ripped out the laces but pulled and stretched the side stitching to allow the poor, swollen, terrible feet to be sufficiently encased in leather to meet his standards. Chic was never a man to be seen in tracksuit and runners: he saw no reason to lower his standards at this point.

I pushed him in the wheelchair into the oncologist's consulting room, and Chic told him an abbreviated version of what I'd discovered. The oncologist asked to look at the sores. Having seen the most accessible one, Michael stood up:

I think we need to get you into a hospital bed…

he said; and I was immediately torn between enormous relief and overwhelming terror. I said something about how I agreed entirely, how desperately worried I was at not being able to give Chic the kind of care he needed; for

I felt deeply guilty about wanting him to be looked after by someone else.

A bed was organised in a kind of temporary ward, and I went home to bring back the necessaries.

§

What followed is hazy – my mind has taken refuge on many issues, and I'm simply unable to remember clearly everything that happened. One thing I have no difficulty in calling to mind is that, from the moment he lay down on that bed, his voice changed. I never again heard the deep, beautiful Stringer voice; for from then on his speech was slurred. The brain tumour had cut in.

I know, too, that the pleura around Chic's right lung was drained, as it had been found to be filling up, which had caused the breathing difficulties. In fact, it was drained twice, and after both occasions he felt greatly better. But it seemed the pleura was only going to fill up again, and the draining could not be a daily event. Once he was in an actual ward – in which he spent two weeks – a permanent drain was inserted: there was a large plastic tube coming out of his back and emptying into a container under the bed. They said this process would eventually finalise the draining.

I would arrive at his bedside at around six-thirty every morning, and would leave somewhere around seven every evening, when the nursing staff had become heartily sick of the sight of me and wanted to have everyone lying neatly in bed, ready for sleep. He actually tried to say, on the first day, that I didn't have to spend all my time there with him, but my face told him as much as he needed to know about that – and my replying that there was nowhere else I had the faintest interest in being didn't go anywhere near explaining my desperate need to be with him.

One night during that first week, the telephone rang here at home around two am. My heart leaped into my throat, for, of course, I thought it would be the hospital telling me something unbearable. But it was Chic! He'd found the mobile I'd left with him and decided to give me a call. He told me slowly and clearly that I was to bring him the nail scissors and file the next day, and help him do his nails. When I arrived next morning, he had no memory of having called me, but he was quite pleased to see the nail equipment, and happy for me to give him a bit of a manicure. We laughed about the phonecall – I remember that well. I can remember every time we laughed.

My solitary evenings and early mornings here during those two weeks passed as if in fast-forward – or perhaps I mean slow motion. I don't know what I ate, or what I did once home from RPA. I suppose I watched television ... Oh! – now I recall seeing the first, possibly the second, episode of *The Eagle*, and starting to describe it to him the next day, rather confusedly. And now, in addition, I remember that he asked me not to bother, saying that he had other things to think about – which I made no attempt to follow up on. I weep with shame and misery, having recalled that: I was so terrified of what I pretended wasn't happening that I never offered him an opening for discussion.

Later, when he was back home, I put my head beside his and took a photo of us with the new mobile J-C had given us: in it I am, of course, smiling – my outward focus had long been to keep up his spirits.

A line from the theme music of *The Eagle* is engraved on my heart:

I lay down my head on your pillow and ask for forgiveness.

§

My sister Jo, still in Melbourne, would call me every night. What would have happened without her is unimaginable. I had no strength. I needed hers and she willingly gave it; and she would have done so even were she not herself a counsellor (though she was not using her qualifications, simply continuing to be my loving sister). She loved Chic, and he her; and this knowledge was of immense support to me, hopeless, cared-for person that I had always been, doing my almost useless best to provide some sort of care to he who was everything.

My eldest sister and my youngest provided what support they could from their distant locations; Erica and Sarah sent frequent email; J-C was distraught to be so far away and unable to help at all. I can't pretend I was alone in the world. But half of me was being pared away.

The nadir of the fortnight that Chic spent in hospital, eating virtually nothing and finding it harder and harder to have a conversation, came when a physiotherapist arrived to instruct him how to use a walking frame.

We had been asked if we wanted to put Chic into a palliative care centre or simply take him home – one of the very few times we were consulted about what we wanted. It took us about half a millisecond to say, '*Home!*', which we did in concert, and smiled at each other. What had then to be done was the organisation of a collection of things we would need to help Chic manage: a hospital bed, first and foremost; a wheelchair; an over-bath platform; etc., etc. And the bloody walking frame.

I'm not able to describe the episode of the physio's attempting to have Chic use the thing. I can say only that it was unspeakable. There was no room left for me to pretend any more: I had to admit that he was never going to get better.

He was dying. Only then, after what I had just seen, did those terrible words force their way into my head.

§

Without any idea how I was going to look after him, all I knew was that I wanted Chic out of the hospital and back in his home; and that was all he wanted, too. Someone at the hospital talked to me about whether I felt I could cope, and seemed worried because she'd been told I'd been found in floods of tears by a couple of the nurses (after the walking-frame incident); she gave me her card and said I could call her if I found myself in difficulties. At some point, a couple of weeks later, I did try to reach her; but she was out of her office.

They took the tube out of Chic, and it had indeed finished draining, thank all the gods – for I couldn't possibly have dealt with continuing to use it on him.

His coming home was amazingly complex to organise, but it was eventually done: the bed was in place, and all the other paraphernalia. I waited here that morning, not going in to the hospital.

It was a few days before Christmas that they brought him home to me.

§

I have to go back, very briefly, to that time following his diagnosis of cancer.

Only those who knew him were able to see the weight loss; for it wasn't sudden, and it wasn't appalling. Only those who loved him could see the very gradual diminishing of strength. As far as the world was concerned, he was just the same; the same humour, and wit, and cleverness. Oh yes, for more than two years Chic was a top advertisement for the doctors' care ... except that it had nothing to do with them. It was a result of his absolute determination to deal with everything positively; which he did, without ever once falling into despair. Not in my company.

I want to make this very clear: for the two and a half years that remained of his life, he didn't complain, *ever*. Not one word. Never 'why me?', let alone 'it's not fair!'. His single negative statement was the occasion on which I heard him curse Philip Morris, as he lay imprisoned in his hospital bed in our living room; damning their having sucked in young blokes with their Marlboro 'It's a man's smoke' advertising. No, Chic was totally positive through the whole of his ordeal:

he said he felt privileged to be offered so many treatments that might help him.

There is something I need to write about our very last period together – the five and a half weeks I had him in that bed here at home ... It is about the fact that he had no one but me to look after him. I did it as best I could, but not well: he deserved so very much more. But there was no infrastructure of friends and family to gather around and help: there was just me, as it had been for all our life.

I worried frantically about this. I wished there could be all manner of people to visit him, and talk to him, and provide something or someone other than me to keep him stimulated. I wanted lots of people to come and tell him that they loved him.

I didn't think I was *enough*.

But I know, now, that I was all he wanted.

SILENCE

Those five and a half weeks passed as if someone else was living them. I wish I'd been able to talk to Chic about it: he would have been able to explain.

Nobody at the hospital ever gave me any information about Chic's condition – but in all honesty, I think it was because they believed me incapable of dealing with it.

The man in my charge was, for a short while, a stranger; the day after he came home he became another person. I had no understanding of the fact that the brain tumour was now to be taken into account; I had no understanding of anything, in truth. I remember emailing someone saying that I was afraid he would die without remembering that he loved me. For a day or so I tiptoed around the flat in despair. I could do nothing that didn't make him angry or upset; and as I grew more and more fearful of these reactions and thus increasingly abject, he became increasingly irate.

And then, suddenly, it was over: Chic was back again, love in his eyes. Love, and more: terrible, helpless understanding; enormous sympathy ...

§

Jo came to spend Christmas with us, bringing us each a beautiful little glass bird filled with tiny splashes of colour. One was bigger than the other. They were put where he could see them, the smaller bird sheltering against the larger one. Jo had never lacked comprehension of the Stringer dynamic.

After she'd gone home again to look after her own husband, we were alone but for the district nurse, who came every weekday morning to give Chic a bed-bath and change his bedclothes. She had taught me to do both things, and I was able to perform these tasks; but my problem was in being too tentative. I was dreadfully afraid of hurting him in some way – pinching or bruising in turning him. So I took a very,

very long time, and it became too tiring for him. Far better to have her come during the week, and me do it on the weekends. Besides, it was someone else for him to see, and talk with.

For almost half the time he was at home, his hospital bed was in the bedroom. I have to confess to this appalling fact: my brain, functioning at somewhere around twenty-five per cent, I believe, said to me 'bed = bedroom', and so I had them install him in there. Fortunately, there was a subsequent increase in cerebral functionality: I hired two blokes and had them swap all the furniture around to enable his bed to be in the lounge room – front and centre, as he should always have been.

From then on I went back to sleeping in my recliner chair, next to him: there's no way I can possibly explain why I didn't think of all this from the beginning.

§

Although the man I knew had returned, he wasn't able to stay with me all the time. There was no pattern to the personality change, as the pressure on his brain was doing something to its chemistry in an unpredictable manner.

Most of the time I had Chic, but occasionally he was an almost unknown person – nearly always like that when he had been given a morphine drug for pain alleviation. He'd started to work this out while still in the hospital; but that had been just before he came home, and the move was a distraction. He did arrive at the correct conclusion once settled in: he didn't like the morphine, as it was causing him to hallucinate. One night he insisted I give him the digital camera so that he could take a photo of what he was seeing in the corner of the ceiling – even though aware that it wasn't really there. I can't imagine what it must have been like for him, with his mind, a man of a lifetime of ordered and logical thinking, to have to acknowledge to himself that his brain wasn't making sense. And yet all I could do was hover anxiously next to him, fearful of his dropping the camera – and he knew it ...

Geraldine, his erstwhile (and small) CEO, came to visit him more than once. It brought us great joy to see her, reminder as she was of times so much better. She spoke to him of things to do with the network he had set up, and asked him questions about it. It was of huge importance to him, having meaningful conversations with someone who wasn't talking to him just because he was the centre of the universe, because he was completely loved, because he was himself the answer to every question ever asked. Yes, the importance was immense; even though he struggled to respond as he wanted.

During our first week, the wife of the couple who used to own a little greengrocery a couple of blocks away brought me an order I'd given her by phone. She put it on the kitchen bench and asked if she could say hello to Chic. I took her through to the bedroom and told him how kindly she had brought the fruit and vegies, and that she would love to say hello. Fay took a step into the room. He looked up. Without a second's hesitation she moved to him, bent down and kissed him on the forehead. It was one of the most moving things I can remember of that terrible time; dear Fay, overcome with sorrow and unable not to do what sprang from her heart.

§

At the beginning of the second week, someone from the oncology team at RPA did phone, to say various fairly meaningless things to me. I think the intention was to raise my spirits: the woman told me how impressed she was that I'd looked after Chic on my own for a whole week, without respite. That was my first introduction to the word – in that context, I mean – and it was mentioned again, more than once, in the week that followed.

There were a couple of people from the palliative care section of some hospital* who turned up early to check on Chic: one was an admin woman and the other a male doctor. We saw him but twice, as he then left Sydney and went – somewhere else. Chic, having taken a great shine to him, was deeply distressed to learn he wouldn't be coming back; and I HATED them for doing that to him. The woman came again at some stage, but her arrival wasn't something looked for. Anyway, she talked a good deal about my getting some respite, and the day nurse also took up this thread.

Before long I had to acknowledge that it wasn't possible for me to attend to him nonstop: I was becoming stir-crazy. I needed to be under the sky. I would like to be able to make that statement appear less superficial or pretentious, but anyone who has had to stay inside a small flat for a long time will understand. I was so mad for the outside that I was even prepared to turn my back on Chic for a while.

Some strange organisation of beneficent purpose arranged for someone to look after Chic while I went out and did some shopping; the young woman provided was Spanish-speaking, and had very little English. My heart was already sinking as I reluctantly closed the flat door behind me to walk into town ... and I returned in less than an hour, having rushed madly through the shopping with anxiety mounting about the 'respite care'.

The first thing I saw as I opened the front door was Chic, lying on the bottom – the *base* – of his hospital bed, naked, clutching to himself the plastic mattress liner. The rest of the bedclothes, his gown and the mattress were folded neatly in a pile on the floor; the respite carer was sitting primly on a chair, ankles crossed.

Had it been the erstwhile me, I would have leaped down her throat without a second's hesitation. But that M.R. had gone, once she finally understood that the Chic of old would

---

* the manner in which palliative care services are shared around between State institutions is a complete mystery – and I mean it would be one to me *now*, let alone in the mental state I was in at that time

never come back. I wanted to fall on the floor and weep. I wanted someone else to solve this frightful problem. I helplessly asked her why she had done it, and she got across that Chic had told her to. I pointed silently to the door. She left.

Chic was slightly feverish but he abandoned the mattress liner once she was gone, and I helped him back into his hospital gown.

He had wanted her to make his bed, not realising – and no more had I – that she was completely unsuited to even be there, and could do nothing at all for him. She had interpreted his words and his gestures as meaning that he wanted his things removed – so she did this (to a quite insane degree: I was in a raging passion at the thought of her having taken his gown off) down to the last item on the bed, the mattress; and she had banged him around fairly severely to get at that – when I saw the bruises, later, I wished I'd bashed her face in.

How to solve the problem facing us? Chic could certainly not lie overnight on the base of the bed and, equally, I could certainly not get the mattress back underneath him. In desperation, and with no expectation of finding her in the office, I phoned the day nurse, and the gods were kind – she was there! She arrived in no time, and together we made his bed again, with him in it, the dear thing ... smiling, happy to be back in what had become his familiar environment.

I was consumed by wanting not to have to feel compassion for the one who had been, all our life, the leader, the strong one, but I was filled with it. I could scarcely bear his helplessness.

§

One Saturday morning, I had a barber come 'round to give him a shampoo and a shave.

It was delightful, and so was the barber – a middle-aged European called, if I remember correctly, Karl. I'd found him by the simple expedient of calling every barber in the CBD in the Yellow Pages and asking if they would do a house call: happily for us that Karl's place turned up fairly early on the list. He went about his job without any fuss or anxious trepidation regarding the invalid, and Chic loved the whole process. Perhaps I should have poured a libation to those gods who gave me the idea: looking back on how I was during all those weeks, it seems astonishing I was able to come up with it.

I took a photo with the digital camera when Karl had gone, so that I could show Chic how handsome he was with his newly barbered head. My bereavement counsellor says it is the most beautiful picture of a dying person she has ever seen. I am totally unable to look at it: I can't bear the knowledge in his eyes. Or the acceptance.

§

Our GP had taken to visiting him twice a week. I asked him to because I was completely consumed with terror that Chic might start to die, that this process could be stopped but I would be unable to do so. I wanted Maahir to keep telling me how Chic was doing. He could see how wild my thought processes had become, and there was some chat about giving both Chic and I a weekend of respite by putting him into a hospital's short-term palliative care ward. It would do us both good. I went along with the idea, as there could be no repetition of ignorance of care.

On a Friday afternoon we were taken by patient transport to the city hospital. Everyone there was pleasant. Chic was put into a bed in a four-bed ward (how stupid was I to have thought he would be in a private room?!) and we were left to talk for a bit. Fairly soon he needed to throw up, so I emptied a container of odds and ends and helped him to use it. A nurse arrived pretty smartly, and to my amazement inserted a kind of cannula into his forearm and attached a drip to it. When I asked what was in the drip, the answer made me even more amazed, as it was a drug I knew to be an antipsychotic. They assured me smoothly that it worked well as an anti-nausea treatment.

Once again I was reluctant to leave him, but my misgivings could not be voiced in any sensible way: how could I possibly suggest they were ensuring their temporary patients would give them no trouble by turning them into short-term zombies?

So early the next morning I went in to see him: he was propped up in his bed, arms neatly by his sides under the covers, staring straight ahead. I kissed him and asked him how the place was, and he replied 'All right'. Me being me, I pressed him: he responded with a single word: 'Unspeakable'. I kissed him again and said I'd be right back, then went straight to the front desk to say I needed the patient transport again, immediately, to take him home. It was very strange: no one turned a hair; no one asked why; no one behaved in any way other than as if this was perfectly normal. They removed the little cannula and prepared him for departure; the transport arrived in about twenty minutes, and off we went.

As I brought him back home, my hand resting on one of his as he lay in his wheeled stretcher, I was exalted.

§

Chic had quite a lot of severe pain in his right upper arm – something to be expected, I now know, because of the tumour. Of course, I had no idea of this at the time: nobody had talked about it. I did my best to help with the pain by using the rather large massager we had bought, long since, for him to use on my lower back (in the days when I could lie face down on the bed). It's a great heavy lump of a thing; and holding it up in front of me while working it to and fro on his arm ... well, I didn't do it very well at all. In fact, I rarely lasted more than fifteen minutes before giving up because of aching in my own arms. He really liked me doing it, but he didn't complain when I had to stop (that other Chic did, a few times).

As well, he liked to have his calves, ankles and feet massaged by hand, with something like Skin Repair. Jo had been particularly adept at this, and seemed tireless. After her visit, he was sulky that I couldn't match her expertise; but that was only the other fellow; in the end he forgot that Jo had been so much better, and complimented me on my skill.

The other person was seen less and less, and I had the real Chic with me almost all the time. We had some wonderful exchanges, and we laughed quite often. He said many beautiful things to me, and on one incredible occasion, he sang me a love song.

The mighty Stringer brain performed at its best for as long as it was under his control.

By now each knew what was happening and each knew the other knew, but we were utterly unable to discuss it.

§

As he grew still weaker, it became an enormous challenge to give him his medication; and it had to be done because it included Endone, bringing some relief from pain. We worked out that giving it to him one pill at a time was too slow and too demanding, and giving them to him all at once was totally impossible, so he selected those to give him at any one time. And even if it took a very long time to do, it was so much better for him to have set the situation up than for me to use some kind of warped logic like 'How about you take all the littlies at once?'.

On the afternoon of Friday 27th January, I spoke by phone to Jo, telling her that he had been growing strangely absent over the previous forty-eight hours, and that I was deeply anxious about trying to give him his pills that evening. She did her best to make me be sensible about it, pointing out that there had in fact been some evenings when the medication had gone down without problem. And when Maahir came by, he said much the same thing.

At somewhere around six o'clock I began the process of delivering the pills in hope of his being able to consume them. It was hopeless. He couldn't even begin to take them into his mouth: first he choked, and then he would spit them out as if he were refusing to take them – although I know that was not the case. It was that he had no longer any mechanism for taking them.

But I, being the all-too-imperfect woman I was – and am – could not seem to grasp this. I grew frantic with anxiety: I couldn't handle the thought of his not getting relief from pain. As this horrible time went on and on, Chic somewhere else and unable to talk to me, I became mad. I shouted into his ear

    I know you're in there, Stringer!

and stamped away from his bed, going into the study and crying out, over and over, to no one at all

    Oh, please help me! Why is there no one to help me?!

I called Maahir and shouted at him, too, in spite of the fact that he was taking my call during his surgery hours. He couldn't advise me how to deliver the pills, but explained that it wasn't vitally important, I should just let things be.

Alone, Chic most dreadfully ill and unable to communicate with me, I understood madness. But before too much longer, Maahir turned up again: for a while I was so relieved I could hardly speak. He tried to explain what was going on with Chic, and told me what I must do in order to keep him alive.

I was out on my feet, and my brain was … useless. I knew I couldn't do it, for it was a complex series of things that needed to be carried out throughout the night. Chic would need, then, Maahir pointed out as the only alternative, to go to a hospital.

It had been to our GP that I had conveyed my opinion of the city hospital Chic had gone into so briefly for 'respite care'; so, before telephoning for an ambulance, he arranged for him to be taken to the only other palliative care hospital ward within a reachable distance of us. But in the first instance Chic was to go into RPA, simply because calling an ambulance meant he must be taken to the nearest hospital, regardless of any other intended destination. Public service methodology is not to be meddled with under any circumstances. There's no point in describing what happened, in all its amateurish horror, once the ambulance arrived: it was scarcely credible. And it was appalling. But eventually I was in the ambulance with Chic, and Maahir was outside closing the doors, so that at somewhere near ten pm he would be able to go home.

I've come to understand that I can write about everything except the bad treatment that the health system handed out. I don't have a problem describing my own behaviour in looking after Chic; for I comprehend, now, that when I lost control and screamed at him, it was because of loving him so, and the madness caused by knowing I was losing him. But the hospital people had no reason to treat him as they sometimes did, and I cannot forgive them for it. Nor can I ever stop blaming myself for having stood by without preventing it on those occasions when they did impersonal and heartless things to him. I can't write of the ambulance journey to the hospital, or of what happened once Chic had reached the emergency ward. It was, simply, the most terrible night I ever spent.

Somewhere after two-thirty on Saturday morning, they were at last able to provide him with a bed rather than the trolley he'd been on for so many hours. No one offered me the opportunity of going with him – in fact, they told me to go home. By then I had lost all vestige of normality, so I simply went.

I'd already called Jo on my mobile and told her that Chic was back in hospital, and dying.

§

Very early on Saturday morning there was a knock on the flat door, and it was my sister: I wept to see her, accepting her huge generosity, and all associated complications in getting up to Sydney almost instantly, without surprise.

We were breakfasting when the hospital called, but it was to say that Chic's condition had improved, and that he had slept. I wept again; I asked the woman to tell him I loved him, and said we would be there very soon. She asked, ready to be scandalised,

You *are* his wife?

and Jo and I could laugh.

When we were shown into his room, I could think only that I could have been there with him: there were two large recliner chairs, in either of which I could have slept for those few hours, and been in his company.

Chic's condition was such that I wondered if everything about the night that had just passed had been only a hideous nightmare, a figment of my overwrought imagination: he was really pleased to see Jo, and they had a bit of conversation – in terms of his most recent days it was wonderful. We spent the morning in an almost normal environment, waiting for the ambulance that was to take him to the other hospital. I kept asking why Chic couldn't stay where he was, and the only answer was that RPA is not a palliative care hospital. I suppose they had no idea for how long he might live.

When the ambulance men arrived and started to move him, he was quite angry, suddenly, wanting to know what was happening. I tried to tell him about the change of hospitals without including the reason, but he was starting to go away somewhere.

I asked Jo to sit next to him in the ambulance, as he seemed to be responding better to her than to me.

§

The initial handling of him at his final destination is yet another thing not to be written about. It wasn't from everyone – just from the nurses, who should have been those most caring. They were not. I wanted to kill them. I was beside myself: had Jo not been there I would have created an hysterical and demeaning scene. But finally all the terrible behaviour was over and they had gone away, and we were with him in his room. We talked gently, to him and about him, and he lay looking out the window onto some trees.

Jo was out of the room when it was indicated that we should go home. I kissed him many times and told him I'd be back tomorrow, and wandered to the door, waiting for my sister. She turned up very shortly, and went in to say goodbye to him for the day while an admin person spoke to me. When Jo came out, she told me that Chic had asked her if she was going back to Melbourne now, and when she replied that she was staying here with me, he smiled beautifully. He said

That makes me very, very, very, *very* happy!

§

On the morning of Sunday 29th January 2006, Jo and I took a taxi back to the hospital. She had made me take a Xanax; I realise now that the nurses must have warned her Chic would probably die that day, and she wanted to help me in whatever way she could. Since that day I have cursed her for it, and I have blessed her.

They had called from the hospital to say that his condition was deteriorating, so I was in a fever to get there.

I remember muttering

Please don't die…please don't die…

– and he didn't. When we went into his room, he seemed much as he had the day before, and we sat by his bed in comparative peace. Jo's mobile rang: it was one of her patients. She'd left her diary behind at our place, and she really needed to be able to give this person an appointment. So she took a taxi home, to return as soon as she could.

I was sitting there, my left hand on his bed, his hand lying on it, and I fell asleep. It would be only excusing myself were I to offer any explanation for this, because there should have been *nothing* in this imperfect world that allowed me to do that. He was everything. He was life. He was knowledge. He was love. And yet I fell asleep while he was dying. I was woken by two of the nurses coming in, laughing with each other. My head jerked up and I saw that he was still with me. I don't know what they came in for, but soon they had gone and we were alone again. I knew I wouldn't fall asleep again, for into my head, unbidden, came something I had to do: I started to talk to him; slowly, quietly and with all the love in my heart. I will never know if he heard me. I spoke to him about the wonderful, amazing things he had done for us, during all of our life. I went through, in a kind of order, the places where he'd made things, and built things, and improved things. I spoke about the loved house he created for us, all on his own. I talked of how fantastic he'd been as a director and a producer in our business. I believe I remembered to tell him how he had supported me in everything, in health, in sickness ...

When I finally came to the end, I had only one thing left to say to him, my loved– my *beloved* soulmate. The words just came out:

I have never spent a boring moment in your company.

And soon, somewhere between the beginning and the end of time, he very quietly died.

EMPTINESS

Jo came back then, and she helped me say goodbye to Chic. I wanted nothing but to lie down on that bed and go with him: he had never gone anywhere without me.

But I had to turn and walk away from the body of my husband, he who was half of me, knowing I would never see him again.

My sister stayed with me for most of the next week, while I alternately snarled and shouted at her or told her how grateful I was and how much I loved her.

§

Chic's brother Reg, when I called to tell him Chic had died, had asked me at what time he'd gone. When I told him it was shortly before one-thirty, Reg's breath caught in his throat: he and Jill had been with friends for lunch, and at much that time Reg had felt, suddenly and briefly, terribly ill. I didn't know how to respond, for I felt only a jealous rage that in his veins ran blood shared with my husband that enabled this fraternal sympathetic reaction.

Reg arranged (and paid for) what he and I would do for Chic, that Thursday: we called it The Gathering, and it was a small group of those within travelling distance of Sydney who had loved him. There was never any kind of service – the very idea! I almost managed a smile at the thought of his reaction to one. We simply came together to talk about him in remembering him; and it was as good as something like that can be.

That evening, we four remaining sisters were together for a meal – the first and the last time. There is no end to sadness.

§

During the week, Jo did all kinds of organising for me, but at the end of it she had to go. She'd been away from her own household for much longer than anticipated, and her clients were backing up. She was most dreadfully reluctant to leave me but she also saw that at some stage I was going to have to be let sink or swim. I was sitting in front of the TV, full of terror, when she left: the cricket was on. I must have turned it off at some stage. I must have eaten something. I must have gone to bed. I must have got up again the next morning ...

One thing I know is that for a long time I would spend the first part of the night in bed, and then get up and move to my recliner chair in the lounge room where I'd spend the rest of it, in dread of morning.

For a long while there, I have no idea how my life passed. But I do remember, and clearly, the killing rage that seized me when a phonecall came in, the day before I was due for the first of a series of bereavement counselling meetings at the hospital (one of the things Jo had arranged for me), to say that the doctor wasn't well and it was cancelled. I stamped around the house pulling things off shelves, throwing things, screaming and crying. I couldn't take in that I had so little meaning for them that they couldn't find anyone at all to see me, alone as I was and so dreadfully needy of help, of someone just to *talk* to.

But it was a blessing, I was to discover – this last, typical gesture from the NSW health system.

I went on-line in search of help, and found there the transcript of a totally excellent interview in which Norman Swan talked with a bereavement counsellor in Sydney. I could see that the way the counsellor approached his subject was precisely that in which I wanted it approached; and it was only sensible to believe that the method he discussed would be used by everyone in his practice.

When I called his rooms I found myself talking to a woman with a lovely voice; but she had to listen to me for a good while, so didn't get much chance to use it. Once I'd stopped raving, she asked me how long it had been since my husband died. I counted on my fingers: two and a half weeks, I told her. She was appalled that I was alone, with no infrastructure, no family bosom to fall into, but had to tell me that counsellors need bereaved people to come to them after a month has passed since the death that brought with it the grief. She asked me to call her back that afternoon: she would look into the best way to handle things.

Shortly, Jo called, and said she'd be coming up for the weekend. I was *very* pleased – and also inspired: I suddenly decided I'd go back down to Melbourne with her. And it wasn't a case of my burdening her unfortunate husband with my grieving presence, for he had just flown off to Spain to help a colleague by standing in for her at her university. Jo was happy to have me – relieved, even. I reckoned a couple of weeks would take me to the thirty days required by the counselling people, and so we set the timeframe. I was able to tell the lovely lady, whoever she was, that I would indeed be spending some time in the family bosom; and she too was relieved, giving me an appointment that followed immediately upon my return to Sydney.

And thus began a relationship that has lasted from that day to this, and I hope very much will last until one or other of us drops off the twig. She is my counsellor, my life mentor and my refuge: I admire, trust and love her. Most importantly, she is the only person to whom I can talk about Chic with absolutely no holds barred: and I do, at length, whenever we are together (fairly seldom, now). If I were not able to talk of him like this, totally unfettered, they would have to institutionalise me: that it is to her, beautiful and worthwhile person that she is, is my good luck.

I believe I deserve some.

§

When I was staying with Jo, I suddenly realised something terrible, terrifying: I would have to remove the 'home' entry from my mobile.

When this truly hideous awareness hit me, my brain stopped functioning properly: I wept and screamed for several hours, until I became sick. The fact struck at the fundamental basis of my life: home *was* Chic – my centre, where my heart was. The deletion of our number from the mobile's list thrust reality in my face: there would never be anyone at home for me, ever again.

There were a lot more instances of having to take refuge in Xanax over the next weeks, and then, via Maahir, to longer-term medication – there had to be. You can't lie indefinitely on the ground and weep – the world doesn't let you. So it's mindless not to grab hold of whatever available chair leg enables you to stand up again; rather than scrabbling, largely ineffectually because there are no handholds, up the wall.

The days have to be got through. You need to accept whatever help is there for doing that – unless, that is, you've decided to bring them to a halt. And it is to be admitted that if I'd had available any tried and tested methodology known to be quick and absolutely foolproof... But knowing what Chic would have said to that made me do away with any further thinking along those lines. Still, although I had come down on the side of doing myself no harm, it didn't stop me wishing, *longing* for harm to do itself to me, somehow or other. My outlook had changed forever on that frightful January day.

For a very long time I had a real problem with one-twenty-five on Sundays.

When I awoke I would have a background headache, and as the morning progressed I would become more anxious and angry, and the pain would escalate. By noon I was to be found huddling in a chair, staring at nothing, stressed to the point of screaming. The ten-minute hurdle from one-twenty onwards was terror, blackness. Several hours later, by one-thirty, I was reprieved.

This went on for a rather long time; but eventually it simply... passed.

All things must.

§

I sent a long email to someone who was, I thought then, a friend. Later I forwarded it to my bereavement counsellor, and then deleted it. I had kept it for a while because it was a kind of summation of a grieving person's trying to deal with *self* – with all those issues of guilt and fear and raging grief that coalesce only into utter confusion ... And I'd thought of including it here because, after all, part of my reason for writing is to travel all the roads and pathways and side alleys leading to and from grief. I can only think this was to make them less ... unknown.

But you don't have to struggle through it, after all. It's gone. And in its place I want only to write a small part of those unspeakable days, those days of absence of reality when my beloved husband lay here in his hospital bed, slowly taking leave of me though he never wanted to and would have fought to stay with me – were he not under the influence of all manner of very strong medication – with every ounce of strength he had.

Amidst the searing regret I can't seem to get over, regret of knowing that my care of him was done so poorly, there is a faltering spark of pride that flares a little when I'm forced to acknowledge that at least, at the *very least*, I did as well as I was able.

And there remain memories of that time that can actually make me smile! – can you believe that? Oh yes; Chic's sense of humour lived almost as long as he did:

INT.	LOUNGE ROOM	DAY

She is sitting beside his bed, reading a book she's read twenty or so times before so as not to need to concentrate on it.

He lies there, restless, not at ease. And finally he speaks:

C.S.

OK, time for an enema ...

She's on her feet, as this occurrence is generated by great discomfort and not to be dealt with other than instantly, and she reaches under the bed for the assorted paraphernalia.

M.R.

(somewhat muffled)

Have you been sneaking out of bed and hiding all the stuff?

C.S.

You guessed.

She continues to chuck things about until eventually laying hand on the necessary articles, and both that procedure and the one that ensues as a result of it are carried out.

He, greatly relieved - in all senses - is now lying on his side, facing away from her as she works.

M.R.

You think I'm here to wait on you, hand, foot and finger whenever you snap your fingers?!

C.S.

(sniggering)

Kiss my arse!

And, with immense love, she does.

It wasn't always like that: he was mostly not well enough to be light-hearted about things like the need to pooh while lying in bed, and enemas, and bedpans. But something really positive I can relate about it all is that whereas many, many men would have seen it as an unacceptable loss of their dignity and behaved as badly as they felt that warranted, Chic was never once difficult in any way on the matter of dealing with the functioning (or, in truth, non-functioning) of his bowels. Whilst he'd never been one to sit on the lav with the door open, having been raised as conservatively as I, from the time he was consigned to the prison of the hospital bed he allowed me to look after him without a single word of anything but ordinary, unfussed gratitude, like

```
Ah, thanks, darling - much better!
```

even if we hadn't been entirely successful. And, of course, that happened.

Is all this TMI? – I hope not: I'm not supplying colourful detail, after all. I want to show only his total acceptance of me as his carer in spite of my lack of ability, and my occasional success at being that person.

If I didn't have those two things to hang on to, I wouldn't be able to live with the bad parts.

AFTERWARDS

Out of the unending misery, the acrophobia that comes from standing on the edge of a pit of despair, the fear of madness...out of all these terrible things one or two good ones emerged. I understand they always do, and that they furnish what's needed to go on.

In my case, they're represented by a couple of tangible assets, and prime amongst these is Lui Stringer.

One evening when Chic was lying in his bed in the lounge room, his gaze moving about so that I could see he was engaged in thinking about something, he suddenly announced

```
What this house needs is A CAT!
```

I was amazed and charmed, thinking he must be remembering The Captain, our beautiful and deeply loved Russian Blue. We talked only a little about cats in general – I was anxious that if he really was thinking of The Captain he might become sad.

It was months afterwards when I realised: it had been an example of his advice for after he had died, while being determined not to reveal the terrible secret. As if during our life, even when it was nearly over, he continued to build up in me the strength to be able to live without him.

In my usual way, the moment I understood I rushed to act on it, and thus brought down on me a couple of instances of what happens when you don't think things through. I purchased from a breeder not one but two Russian Blue kittens – one after the other!, I hasten to clarify – but neither was at all suitable for flat-dwelling. I suspect she allowed her kittens out into her garden, or some such thing; for there was no way either she sold me was going to tolerate being cooped up in a little flat, regardless of the fact that Russians are meant to be the best cats there are for living in just such circumstances. I onsold each after a short time.

Some months after that, a neighbour a couple of flats away knocked on my door and offered me a marmalade tabby from a litter of kittens she'd just saved from being put down. I must confess to giving her offer about the same amount of consideration that I gave the purchases of the Russians: I rushed back to her flat with her to collect him. I called him Lui, because that means in Italian 'he' or 'him' – and it means the same in French, but is pronounced quite differently. Lui is now an adult, in both cat years and the human equivalent. He is, it may not be surprising to learn, more than a little neurotic: but what domestic animal could avoid becoming so when cared for by an ageing, solitary woman of uncertain (not to say unpredictable) temper, and never setting eyes on others of his kind? He is very large, but also very beautiful, and he is my constant companion; he follows me about the flat and lies at, and often on, my feet. I love him.

Lui Stringer

There is nothing as wonderful as discovering that while you are only half a person now, the only one from whom you could ever readily accept advice, the other half, is still providing it.

The little balcony garden is another asset. Chic had maintained lovely plants out there, almost from the day we moved in to our flat, but joy in it faded when we returned from our Magical History Tour to find that the cat-sitter had neglected to water the four planters of red geraniums until the day before we got back, when he drowned them. After that it was just going through the motions, with Chic less than motivated for reasons I had no wish to understand.

So I went to work on it with a will to recapture something of its former glory under his reign. There are once again red geraniums, this time in hanging pots; and those same plants have been there, flowering regularly, bless their hearts!, since first I found strength to begin again.

§

Friends have had to be...I suppose the right word is 'rationalised'. This is a subject that bewilders and frightens everyone who has known terrible loss.

Anthropologists write of primitive tribes who, upon the death of one of their own, remove the remaining spouse to somewhere far away in long-term coventry, and often until the outcast dies. It's done for fear of the associative aspects: they think it likely, in their unsophisticated savagery, that they will be contaminated by death if the widow/er remains in their midst. But it might be written of our own society, for it's more or less what goes on still.

It happened to me: people simply vanished from my radar. For a while I tamped down my paranoia and continued to make contact, but eventually admitted I was forcing the issue and left it to them – who were thereafter never heard from again. A bereaved person is largely shunned, and that's it: even close friends may be unable to handle another's grief.

On an oblique note, I realised only recently a rather strange thing: those who were my friends *before* Chic came into my life and who then became his friends, too, largely remain. Some have taken the trouble to chase me up, even after years and years of being ignored when he and I turned in on each other. But with a single exception, those who became our friends while we were a couple have exited without trace. If it's because they loved him so much better than they did me, I'm really happy!; but it might be that I am a reminder of what they knew having become now (and forever) unfamiliar – and a pointer to mortality.

§

In the first months of loss, it was a toss-up whether I'd go completely mad and be put away, or simply become a shapeless weeping wreck. Luckily for me, my younger sister, a professor (since retired) at one of our universities, arranged to divert some personally generated incoming funds and was thus able to provide me with some real research work. I found out why they say you need to go back to work in this situation: you do. Or, in my case, you need to find some and do it. She saved my sanity: my brain was largely occupied for months.

Later, I decided there were two things I could do, so I would do them. One was to lose weight (I lost twenty kilos over nine months; put back on thirteen; and eventually lost another sixteen – *plus ça change*, eh?), and the other to do some postgraduate study. How was that possible for me? –

University of Technology Sydney admission requirements: Applicants must have completed a recognised Australian bachelor's degree in a related field of study, or an equivalent or higher qualification, **or submitted other evidence of general and professional qualifications that demonstrates potential to pursue graduate studies**

– that's how (emphasis mine). The Editing Certificate I undertook was something completely practical, unlike all the other postgraduate activities I've since thought about doing. And having it under my belt brought me some work[*],

---

[*] I used to edit PhD theses, when I could bear it; then, eventually, I couldn't

which meant my brain was occasionally forced to be active.

In truth, it's been quite often active when you take into account my reading – the first thing that Chic helped me with after he died. I shall never forget it … I was sitting in my recliner chair, as always completely focused on my grief, when something impelled me to get up, go to our bookshelves and take out Michael Crichton's *Timeline*.

This is a book we enjoyed greatly while travelling in Italy in 2002: it set part of our itinerary for the Magical History Tour; I wrote of it on our travel website. *Timeline* is a book of Stringer significance.

I took it back to my chair, sat down, opened it cautiously and guiltily and started to read. Hours later, I looked up at the nearest photo of Chic, smiled, wept, and said

`Thank you, Stringer darling!`

for it was as if he'd given me … not permission, no: more like *the thumbs-up* for reading

`That's it, me old-I knew you'd work it out!`

Functionality lifted an uncertain head.

§

That guilt is something no one can possibly understand without experience of deep bereavement.

It was nonsensical for me to think for a split second that I had to weep without pause, but the real truth is that my brain chemistry, rendered into a kind of mad soup, persuaded me that to do anything at all would be, somehow, indicating (to whom, I have no idea) that I hadn't loved Chic. In addition to its having ordered me not to read but to simply *sit*, it dictated I must not change a single thing in our house; must not throw out anything at all that he had ever touched; must not reorder things he had arranged.

I partook of the mad soup for a very long time: it was a diet of single-minded activity. No! – not activity at all!: of *non*-activity. My life was governed by it, during which time I didn't seem to evince any symptoms at all of wondering if there weren't anything better to consume. Chic's thumbs-up to reading showed that the supply of mad soup was beginning to run out. Hallelujah.

But let me add something in defence of myself: mad soup is the norm. It's the grieving person's way of maintaining contact – or as near as possible to it. New and terrible grief is gripping on blindly, when there is no other choice. Eventually, grief is holding on for love, and the soup-plate can be pushed away.

As for those things that I shouldn't do – I've done all of them. I swapped over the bedroom and the study, understanding why Chic set them up as they were – couldn't fit the beds side-by-side in the other room – and I gave one away. I let Chic's video editing suite go, to ensure it gets used. Just before their increasing inclination brought them down I threw out the wooden shelves he'd erected for our plants on the balcony. I've even given two or three items of his wardrobe to men who were our friends, but I keep most because I enjoy seeing it, just knowing it's there in the cupboard. And now, many kilos lighter, I can wear a lot of his shirts!

But there's actually no need to provide rationales: I'm not guilty any more, because it finally percolated through that there's not a single person in the world I need to convince of my love for Chic.

§

One thing I've done has caused raised eyebrows, but my few visitors are not brave enough to comment. I've filled the place with photos of him – that is, photos of and by him.

The latter need no defence: they're some of the stills he shot while we were travelling, and *anyone* would be happy to have them on the walls. The former – well, I gain more enjoyment out of them than the travel photos. To be able to turn my head in any direction and see Chic's face ... I can't think of why I wouldn't set up this environment!

And yet, it took me until recently to put up in the living room the big print of J-C's lovely photo of him (posted from Lausanne by J-C himself, with his usual kindness), because I felt it might be just a bit over the top. It was when I was rearranging the furniture, a few months ago, that some wall space was revealed, demanding to be filled, and it was only logic to fill it with the best photographic subject there is. Now, when I'm watching TV and it loses my interest, I just let my gaze slide off and up, and there he is, camera in hand, Annecy behind him, looking directly at me.

I know there are some who can't bear to see their lost loved one's image: all I can say is that I am not amongst them.

§

Am I happy ...?

I don't think the word is meaningful, not any more. I've come to terms with my situation. I am no longer terrified, or even afraid; and that's a real blessing. I can laugh, and I often do. I saw on television the other night a comedian whose presentation was one of gentle and understated wit that crept up behind and bit you on the bum: he made me laugh uproariously.

I've long since taken myself off the medication prescribed to help me 'get through'. I'm proud of having done that. The SSRI turned out to be addictive stuff, and I tried once under Maahir's direction and failed, before managing to do it a couple of months later, without telling him of my renewed efforts until I'd been successful.

All this is possible because I've arrived at a simple formula for living: when I have doubts about anything, I ask Chic.

By this I mean that I have only to apply his standards to whatever requires judgement, and I have a response ... and

I'm never without one, for I know how his mind worked. Would Chic be grumpy with me for not weeping 24/7? – he'd be awfully grumpy to think I was doing it. Would Chic have minded me putting back so much of the weight I lost? – he'd smile, and give me a comforting hug, and tell me how unimportant it was. There's nothing with a question mark at the end that Chic wouldn't have had an answer for, so all I do is work it out.

In this fashion am I still supported by the one who was half of me, even though I shall never see him again ... and the ability to draw on him still is what sustains me, enabling me to write that terrible clause without collapsing in black despair.

But there are some streets where I cannot walk, where the misery and horror of his last journey through them can't be forgotten, nor ever will. These are ugly places, though ... there are other ways I can use, and many where I can rejoice in, the memories they give rise to.

I have to add that I'm *instantly* angered when I do something stupid: when I break something, or forget something important, say. I rage, impotently, and often throw things around ...

I wish I could show the world a person without all these very mundane flaws, in honour of the husband who kept my brain working.

§

She died, too, the woman I loved most throughout my life: my second-eldest sister, my helper through thick and thin, through blood and tears – Jo, my surrogate mother.

She died from motor neurone disease that came upon her like a thief in the night. No one knew why she contracted it, and no one could save her from it.

I couldn't go down to Melbourne to see her while she was dying: it was *too soon*. She was too tied up with Chic's death for me to bear seeing her lying there, unable to speak, eyes full of love. I wrote and told her of my cowardice, and she understood. She always understood.

Not all that long ago, then, I lost the other person I knew and who knew me.

When I was at her funeral, it came to me that it was she and Chic who, in my adult years, had each brushed my hair and kissed me.

BOUND

Something important has happened in the time since I was reduced to half a person: a few months ago I realised that I can no longer remember what it was like to love and be loved. That glorious luxury went from my life when Chic left me; now it is also gone from mind.

In my heart I believe the memory left me at the moment of his death, or at whichever moment it was that his wonderful brain lost the ability to operate under his direction ... as if the terrible occasion of his ceasing to be able to choose to love me brought with it, for me, the impossibility of remembering what it was like when he did, so greatly and for so long.

And the saddest and yet best part of the memory's leaving me is that I couldn't go on if it hadn't: I *had to* forget what love was like. Acknowledging that I would remain in the world meant that there could be no struggling to cling on to that magic.

I don't mean to convey that what I felt for him has gone from my heart – that's the furthest thing from reality I can think of. No: what I've lost is what love is supported by – an *understanding* of it.

All I can claim to know now, and beyond all doubt, is that there were thirty-one years during which our love for each other was the predominant thing in the world for us both.

Nothing can ever change that.

§

A while ago I heard from an Englishwoman living in France, whom we'd met on one of our journeys. She told me of her brother: less than a year earlier he'd lost his wife of twenty years to cancer, but he had just met another woman at a bereavement group and was about to marry her.

I can only think he wasn't sixty-two when his wife died.

Age is far from the whole of it, of course. Further clarification comes with the following – part of the Stringer dialogue held many, many times in a variety of settings:

| INT. | KITCHEN | DAY |

C.S. is at the stove, stirring something. He speaks over his shoulder without turning or ceasing to stir:

C.S.

I love you.

She is reading, in the living room part of the big, open-plan area.

M.R.

(looks up smiling)

Thank you, darling!

C.S.

(a careful taste from the spoon)

You don't have to thank me.

She holds up an admonitory finger.

M.R.

Yes I do – it's good manners! And besides, I'm grateful!

He stops stirring, turns to look at her.

C.S.

There's nothing to be grateful for. I love you, and that's it.

                          M.R.
          (faint hope that maybe this time…)
      But WHY do you love me?

                          C.S.
          (smiling, turns back to stirring and
          tasting)
      Because you're you.

She gives a small sigh of joy and frustration: once again
the answer has not been forthcoming.

_____

   Not another soul could ever, conceivably, have loved me
because I am me, nor have told me so.
   But there was another frequent scenario – equally
important though radically different in tone and mood:

_____

INT.   LIVING ROOM   EVENING
_____

She's glaring at him: his expression has a tinge of the
sanctimonious.

                          C.S.
      You're not being rational.

                          M.R.
      Fuck being rational!

                          C.S.
          (patient)
      I'm just trying to make you think
      sensibly.

The patience is as irritating as the stance.

M.R.

No: you're just TRYING. Very!

C.S.

(shrugging)

I don't know why you're so angry about it.

M.R.

At times like this, I don't love you a bit!

She turns and starts to walk away.

C.S.

(to her back)

I love you all the time.

A couple of years ago, when I was reading *Stone's Fall,* the latest marvellous novel from my second-favourite author, Iain Pears, these words leaped out at me:

> *Only when you can know someone's every fault, failing and weakness and not care do you truly know what love is.*

and, before another breath had entered my body, understanding flooded me regarding what my husband had meant whenever he said that he loved me all the time. It was a wonderful — no, a *thrilling* discovery!

There is, of course, no possibility of anyone else in my life: there aren't two Chic Stringers on one planet. As well, I've only ever been full-on about what's important: there's never been any middle ground. Always and forever my driving passion is that comprising the motto of my historical hero, Richard III of England: *Loyaulté me lie.*

Loyalty binds me.

§

A TV series from the BBC called *New Tricks* is one of my best-loved dramas. Three of its four main characters are ageing policemen brought back into the force: their backgrounds are very different, but shadows lurk in all.

There's an episode in which one of the leads, a widower deeply bound to the memory of his murdered wife, is being cross-examined in court: the barrister, seeking to show him as an unreliable witness, asks question after question regarding his home life, revealing that it's focused on celebrating the former presence of his wife.

The barrister makes him admit that he sits, every evening, in a little garden arbour where Mary's ashes are buried and talks to her – at which point the silk utters the incontrovertible truth

```
But she's dead, Mr Halford – she's DEAD!
```

and his (script) point is made.

Part of the brilliance of this series is that its writers show us a man with real grief, behaving in a way completely recognisable to those of us who share it.

Whoever wrote the character of Jack Halford has either experienced grief or talked about it at length with someone who has; for a portrait is drawn of a man living a pseudo-normal life and behaving to all intents and purposes like everyone else ... But in fact he is entirely concentrated on that part of his life when his wife was alive, and extrapolating from it.

We're not entirely sane, we who have lost our soulmates.

THIS IS HOW IT IS

Tonight I'm going to cook a recipe of Chic's that he called *pasta coi fagioli* – and it is indeed a pasta dish that has beans in it. It is also utterly yummy, although not quite as yummy as it was when he made it. My cooking has got to where it's fine – guaranteed not to upset anyone and even worthy of a word or two of praise. But Chic in the kitchen was something else: without concentration and with consummate ease he would produce the most delicious dishes, none of which was in any way complicated or *nouvelle cuisine*–like, which we would consume with gusto and, where possible, Italian bread (as I believe I may've mentioned?).

Last weekend it was cool enough for me to make a huge pot of minestrone. The idea came to me when doing the vegie shopping and realising that it's broad bean season. This is a Keith Floyd recipe that Chic loved to make, because of its simplicity and stunning flavour. So there are several plastic bags of it in the freezer, now, which means I can watch my pre-dinner TV programs on the ABC in peace, with a large serving of what we always referred to as 'mine strohn' warming up very slowly in a saucepan. No microwave for me! – I hate the bloody thing. Chic never used it except to thaw cat's meat, and I do that too. But I do also use it now, I must confess, to defrost the occasional pea, or to make porridge. Talk about a great technological leap forward ...! Very unlikely I'll venture further but.

One thing he made for me as a treat – which means we ate it about monthly – was *spaghetti alle vongole*, a dish I would once have killed for. The other special meal, a real treat, he made on my birthday without fail: roast beef and Yorkshire pudding, with roast potatoes, pumpkin and parsnip, and cabbage and beans – all served with his divine red wine gravy. We never bothered with birthday presents, but that meal was better than one – like a kind of benison; and I looked forward to my birthday on account of it.

I'm completely vegetarian, now. But even though I can no longer live with the concept of any helpless, terrified creature's being slaughtered in unspeakable circumstances (for that is virtually a given) so that I can eat some of it, that doesn't stop me reminiscing and smacking my lips. I don't extrapolate backwards (is that even possible?!).

Penne alle melanzane was our staple, you could say: Chic started cooking it after we found Gennaro's eponymous *ristorante* in Leichhardt and took to going there for lunch at least once a week (it doesn't exist any more, having been in that part of Norton Street obliterated to make way for the Italian Forum). When Chic made it, it was quite different from Gennaro's version, but totally and gob-stuffingly delicious. I never asked him his secret for cooking eggplant, for I didn't know I'd ever need it: and I've not been able to replicate it. When Chic cooked it, *la melanzana* was my favourite vegetable of all.

I think of my efforts as *una che prova cuocere* (a woman who tries to cook), because it's the Italian *cucina* I stick to. It's tested and true; it's simple; it's absolutely delish; and, most of all, it brings Chic back into this little kitchen.

I have the best photo of all stuck on the door of the kitchen cupboard next to the stove*: he's in that very place, smiling, his favourite *padella* in his right hand – the photograph of him that I love most of all. No, not because he's in the process of producing a meal! – but because he's smiling at me, his wife, with a beautiful and loving expression. I've never in all my life seen a photograph in which can be seen so clearly a heart both giving and accepting. This is, of course, the photo you've seen among the colour plates: you won't have missed Chic in his 'jamies. :-)

I took it some time during his last years, after he had been diagnosed with cancer. It seems to me that he is telling me something... telling me to be strong, telling me how much he has always loved me. I think he's telling me that if

---

* I had to laminate it to protect it from culinary splashing – I feel fairly sure I'm the world's *messiest* cook

he had anything to do with it he would love me till the end of time – something he couldn't say while he was alive. He is looking as if at his best: that choice still very much his, and he still very much the head of the household. To see him there in the kitchen, the pan in his beautiful and capable hands, brings me comfort – trying to understand how it is I am an old woman now, working at just ... *being*, without him here. Still learning how to do almost everything. (And often wishing I'd been a better photographer myself, so that I wouldn't've made him look foreshortened ...)

I talk to him all the time about what I'm doing.

I spent a lifetime talking to Chic: I can't stop just because he isn't here any more, and whyever should I? See, with my favourite photo of all right there near the stove, it's as if he's actually waiting for me to start yakking!

But then, all Chic's photos have to put up with the occasional monologue.

§

This morning, for reasons of which I have zero understanding, I got out the kitchen steps. I put them in front of the set of shelves he built on one end of the kitchen bench (it reaches right up to the ceiling – which, he told me, would've collapsed unless he'd built it, and grinned), so that I could access the very top shelf whereon are stored twenty or so jars of marmalade – the last batch he made. I'd been told they couldn't possibly have remained sound, even after a few years, let alone all those that have passed, but there was no way I was going to rissole them.

I brought one down, cleaned its lid and put my efforts to getting that open. Took a while and several implements: Chic was really good at creating a vacuum when he bottled his marmalade.

I know you're ahead of me on this, but it has to be said: that marmalade is, quite simply, as delicious as any of the dozens and dozens of batches he ever made. The people who manufacture Cooper's Oxford would give their back teeth to be able to produce stuff like this – dark, bittersweet and wonderful! And *at least seven years old* ...

You may not be surprised to learn that I burst into tears. I told him I should've trusted him, and why in the name of all the gods had I not done so? Of *course* his marmalade would be still perfect! Of *course* it would not have been affected by the passage of years!

It's hard not to wonder at such moments if he isn't reaching out lovingly to touch me ...

§

That's it, then: I'm here with all that in my mind and my heart, doing some of the things he used to do. Trying my best to keep going as he would want me to.

I created the final site within the travel portal Chic created (to be found at stringertravelling.com.au), which I called *The Hero's Reward*. We'd decided it was going to be called that from the time he started planning it, before we took off for our last French journey, and he was working on it afterwards, during the last month he was here at home.

Took me a while to bite the bullet. In 2008 I attended two short USyd courses to learn the basics of his chosen software, Dreamweaver 8, and was thus able to create the site from the background photo enhancement he'd made as the beginning of his version. I wish I knew how he'd meant the completed site to look, but I think he'd be happy with what I did with his initial work. It was one of the things that kept me going, knowing that I was putting on-line something he'd started, that would never have been seen without my having learned how to utilise his favourite software.

And I've been writing this story, which has taken me such a long, long time ...

It's brought me equal happiness and pain. I need never be anxious again about any memories of our life fading beyond my reach: even those that you don't read about here, once having been summoned back to mind, are with me again and now always will be.

Chic would have encouraged me throughout: he told me many times that I should be writing, though I never had any idea why.

The joy, the bottomless sorrow, the laughter, the grief that can't be assuaged ... while I've been putting down these words, my emotions have been hard to separate. There's been something terrible about this journey – terrible, but at the same time ... I have to look for a word, here. I think it's 'valuable'. What a pity: I wish it were a more exciting word.

There's something else, too ...

The final colour photo is the last he ever set up. During our final French odyssey we rented a *gîte* in Saoû that had a little tower on one side; and he was enormously taken with the small round room on the upper floor that the owner called, somewhat exaggeratedly, *la salle de rédaction* – the writing room. Chic loved the great plume standing in a little inkwell, and though there was no ink in it nor any available, he wanted a picture of me writing at the little desk with him in the background looking out of the window. He went on and on about it, until we finally went up there and put ourselves into the pose, and after the camera had fired the second time (the first shot was dark), the tripod fell into a hundred pieces, never to be used again.

It's another thing I can't pretend to understand completely. But I know now that he was aware he didn't have long to live and I believe he wanted to create for me anything he could of significance. The photo is another visual message, like the beautiful road in the tunnel of trees.

This one is an analogy of two periods of time in one frame: there he is at the end of his life, looking away into the unimaginable; and there am I, writing a travel diary that will perhaps one day turn into his – I should say, *our* story.

§

A while after he'd gone from me I found in his files one of his drawings. I remembered when he did it, years and years ago, for a plotline he was developing; and now it leaped off the page, so moving and so pertinent. It was this drawing that gave me the idea of writing about him – about us ... about me ... Oh, about *everything*!

For a while, though, I wondered: had there been some kind of premonition before any shadow loomed?

Could he have been unsurprised when cancer was diagnosed ...?

Was it possible he believed all along that he would one day be in the irresistible grasp of the disease that consumed his father's family ...?

No. It wasn't like that. Among all the leafy green boughs of my truth tree, one of those that stands out points to an absolute certainty:

T³ *Chic Stringer was the most genuine person I have ever known. Artifice had no place in his life.*

Not until his last two and a half years did he present to me anything other than the whole of the person he was, and that was for his private and completely unselfish reason – and he was able to do it then only because I had immersed myself in denial.

It may well have occurred to him at the time of his diagnosis to reflect on the number of Stringer men taken by cancer, but before that? – no.

There is no doubt in my mind that he lived and loved without any fear of the future; giving himself to me with laughter, with music and with joy.

AND THEN LIKE MY DREAMS

In the hollow nights I am a comet, racing through space and time in my uneven orbit around him, drawing behind me the beautiful comet tail of our life – crystal, shining.

I have come from somewhere unimaginably distant, somewhere gone from memory, in search of him.

He is glowing... knowing... agleam with understanding...

He will be able to tell me if the solution to curing the world of greed and rage and hate is love, simply love: accepting, not resenting; filling every cup; answering every need.

§

My sister Jo wrote to her family just before she died, 'Love is all.'

I had that: I had love wrapped around me for what I look back on as my life.

The one who loved me, who gave me all that ... he is gone. He who was mine belongs to history.

But once there was a magical, arcing spasm of light that hung and glittered over all the world as it traversed it, horizon to horizon, revealing to me knowledge and purpose and happiness. It was a lifetime in the passing.

Now, within head and heart, my husband lives; with all his love, his humour, his wisdom, his kindness and his *astounding* brain.

You see, at last I understand ... He bequeathed me everything he ever was.

PRAY, LOVE, REMEMBER ...

INT.	OFFICE	DAY

He has desk drawers out, filing cabinets open. There are
cartons, boxes and files everywhere, and it looks like
he's been tearing his hair...

C.S.

(flummoxed, calls out)

In all this STUFF we've accumulated as
resource material, I'm unable to find a
single piece of artwork even remotely
resembling the imagery I want for the
storyline I'm writing, bugger it!

He listens as she responds from somewhere else, and
smiles.

C.S.

No, I'm not going to tell you what it's
about; you'll just have to wait and
see...

Turns back to the mess: a pause while he mentally
scratches his head.

C.S.

(logical as ever)

Well...I s'pose I'll just have to draw it
myself - *if* I can find the Indian ink...

(faintest of hopes, calls to her again)

You don't know where it is, do you,
darling?

while he opens another cupboard, cheerfully...

APPENDIX 1

To my amazement and ecstatic joy, I was able to ensure there is and always will be a place where people can look up Chic's name and his work – or come across him by chance! – when I put something in place that means he will never be forgotten.

The National Film and Sound Archive in Canberra now has in its document and artefact archives some of his film industry output. It's a representative collection, as he kept scarcely any of his stills, considering it a matter of honour to ensure the production company got the lot. And as production companies cease to exist once a film's post-production and distribution are done, the task of tracking down stills from old Australian feature films is virtually impossible. But those very few of his colour stills that I had, and a lot more B&Ws, are now down there in the NFSA forever, along with his work from Oz features that was previously catalogued only under various directors' names.

You can research him on-line! This is how he should be remembered (and I'm pretty sure it's what he would've wanted, if he'd ever been asked) – as part of the Australian film production industry's history.

- Go to the NFSA website's home page: nfsa.gov.au
- click the COLLECTION item in the menu bar across the top
- in its dropdown click on SEARCH THE COLLECTION
- in the SEARCH FOR slot enter 'Chic Stringer' – there are a few items, as well, under 'Charles Stringer'
- tick the check-box for DOCUMENTATION[*].

The references the database brings up are only a small percentage of the photographic work done by Charles 'Chic' Stringer on Australian feature films in the '70s and the early '80s, when he was the best stillsman in our industry.

---

[*] they keep changing the site search terms: this is current as at March 2013

APPENDIX 2

And here's how it happened.

I wrote – as a travel writing assignment for the non-fiction writing unit of my postgraduate editing studies – the story of my Canberra journey, and it was given the top mark. That very satisfactory result, together with its being an early step in my journey back to the world, explains its presence here. (Unhappily, the passage of time has wrought change of text on the Lonely Planet site: you'll just have to accept that once it said what I reckon it did!)

§

A Capital Day

'*A smooth lake, a glamorous gallery and a whole lotta politics*' – Lonely Planet's opening spiel (italics included) on the webpage it dedicates to our nation's bureaucratic centre. It goes on to state, admonishingly but indisputably, that 'Canberra is often described by Australians who haven't been there as a boring town, full of politicians, bureaucrats – and not much else'; and in intended comeback finishes 'but those who go there find beautiful galleries and museums clustered around a lake and cupped in bushland'. Oh wow.

Let's face it, everyone knows that Canberra isn't the most exciting of travel destinations: only a sad git would go there, right?

Right. I went there. I even had a choice; for I could have carried out my business by email rather than by briefcase. But I decided to make the trip, having to take on eight hours on the road in one day so that my cat wouldn't expire from starvation overnight (who can afford to *fly* anywhere?!).

At a somewhat unearthly hour I took the Light Rail to Central, where I found a Greyhound, very tall and very narrow, seemingly waiting just for me. But inside the depot building – why is it that bus station waiting rooms are so dispiriting? – there were other would-be travellers, their various attitudes indicating that their seats were signally uncomfortable. I was filled with anticipatory gloom: *This does not augur well*, I told myself pessimistically, intoning it solemnly into my little Sony MP3 recorder for good measure.

We boarded eventually – a tricky ascent, for the steps seemed each about thirty centimetres, and there was a mean right-angled turn – and the bus pulled away half-full from Eddy Avenue.

A Chinese-Australian girl across the aisle spent some time fitting herself and three huge bags into her seat and the one beside her, then started rustling in them to extract food – and this she did throughout the journey, it transpired. Each item withdrawn noisily from one or other bag proved to be a collection of tiny objects, looking from where I sat rather like pipis, on a polystyrene tray; and she dealt with them one by one, lips pursed delicately, removing something from her mouth and putting it into a plastic bag every time.

I wanted to lean over and ask her what the devil was going on; but propinquity might have led to my striking her forcefully, for the endless rustling threatened to become intolerable. When we stopped at the domestic airport terminal to almost fill up the bus, one of the few seats left empty was that beside me; but unhappily another was The Eating Girl's multiple bag storage spot, so there remained no aural impediment between us. She ate on.

The NSW countryside, brown and unexciting, passed at numbing speed. Every so often our respectable, middle-aged driver would fall prey to white-line fever and sneak over the limit by a couple of klicks, and a governor would cut in, peeping loudly and dropping us back with a jerk. One gets used to anything in the end: within forty minutes or so many of us were dozing fitfully in seats that were actually quite comfortable. I had been making some quiet 'travelling' comments into the Sony, but gave up when those passengers still alert eyed me suspiciously; and with nothing else to do, I'd meekly joined the would-be sleepers.

It's a mixed blessing, the upgraded highway between Sydney and Melbourne – faster, but now stultifyingly boring. One no longer goes through Goulburn, stopping and rushing over the road for face-stuffing at the Paragon, as Chic and I always did with huge glee: one doesn't go through – well, anywhere ... sadly reflected by the fact that turning onto the Federal Highway, a far bumpier stretch of road, did at least provide something to look at whenever The Eating Girl's rustling woke me. The autumn trees were in evidence almost immediately, doing their gold/orange/brown thing above horses wearing car-coats – several at a time; was it that cold already? – as well as those famous poplars ... yes, they were leafless: *really* cold, then!

I waited to see Lake George, remembering it from all our joyful trips (travelling with Chic was always fun). We used to have guessing competitions about how much of the fence posts within it would be showing; he always won because he had an active and enquiring mind and remembered rainfall patterns, *inter plura alia*. I still have a clear memory of the huge lake stretching away into the low, distant range behind it, smooth but for those fence posts; but on my Greyhound day it was just an enormous, dry, grey-brown expanse of ground, dotted with sheep and the occasional strangely bright green patch that was definitely not grass. Unidentifiable stuff: Chic would've known what it was. I hoped, perversely, to see a sheep crop some and fall over, legs jerking; but none of them went anywhere near the bilious growths.

The farming area ended and became the city of Canberra; no gradual transition but an end and a beginning side-by-side. We passed the ABC and its plinth telling the time and temperature: hello? – did that say SEVEN DEGREES? Thank all the gods for the large German overcoat we bought me in Madrid! – and I was immediately back there with him in late '89, blown away by the thrillingness of being in Europe ... Our first venture outside Oz but by no means our last; for we became instant, permanent and determined Europhiles upon landing, and got to make another four trips. Now, as the

Greyhound trundled down Northbourne Avenue, I struggled fruitlessly to recall the coat's cost in pesetas, masochistically (and unrewardingly) testing my powers of memory.

And then the journey was halfway over, and I had arrived at the business end.

It was not the Greyhound's attractions that had beguiled me, nor did I seek those galleries and museums: I was there on a mission. With the local map I'd printed out in my pocket, I disembarked German-overcoated, and strode off, briefcase with its precious contents clutched firmly in one hand, and much swinging of the other arm.

The low, round and once-famous Canberra sight that's the Australian Academy of Science still looks like a landed spaceship, I noted as I passed; it squats over the road from the National Film and Sound Archive, once the Anatomy Department of the Australian National University's School of Medicine! The Academy has long been forgotten as something to check out, for the wonders of architecture are just as transient as every other part of our modern existence; still, I suspect Lonely Planet has it ever in mind. Unsurprisingly for the ACT, gentle rain started to fall, but it was a matter of no import for I was by then climbing marble steps.

I had arrived at my destination – the aforementioned National Film and Sound Archive. My contact, Curator of Documents and Artefacts (mentally labelled 'Sonia the Senior'), soon collected me from the enormous and beautiful entrance hall, and something magical began.

My mission was to carry out the most important thing in my life: to create an archive of the work of my husband, so that he will never be forgotten or overlooked by the industry he loved. For Chic – or Charles, as he had begun to have people call him[*] – was a stillsman, a photographer on feature films and TV drama. He was a true great in the twenty or so years he spent with cameras and meters around his neck, seeking out the best positions from which to get his

---

[*] he wanted to move away from the appellation he associated with his youth

shots – frequently ousted from them by later-arriving camera operators – and never having action re-run for his stills needs. While he went on to do many other things in his sixty-eight years, this was the time he was the most fulfilled in his work; and the possibility of setting his name into the national archive of our production industry I had only recently, with tremulous and incredulous joy, come to understand as being within my realm. And, as my bereavement counsellor pointed out practically, *no one else could do this*!

Email and phone correspondence with the NFSA had resulted in my Greyhound journey. I'd brought scans of the contents of an old folder in which Chic had kept a small amount of his professional output, and more of many crew shots in our photo albums: I was here to seek pronouncement on what they could use. It was a win–win situation, I'd persuaded myself over the past weeks: no matter whether the curator chose a large or a small percentage of the items, an archive would be created. Charles 'Chic' Stringer's work would be there, an acknowledged and researchable part of the Australian film production industry, forever.

The day could only be described as wonderful. She wanted everything and more ('But we archive only originals ...' – '*Oh, no worries!*'); a great number of his stills was already there under their various productions' titles and could be cross-referenced for the augmenting of his collection; everyone in the section was speaking admiringly of his work ... I had begun to glow soon after my arrival; before long I was incandescent.

Later, I came away with a big programme of activity: the handover of everything Chic had kept and some more items from our albums, identified from discussion as equally relevant. All would need to be packaged safely and individually, and fully labelled with identities of those in frame – good grief! can I remember all those people? – but, fortunately, the deadline was mine alone. I drifted back onto the bus in a daze, happier than I could have imagined myself to be since my husband died.

The sun, cognizant of the day's import, was waiting politely on the horizon: off we lurched, governor giving a brief premonitory throat-clearing whilst awaiting its first serious opportunity, and the fading orb started to descend slowly from sight. The car-coated horses paled gradually into indistinguishable blurs amongst the leafless poplars still pointing coldly at the now darkening sky. With no Eating Girl across the aisle, I pummelled the German coat into a pillowish shape and fell into the exhausted sleep of achievement.

I went to Canberra, that boring town, and found a reason to live.

I saw him on TV last night.

It was a sweet, joyous but in the end sad documentary about ABBA in Australia. He was shooting stills for Grundy's, who were making a movie about the group as it toured the country; and the movie crew was occasionally seen in the news footage used by the doco makers.

Three all-too-brief times I saw him in the mêlée surrounding the Swedes – always with one of his cameras in his hands, looking for a position in the ongoing madness.

There was no grief; only unutterable joy at the sight of him – young, beautiful, professional ...

He was the most exciting person I have ever known.

§

the Stillsman

ACKNOWLEDGEMENTS

Every reasonable effort has been made to obtain permissions for all copyright work. Please forward enquiries to Fremantle Press. The author gratefully acknowledges permission to use the following: *Stone's Fall* by Iain Pears, published by Jonathan Cape. Reprinted by permission of The Random House Group Limited. The line from the title track to *The Eagle* is from Jacob Groth's song 'Forgiveness'.

The photographs in this book by Charles 'Chic' Stringer appear on pages 106, 166, 227, 233 (lower), 236–8, 240–246 and 248; and he drew the image on page 313.

§

Assessment of my manuscript was first carried out by Barbara Brooks, who provided input on a very early, unfinished version and told me it was worth completing.

Much later, Life Stories Workshop entered the frame: Patti Miller went exhaustively through each of the first two drafts and Anthony Reeder the last, over quite a long time. The resulting reports and annotated mss were essential to progress: in fact, I could not have got to a publisher without them.

And it was at that point that the final contribution was made: my heartfelt admiration and gratitude go to Georgia Richter, editor *extraordinaire*.

§

But after all that, I feel I should add that it really was me who wrote it ...

First published 2013 by
FREMANTLE PRESS
25 Quarry Street, Fremantle 6160
(PO Box 158, North Fremantle 6159)
Western Australia
www.fremantlepress.com.au

Also available as an ebook.

Consultant editor Georgia Richter
Cover design Ally Crimp
Cover photograph Charles 'Chic' Stringer
Printed by Everbest Printing Company, China

National Library of Australia
Cataloguing-in-Publication entry

Stringer, Margaret Rose
And then like my dreams / Margaret Rose Stringer
9781922089021 (pbk)

Stringer, Charles.
Stills (Motion pictures)—Australia—Biography
Photographers—Australia—Biography
Motion picture industry—Australia—Biography

Government of **Western Australia**
Department of **Culture and the Arts** | lotterywest | Australian Government | Australia Council for the Arts

Fremantle Press is supported by the State Government through the Department of Culture and the Arts. Publication of this title was assisted by the Commonwealth Government through the Australia Council, its arts funding and advisory body.